Kaplan Publishing are constantly finding new ways to make a difference to your studies and our exciting online resources really do offer something different to students looking for exam success.

This book comes with free MyKaplan online resources so that you can study anytime, anywhere. **This free online resource is not sold separately and is included in the price of the book.**

Having purchased this book, you have access to the following online study materials:

CONTENT	AAT	
	Text	Kit
Electronic version of the book	✓	✓
Progress tests with instant answers	✓	
Mock assessments online	✓	✓
Material updates	✓	✓

How to access your online resources

Kaplan Financial students will already have a MyKaplan account and these extra resources will be available to you online. You do not need to register again, as this process was completed when you enrolled. If you are having problems accessing online materials, please ask your course administrator.

If you are not studying with Kaplan and did not purchase your book via a Kaplan website, to unlock your extra online resources please go to www.mykaplan.co.uk/addabook (even if you have set up an account and registered books previously). You will then need to enter the ISBN number (on the title page and back cover) and the unique pass key number contained in the scratch panel below to gain access. You will also be required to enter additional information during this process to set up or confirm your account details.

If you purchased through Kaplan Flexible Learning or via the Kaplan Publishing website you will automatically receive an e-mail invitation to MyKaplan. Please register your details using this email to gain access to your content. If you do not receive the e-mail or book content, please contact Kaplan Publishing.

Your Code and Information

This code can only be used once for the registration of one book online. This registration and your online content will expire when the final sittings for the examinations covered by this book have taken place. Please allow one hour from the time you submit your book details for us to process your request.

Please scratch the film to access your MyKaplan code.

Please be aware that this code is case-sensitive and you will need to include the dashes within the passcode, but not when entering the ISBN. For further technical support, please visit www.MyKaplan.co.uk

PERSONAL TAX

TEXT

...ramework

AQ2016

...e Act 2018

...mber 2019

This Study Text supports study for the following AAT qualifications:

AAT Professional Diploma in Accounting – Level 4

AAT Level 4 Diploma in Business Skills

AAT Professional Diploma in Accounting at SCQF Level 8

British Library Cataloguing-in-Publication Data

A catalogue record for this book is available from the British Library.

Published by
Kaplan Publishing UK
Unit 2, The Business Centre
Molly Millars Lane
Wokingham
Berkshire
RG41 2QZ

ISBN 978-1-78740-275-1

CONTENTS

INTRODUCTION

HOW TO USE THESE MATERIALS

These Kaplan Publishing learning materials have been carefully designed to make your learning experience as easy as possible and to give you the best chance of success in your AAT assessments.

They contain a number of features to help you in the study process.

The sections on the Unit Guide, the Assessment and Study Skills should be read before you commence your studies.

They are designed to familiarise you with the nature and content of the assessment and to give you tips on how best to approach your studies.

STUDY TEXT

This study text has been specially prepared for the revised AAT AQ2016 qualification.

It is written in a practical and interactive style:

- key terms and concepts are clearly defined

- all topics are illustrated with practical examples with clearly worked solutions based on sample tasks provided by the AAT in the new assessment style

- frequent activities throughout the chapters ensure that what you have learnt is regularly reinforced

- 'pitfalls' and 'examination tips' help you avoid commonly made mistakes and help you focus on what is required to perform well in your assessment

- 'test your understanding' activities are included within each chapter to apply your learning and develop your understanding.

ICONS

The study chapters include the following icons throughout.

They are designed to assist you in your studies by identifying key definitions and the points at which you can test yourself on the knowledge gained.

 Definition

These sections explain important areas of knowledge which must be understood and reproduced in an assessment.

 Example

The illustrative examples can be used to help develop an understanding of topics before attempting the activity exercises.

 Test your understanding

These are exercises which give the opportunity to assess your understanding of all the assessment areas.

Quality and accuracy are of the utmost importance to us so if you spot an error in any of our products, please send an email to mykaplanreporting@kaplan.com with full details, or follow the link to the feedback form in MyKaplan.

Our Quality Coordinator will work with our technical team to verify the error and take action to ensure it is corrected in future editions.

UNIT GUIDE

Purpose of the unit

This unit is about the key aspects of taxation that affect UK taxpayers. Income tax, National Insurance (NI), capital gains tax and inheritance tax are covered within this unit.

This unit provides learners with the underpinning theory on taxation, such as what makes for a fair and equitable taxation system. Learners then explore three core areas of income that contribute to a taxpayer's income tax liability: employment income, income from investments and income from property. Deductions and reliefs that apply to this income are then covered, so that learners can compute the net income tax payable, or reclaimable, for a UK taxpayer.

NI as applicable to employment income is covered, together with the key principles that are part of capital gains tax and inheritance tax.

Learners are also expected to demonstrate their knowledge and understanding of how, legally, UK taxpayers can minimise their tax liability. For example, investing in an individual savings account (ISA) will mean that interest will be exempt from tax, whereas an investment in a building society will usually give rise to a tax implication. The ethical issues that surround this complex area will also be considered.

Taking all areas together, learners will gain the knowledge and understanding on all key areas of UK tax that can affect an individual UK taxpayer.

Learning outcomes

This unit will enable the learners to:

1   Analyse the theories, principles and rules that underpin taxation systems

2   Calculate a UK taxpayer's total income

3   Calculate income tax and National Insurance (NI) contributions payable by a UK taxpayer

4   Account for capital gains tax

5   Discuss the basics of inheritance tax

Scope of content

The unit consists of five learning outcomes, which are further broken down into assessment criteria. These are set out in the following table with reference to the relevant chapter within the text.

In any one assessment, learners may not be assessed on all content, or on the full depth or breadth of a piece of content. The content assessed may change over time to ensure the validity of assessment, but all assessment criteria will be tested over time.

Chapter

1 Analyse the theories, principles and rules that underpin taxation systems

1.1 Evaluate the objectives and functions of taxation

Students need to know:

- the principles underpinning tax systems   1

- the features of tax systems, including tax bases and structures   1

- how to compare progressive, regressive and proportional tax criteria used in evaluating a tax system.   1

1.2 Differentiate between tax planning, tax avoidance and tax evasion

Students need to know:

- definitions of tax planning, tax avoidance and tax evasion   1

- ethical implications of avoidance and evasion   1

- requirements to report suspected tax evasion under current legislation.   1

1.3 Discuss the roles and responsibilities of a taxation practitioner

Students need to know:

- AAT's expectations of its members, as set out in the *AAT Code of Professional Ethics*   1

- principles of confidentiality, as applied in taxation situations   1

- how to deal with clients and third parties.   1

Chapter

3.2 Apply relief for pension payments and charitable donations

Students need to be able to:

•	apply occupational pension schemes	8
•	apply private pension schemes	8
•	apply charitable donations.	8

3.3 Perform income tax computations

Students need to be able to:

•	calculate income tax, combining all income into one schedule	2
•	utilise losses on property	5
•	apply tax rates and bands	7
•	deduct income tax at source.	7

3.4 Calculate NI contributions for employees and employers

Students need to be able to:

•	identify taxpayers who need to pay NI	9
•	calculate NI contributions payable by employees	9
•	calculate NI contributions payable by employers.	9

3.5 Advise on tax planning techniques to minimise tax liabilities

Students need to be able to:

•	maximise relevant exemptions and reliefs	Throughout
•	change benefits in kind to make them more tax efficient	4
•	change investment incomes to make them more tax efficient	6
•	make other changes that can minimise tax liabilities.	6, 10, 11

KAPLAN PUBLISHING

THE ASSESSMENT

Test specification for this unit assessment

Assessment type	Marking type	Duration of exam
Computer based unit assessment	Partially computer/ partially human marked	2 hours 30 minutes

The assessment for this unit consists of 13 compulsory, independent, tasks.

The competency level for AAT assessment is 70%.

Learning outcomes		Weighting
1	Analyse the theories, principles and rules that underpin taxation systems	10%
2	Calculate a UK taxpayer's total income	28%
3	Calculate income tax and National Insurance (NI) contributions payable by a UK taxpayer	23%
4	Account for capital gains tax	27%
5	Discuss the basics of inheritance tax	12%
Total		100%

Sample assessment

The sample assessment has 13 tasks.

An analysis of the AAT sample assessment is set out below.

Task	Learning outcome	Topic
1	1.2, 1.3	Professional conduct in relation to taxation
2	2.1	Employment income benefits – provision of cars
3	2.1	Employment income benefits – other benefits
4	2.2	Investment income
5	2.3	Income from property
6	3.1, 3.2, 3.3	Calculation of income tax liability
7	3.4	National insurance contributions
8	3.5	Minimising tax
9	4.1, 4.2	Knowledge of capital gains tax
10	4.3	Chargeable gain on a disposal of shares
11	4.4	Calculation of capital gains tax
12	5.1	Knowledge of inheritance tax
13	5.2	Calculation of inheritance tax

STUDY SKILLS

Preparing to study

Devise a study plan

Determine which times of the week you will study.

Split these times into sessions of at least one hour for study of new material. Any shorter periods could be used for revision or practice.

Put the times you plan to study onto a study plan for the weeks from now until the assessment and set yourself targets for each period of study – in your sessions make sure you cover the whole course, activities and the associated test your understanding activities.

If you are studying more than one unit at a time, try to vary your subjects as this can help to keep you interested and see subjects as part of wider knowledge.

When working through your course, compare your progress with your plan and, if necessary, re-plan your work (perhaps including extra sessions) or, if you are ahead, do some extra revision/practice questions.

Effective studying

Active reading

You are not expected to learn the text by rote, rather, you must understand what you are reading and be able to use it to pass the assessment and develop good practice.

A good technique is to use SQ3Rs – Survey, Question, Read, Recall, Review:

1   **Survey the chapter**

    Look at the headings and read the introduction, knowledge, skills and content, so as to get an overview of what the chapter deals with.

2   **Question**

    Whilst undertaking the survey ask yourself the questions you hope the chapter will answer for you.

3   Read

Read through the chapter thoroughly working through the activities and, at the end, making sure that you can meet the learning objectives highlighted on the first page.

4   Recall

At the end of each section and at the end of the chapter, try to recall the main ideas of the section/chapter without referring to the text. This is best done after a short break of a couple of minutes after the reading stage.

5   Review

Check that your recall notes are correct.

You may also find it helpful to re-read the chapter to try and see the topic(s) it deals with as a whole.

Note taking

Taking notes is a useful way of learning, but do not simply copy out the text.

The notes must:

- be in your own words
- be concise
- cover the key points
- be well organised
- be modified as you study further chapters in this text or in related ones.

Trying to summarise a chapter without referring to the text can be a useful way of determining which areas you know and which you don't.

Three ways of taking notes

1   Summarise the key points of a chapter

2   Make linear notes

A list of headings, subdivided with sub-headings listing the key points.

If you use linear notes, you can use different colours to highlight key points and keep topic areas together.

Use plenty of space to make your notes easy to use.

3 Try a diagrammatic form

The most common of which is a mind map.

To make a mind map, put the main heading in the centre of the paper and put a circle around it.

Draw lines radiating from this to the main sub-headings which again have circles around them.

Continue the process from the sub-headings to sub-sub-headings.

Annotating the text

You may find it useful to underline or highlight key points in your study text – but do be selective.

You may also wish to make notes in the margins.

Revision phase

Kaplan has produced material specifically designed for your final assessment preparation for this unit.

These include pocket revision notes and an exam kit that includes a bank of revision questions specifically in the style of the new syllabus.

Further guidance on how to approach the final stage of your studies is given in these materials.

Further reading

In addition to this text, you should also read the 'Accounting Technician' magazine every month to keep abreast of any guidance from the assessors.

TAX RATES AND ALLOWANCES

The following tax rates and allowances will be available for you to refer to in the assessment.

Tax rates and bands

Rates	Bands	Normal rates %	Dividend rates %
Basic rate	£1 – £34,500	20	7.5
Higher rate	£34,501 – £150,000	40	32.5
Additional rate	£150,001 and over	45	38.1

Allowances		£
Personal allowance		11,850
Savings allowance	Basic rate taxpayer	1,000
	Higher rate taxpayer	500
Dividend allowance		2,000
Income limit for personal allowances[1]		100,000

[1 Personal allowances are reduced by £1 for every £2 over the income limit]

Property allowance

Annual limit	£1,000

Individual savings accounts

Annual limit	£20,000

Car benefit percentage

Emission for petrol engines	%
0 g/km to 50 g/km	13
51 g/km to 75 g/km	16
76 g/km to 94 g/km	19
95 g/km or more	20 + 1% for every extra 5 g/km above 95 g/km
Diesel engines[2]	Additional 4%

[2 The additional 4% will not apply to diesel cars which are registered after 1 September 2017 and they meet the RDE2 standards.]

Car fuel benefit

Base figure	£23,400

Approved mileage allowance payments (employees and residential landlords)

Mileage	Payment
First 10,000 miles	45p per mile
Over 10,000 miles	25p per mile
Additional passengers	5p per mile per passenger
Motorcycles	24p per mile
Bicycles	20p per mile

Van scale charge

Basic charge	£3,350
Private fuel charge	£633
Benefit charge for zero-emission vans	40%

Other benefits in kind

Working from home	£4 per week / £18 per month
Staff party or event	£150 per head
Incidental overnight expenses: within the UK	£5 per night
Incidental overnight expenses: overseas	£10 per night
Removal and relocation expenses	£8,000
Non-cash gifts from someone other than the employer	£250 per tax year
Staff suggestion scheme	Up to £5,000
Non-cash long service award	£50 per year of service
Pay while attending a full time course	£15,480 per academic year
Health screening	One per year
Mobile telephones	One per employee
Childcare provision (voucher): to 6 April 2017	
Basic rate taxpayer	£55 per week
Higher rate taxpayer	£28 per week
Additional rate taxpayer	£25 per week
Childcare provision (account): from 6 April 2017	
25% of payments into a childcare account:	
Qualifying child	Maximum £2,000
Disabled child	Maximum £4,000
Low-rate or interest free loans	Up to £10,000
Subsidised meals	£Nil
Provision of parking spaces	£Nil
Provision of workplace childcare	£Nil
Provision of workplace sports facilities	£Nil
Provision of eye tests and spectacles for VDU use	£Nil
Job-related accommodation	£Nil

Other benefits in kind (continued

Living expenses where job-related exemption applies	Restricted to 10% of employees net earnings
Expensive accommodation limit	£75,000
Loan of assets annual charge	20%

HMRC official rate

2.5%

National insurance contributions

		%
Class 1 employee:	Below £8,424	0
	Above £8,424 and Below £46,350	12
	£46,350 and above	2
Class 1 employer	Below £8,424	0
	£8,424 and above	13.8
Class 1A		13.8

Employment allowance   £3,000

Capital gains tax

Annual exempt amount   £11,700

Tax rates	%
Basic rate	10
Higher rate	20

Inheritance tax – tax rates	£
Nil rate band	325,000
Additional residence nil-rate band[3]	125,000

Excess taxable at:		%
	Death rate	40
	Lifetime rate	20

[3 Applies when a home is passed on death to direct descendants of the deceased after 6 April 2017. Any unused band is transferrable to a spouse or civil partner.]

Inheritance tax – taper relief	% reduction
3 years or less	0
Over 3 years but less than 4 years	20
Over 4 years but less than 5 years	40
Over 5 years but less than 6 years	60
Over 6 years but less than 7 years	80

KAPLAN PUBLISHING

Inheritance tax – exemptions

		£
Small gifts		250 per transferee per tax year
Marriage or civil partnership:	From parent	5,000
	Grandparent	2,500
	One party to the other	2,500
	Others	1,000
Annual exemption		3,000

Deemed domicile	Criteria
Condition A	Was born in the UK Domicile of origin was in the UK Was resident in the UK for 2017 to 2018 or later years
Condition B	Has been UK resident for at least 15 of the 20 years immediately before the tax year

Introduction to personal tax

1

Introduction

This chapter provides a context for the subsequent chapters in this text.

It outlines the features of a tax system and sets out the manner in which a professional tax adviser should behave when giving advice and dealing with clients.

It then introduces the four taxes covered within personal tax and concludes by setting out the rules relating to residence and domicile.

ASSESSMENT CRITERIA

Principles underpinning tax systems (1.1)

Features of tax systems, including tax bases and structures (1.1)

How to compare progressive, regressive and proportional tax criteria used in evaluating a tax system (1.1)

Definitions of tax planning, tax avoidance and tax evasion (1.2)

Ethical implications of avoidance and evasion (1.2)

Requirements to report suspected tax evasion under current legislation (1.2)

AAT expectations of its members, as set out in the AAT Code of Professional Ethics (1.3)

Principles of confidentiality, as applied in taxation situations (1.3)

How to deal with clients and third parties (1.3)

Definition of residence and domicile (1.4)

The impact each of these has on the taxation position of a UK taxpayer (1.4)

CONTENTS

1   Features of tax systems
2   Duties and responsibilities of a tax adviser
3   Tax planning, avoidance and evasion
4   Taxes within the personal tax assessment
5   Tax residence
6   Tax domicile
7   Professional conduct in relation to taxation

1 Features of tax systems

1.1 Tax system

The Government needs tax revenues to finance expenditure such as the health service, retirement pensions, social benefits and Government borrowing.

The Government will use tax to stimulate one sector of the economy and control another. For example, allowances on capital expenditure may develop the manufacturing sector, while high taxes on tobacco and alcohol may discourage sales.

A good tax system is:

- fair (reflecting a person's ability to pay) and transparent

- absolute (certain rather than arbitrary)

- convenient (easy to pay). For example, the UK tax system uses the PAYE (pay as you earn) system to collect tax at source on salaries and wages

- efficient, with low collection costs.

1.2 Direct and indirect taxes

Direct taxes

Direct taxes are imposed directly on the person or enterprise required to pay the tax, i.e. tax on personal income such as salaries, tax on business profits or tax on disposals of chargeable assets.

The person or enterprise must pay the tax directly to the tax authorities. Income tax, capital gains tax and national insurance contributions are direct taxes.

Indirect taxes

Indirect taxes are imposed on one part of the economy with the intention that the tax burden is passed on to another. Value added tax (VAT) is an indirect tax.

VAT is imposed on the final consumer of the goods or services. The more the consumer consumes the greater the tax paid.

1.3 Tax base and tax rate structures

Taxes are classified according to their tax base (i.e. what is being taxed).

- Income or profits – e.g. income tax and corporation tax
- Assets – e.g. capital gains tax
- Consumption – e.g. VAT.

There are three types of taxes:

Progressive taxes

These take an increasing proportion of income as income rises. For example, income tax where tax is charged at 20%, then 40% and finally 45%.

Proportional taxes

These take the same proportion of income as income rises.

Regressive taxes

These take a decreasing proportion of income as income rises. For example, national insurance contributions which are charged at 12% and then at 2%.

 Test your understanding 1

Tax systems

Read the following statements and state whether they are true or false.

1   Income tax is a direct regressive tax.

2   National insurance is a direct regressive tax.

3   VAT is an indirect tax.

2 Duties and responsibilities of a tax adviser

2.1 AAT expectations

The AAT expects its members to:

- master skills and techniques through learning and maintain them through continuing professional development
- adopt an ethical approach to work as well as to their employers and clients

- acknowledge their professional duty to society as a whole

- maintain an objective outlook

- provide professional, high standards of service, conduct and performance at all times.

These expectations are discussed in greater depth in the 'Code of Professional Ethics' that can be found on the website (www.aat.org.uk).

A person advising either a company or an individual on taxation issues has duties and responsibilities towards both:

- his client, and

- HM Revenue and Customs.

An adviser owes the greatest duty to his or her client.

2.2 Professional conduct in relation to taxation

Guidance on how tax advisers should conduct themselves has been published by the professional accountancy bodies in 'Professional conduct in relation to taxation'.

Extracts from this document are available for you to refer to in the assessment. These extracts are set out in the appendix to this chapter.

In the assessment you may be required to use this guidance to determine how a tax adviser should behave in a particular situation. Accordingly, you should ensure that you are very familiar with the matters covered in these extracts so that you are able to find the information you need.

2.3 Providing tax advice

When providing tax advice and preparing tax returns, a person should act in the best interests of his client.

However, he must ensure that his services are consistent with the law and are carried out competently.

At all times an adviser must not in any way impair his:

- integrity, such that he is straightforward and honest in all professional and business relationships; or

- objectivity, such that he does not allow bias, conflict of interest or undue influence of others to override professional or business judgements.

2.4 Providing information to HM Revenue and Customs/ other authorities

The 'Guidelines on Professional Ethics' state that:

'A member should not be associated with any return or communication where there is reason to believe that it:

- contains a false or misleading statement
- contains statements or information furnished recklessly, or
- omits or obscures information required to be included and such omission or obscurity would mislead the tax authorities.'

2.5 Confidentiality

A tax adviser has an overriding duty of confidentiality towards his client. Under normal circumstances a client's tax affairs should not be discussed with third parties. This duty remains even after the adviser no longer works for the client.

The exceptions to this rule mentioned in the Guidelines are where:

- authority has been given by the client, or
- there is a legal, regulatory or professional duty to disclose (e.g. in the case of suspected money laundering).

The duty of confidentiality also relates to dealings with HMRC.

However, the tax adviser must ensure that, whilst acting in the client's best interests, he consults with HMRC staff in an open and constructive manner (see below).

2.6 Money laundering

Money laundering is the exchange of funds acquired through crime for funds that do not appear to be linked to crime.

The AAT and its members are required to comply with the money laundering laws and regulations.

A tax adviser should check the identity of prospective clients via a review of appropriate documentation, for example, a passport.

A firm of accountants must appoint a money laundering officer.

Suspicion that a person is involved in money laundering should be reported to the money laundering officer who will determine whether it needs to be reported to the appropriate authorities.

Test your understanding 2

Which of the following statements is not correct?

A   Accountants need to follow the rules of confidentiality even in a social environment.

B   If money laundering is suspected, accountants are allowed to break the rules of confidentiality.

C   Rules of confidentiality towards a client must be followed even after the business relationship has ended.

D   Accountants must follow the rules of confidentiality irrespective of the situation.

3 Tax planning, avoidance and evasion

3.1   Tax planning and tax avoidance

It has already been noted that a tax adviser is required to act in the best interests of his client. This would include providing advice on how a client's affairs should be structured in order to minimise tax liabilities.

Tax planning is the use of legitimate means in order to reduce a tax liability such as making use of investment income generated by an ISA which would be exempt from income and capital gains tax.

However, some tax strategies have caused controversy, especially as to the moral acceptability of such planning.

Tax avoidance, although lawful, is where planning may not be deemed to comply with the spirit of the law i.e. to divert investments outside the UK to attract overseas tax rates which may be much lower than those in the UK.

Advice of this nature may subject the client and the adviser to scrutiny, investigation and possible public criticism. An adviser should therefore consider carefully when giving tax advice and factor in any potential negative impacts.

3.2   Tax evasion

Tax evasion is unlawful. A taxpayer who dishonestly withholds or falsifies information in order to evade tax may be subject to criminal proceedings or suffer civil penalties.

3.3 Dealing with problems

In spite of guidelines being available, there can be situations where the method of resolving an ethical issue is not straightforward.

In those situations additional advice should be sought from:

- a supervisor
- a professional body, or
- a legal adviser.

3.4 Dealing with errors and omissions in clients' tax returns

Where a tax adviser realises that an error or omission has been made in a client's or employer's tax return he must recommend that the client/employer informs HMRC.

If the client/employer refuses to do so, the member must not act for them in connection with that return or related matters. The member may also have to consider whether to cease acting for the client.

Dishonestly retaining funds acquired as a result of an error or omission amounts to money laundering (see below).

 Test your understanding 3

When an accountant is advising a client, to whom does he owe the greatest duty of care?

A   HMRC

B   The professional body to which the accountant belongs

C   The client

D   The public

4 Taxes within the personal tax assessment

4.1 The tax year

This study text is based on the tax year 2018/19.

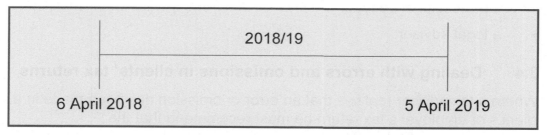

2018/19

6 April 2018   5 April 2019

The tax year 2018/19 runs from 6 April 2018 to 5 April 2019.

This study text will explain which items go into the tax computations for the tax year.

4.2 The taxes within personal tax

The four taxes within personal tax are:

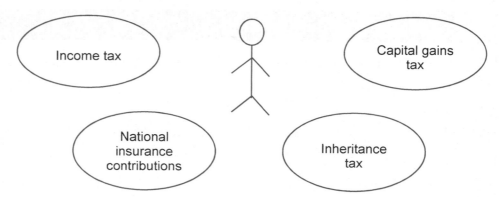

- income tax (Chapters 2 – 8)
- national insurance contributions (Chapter 9)
- capital gains tax (Chapters 10 – 12)
- inheritance tax (Chapter 13)

4.3 Income tax

Income tax applies mainly to:

- amounts earned in day to day work, and
- income generated from assets (for example dividend income on shares).

You will discover how to calculate an individual's income tax payable.

The ways in which the income tax payable by an individual can be reduced are also considered.

4.4 National insurance contributions (NICs)

The personal tax assessment requires knowledge of class 1 NICs, which are payable by employers and employees in respect of employment income as well as class 1A NICs, which are payable by employers in respect of taxable benefits received by the employees.

The NICs payable by the self-employed (class 2 and class 4) are covered in Business Tax.

You will discover how to calculate the class 1 NICs payable by both the employer and the employee and class 1A NICs payable by the employer.

4.5 Capital gains tax (CGT)

CGT applies mainly when assets are sold.

However, certain assets are exempt from CGT and there are other ways of reducing the gains.

You will discover how to calculate an individual's CGT payable.

4.6 Inheritance tax (IHT)

IHT applies mainly on the death of an individual in respect of the assets owned at death. It can also be payable in respect of gifts made by an individual during their lifetime.

Certain exemptions from IHT are available and there are other ways of reducing an individual's liability to IHT.

You will discover how to calculate an individual's IHT liability.

5 Tax residence

5.1 Tax residence status

The residence status of an individual determines whether their overseas income is subject to income tax in the UK.

- individuals who are resident in the UK are subject to UK income tax on both their UK and overseas income

- individuals who are not resident in the UK are subject to UK income tax on their UK income only.

5.2 Determination of residence

An individual is resident for the whole of a tax year if they:

- do not meet one of the automatic non-UK residence tests, and

- meet one of the automatic UK residence tests, or

- meet one or more of the sufficient ties tests.

In order to determine the tax residence status of an individual:

1   Check the automatic non-UK residence tests

- if one test satisfied = non-UK resident

- if not, go to step 2

2   Check the automatic UK residence tests

- if one test satisfied = UK resident

- if not, go to step 3

3   Consider the number of ties the individual has with the UK

- determine whether the individual has been UK resident in any of the last three tax years or has not

- determine how many days the individual has spent in the UK

- identify the relevant number of ties for the individual

- determine how many ties the individual has with the UK

- if the individual's ties are greater than or equal to the relevant number of ties = UK resident

5.3 Automatic non-UK residency tests

An individual is automatically not UK resident if they are 'in the UK' in the tax year for less than:

- 16 days, or
- 46 days, and they have not been UK resident in any of the previous three tax years, or
- 91 days, and they work full-time overseas.

Note that an individual is 'in the UK' if they are in the UK at midnight.

5.4 Automatic UK residency tests

An individual is automatically UK resident if:

- they are in the UK for at least 183 days in the tax year, or
- their only home is in the UK, or
- they work full-time in the UK.

If the individual does not satisfy any of the automatic tests, their residency status is determined by:

- how many of the five 'sufficient ties tests' are satisfied, and
- the number of days spent in the UK.

5.5 Sufficient ties tests

The number of days the individual has spent in the UK, together with their resident status in the three previous tax years determines the relevant number of ties. This is set out in the table below:

Days in the UK	Previously resident in any of the last three tax years	Not previously resident in any of the last three tax years
Less than 16	Automatically not resident	Automatically not resident
16 to 45	Resident if 4 UK ties (or more)	Automatically not resident
46 to 90	Resident if 3 UK ties (or more)	Resident if 4 UK ties
91 to 120	Resident if 2 UK ties (or more)	Resident if 3 UK ties (or more)
121 to 182	Resident if 1 UK tie (or more)	Resident if 2 UK ties (or more)
183 or more	Automatically resident	Automatically resident

The ties are set out below:

		This tie with the UK exists if the individual:
1	Family	has close family (a spouse/civil partner or minor children) in the UK
2	Accommodation	has a house in the UK which is made use of during the tax year
3	Work	does substantive work in the UK
4	Days in UK	has spent more than 90 days in the UK in either, or both, of the previous two tax years
5	Country	spends more time in the UK than in any other country in the tax year

 Test your understanding 4

Residency status

Explain whether or not the following individuals are resident in the UK in the tax year 2018/19.

1   Dieter was born in Germany. He has lived in his home town in Germany until the tax year 2018/19 when he came to the UK to visit on 10 June 2018 until 18 January 2019.

2   Simone was born in France. She has lived in her home town in France until the tax year 2018/19 when she came to the UK to visit for a month.

3   Fred has always spent more than 300 days in the UK and has therefore been UK resident.

He gave up work on 5 April 2018 and on 18 May 2018 he set off on a round the world holiday. He did not return until 6 April 2019.

Initially he spent 5 weeks in his holiday home in Portugal but then did not spend more than 10 days in any other country whilst he was away.

Whilst he was away he kept in touch with his wife and young children who remained in the family home.

6 Tax domicile

The domicile status of an individual differs from the concepts of nationality and residence. It is based on the individual's permanent home. A person can only have one domicile at any one time.

- An individual acquires their father's domicile at birth. This is known as a domicile of origin.

- Until the individual is 16, any change in their father's domicile also changes the domicile of the individual. This is known as a domicile of dependence.

- Once the individual is 16, it is possible to acquire a new country of domicile by severing all ties with the old country and establishing residence in the new country on a permanent basis. This is known as a domicile of choice.

From 6 April 2017 the government has introduced a deemed domicile status. This means that even if an individual is non-domiciled they will be treated as UK domiciled for tax purposes if they meet either condition A or B.

Condition A

- The individual was born in the UK. **and**

- the individual had a UK domicile of origin, **and**

- the individual was UK resident in 2017/18 or later.

Condition B

- The individual has been UK resident for at least 15 out of the 20 tax years immediately before the current tax year.

An individual's domicile status is only relevant for inheritance tax in the assessment, but can impact other taxes.

Test your understanding 5

Domicile status

Explain whether the following individuals are domiciled or deemed domiciled in the UK in the tax year 2018/19.

1   Sunita was born in America. Her father has always been domiciled in the UK. Sunita occasionally visits the UK, and does not have a permanent home in any one country.

2   Francoise was born in the UK and his father was domiciled in the UK at his birth. He moved to France when he was 10, and his father changed his domicile to France at that time. Francoise moved to the UK on 1 January 2018 and lived in the UK throughout 2018/19.

3   Petra was born and domiciled in Spain. She has lived in the UK since 6 April 2004.

7   Professional conduct in relation to taxation

In the assessment you will be able to consult the reference material relating to professional conduct in relation to taxation. This will be available through pop-up windows. The full document has been included in an appendix at the end of this chapter.

Approach to answering written questions

The chief assessor has written a guidance document to assist students with written answers. With the permission of AAT some of the key points of this advice are set out below.

The full document can be found on the AAT website, however, the task discussed covers material which will not be assessed under AQ2016. You may still benefit from reading the advice given regarding how to handle this task, but you will not be able to practise writing an answer to it.

Firstly, it's important you understand that the software in which you are answering the task is not Microsoft Word. So there's no:

*   spell checker

*   grammar checker

*   automatic correcting of typos.

You won't see any different coloured lines highlighting any of these issues. It's quite clear from assessments we've marked so far that too many students are not proofreading their answers, and are failing to correct obvious mistakes.

So, when you type:

"i DON'T LIKE ANWSERING WRITEN QUETSIONS."

… this is exactly how it will look to the assessor. While the sentence can be read and understood, it's poor practice and would certainly not be allowed in the workplace.

You **must** proofread what you've written and correct any obvious spelling and grammatical errors. There's often a mark for presentation of the answer, and the assessor is looking for whether the way you've presented your work would be acceptable in the workplace. This mark is independent of the technical answer, and what we look for is whether a client would find the answer acceptable from a visual perspective.

Length of answer

It may not be obvious when you first look at the answer box on the screen, but this is a never-ending answer box. When you get to the last visible line, you can scroll down for extra writing space. So don't start your answer assuming that it needs to be condensed or short.

You should also remember that in many cases, the model answer the assessor is working from is in much more depth than the answer you'd need to give to gain full marks. It's acknowledged that it can be very difficult to write every aspect of all the areas applicable in a written question, and usually it's not necessary to do so.

Before you start to type:

You must read the question in detail. We've noticed that students often scan read a question, decide what it's about in an instant and then write the answer without giving any thought or consideration to the details. You should:

- read through once to get the general feel of the question

- read through again, slower this time, concentrating on key words or phrases

- plan your answer, ensuring all key areas are covered

- decide the structure of your answer, considering where you'll use things like an email, a memo or bullet points

- type up your answer

- proofread your answer, correcting any errors.

Too many times it would seem that students only follow the fifth of these points. If you do this it **will** affect your marks.

Consider exactly who you're writing to. Most likely it will be a client, so this needs to influence your approach.

Remember, if the client is writing to you for advice, they don't know the answer. We often see students give half answers which the assessor will understand, but which a client would not. As a result, they lose marks.

Similarly, be sure to avoid:

*   abbreviations

*   technical jargon

*   SMS/text message speak.

The following test your understanding questions should be attempted as you familiarise yourself with the content of that document. Do also practice writing out your answers in full sentences, as that is a skill you must develop for the written tasks in the assessment.

 Test your understanding 6

Professional conduct in relation to taxation – familiarisation part 1

Answer the following questions by referring to the extracts from the AAT guidelines 'Personal conduct in relation to taxation' which will be available for you to refer to in the assessment.

You should answer each question by writing a complete sentence.

1   Who has primary responsibility for submitting a correct tax return?

2   What is meant by the term irregularity?

3   What should a member of the profession do if asked to provide information which may be subject to privilege?

4   What is meant when we say that a member of the tax profession must act in an objective manner?

5   What should a member do when advocating fuller disclosure in a tax return than is strictly necessary?

Test your understanding 7

Professional conduct in relation to taxation – familiarisation part 2

Answer the following questions by referring to the extracts from the AAT guidelines 'Personal conduct in relation to taxation' which will be available for you to refer to in the assessment.

You should answer each question by writing a complete sentence.

1 Is it acceptable for a tax return to include estimates rather than precise figures?

2 Is it acceptable to disclose information in response to an informal request from HM Revenue and Customs?

3 Is it ever permissible for a member to be involved in tax evasion?

4 Who is responsible for deciding whether or not a tax-planning strategy is appropriate?

5 Does the concept of materiality apply when completing a tax return?

 Test your understanding 8

Professional conduct in relation to taxation – familiarisation part 3

Answer the following questions by referring to the extracts from the AAT guidelines 'Personal conduct in relation to taxation' which will be available for you to refer to in the assessment.

You should answer each question by writing a complete sentence.

1 When is it permissible to disclose confidential information without specific authority from the client?

2 What should a member do when a client decides to proceed with a tax planning arrangement without taking full advice from the member?

3 When should a member inform a client of a possible irregularity in the client's tax affairs?

4 What is the responsibility of a member when preparing a tax return on behalf of a client?

5 What is meant when we say that a member of the tax profession must act with integrity?

Test your understanding 9

Professional conduct in relation to taxation – familiarisation part 4

Answer the following questions by referring to the extracts from the AAT guidelines 'Personal conduct in relation to taxation' which will be available for you to refer to in the assessment.

You should answer each question by writing a complete sentence.

1   What is the definition of tax avoidance?

2   What should a member do if it appears that the client has used the member to assist in the commission of a criminal offence?

3   When is a figure in a tax return regarded as material?

4   Does the duty of confidentiality apply to information obtained in respect of ex-clients?

5   Is it necessary for the client to review their tax return before it is submitted?

 Test your understanding 10

Barque Ltd

You work for a firm of accountants. Barque Ltd, one of your clients, has told you that they are considering carrying out some aggressive tax planning which you feel is unlikely to be successful.

Using the AAT guidelines 'Professional conduct in relation to taxation', explain your responsibilities in relation to this matter.

 Test your understanding 11

Qual Systems Ltd

You work for a firm of accountants. You have received a telephone call from HM Revenue and Customs requesting information in relation to Qual Systems Ltd. Qual Systems Ltd was a client of your firm until 31 October 2016.

Using the AAT guidelines 'Professional conduct in relation to taxation', explain your responsibilities in relation to this matter.

8 Summary

It is important that you do not neglect this chapter. Much of the information here could be tested in a written question, and such questions are, perhaps, more difficult to answer well than computational questions. So you should learn as much of this material as you can.

Test your understanding answers

 Test your understanding 1

1	False	Income tax is a direct **progressive** tax.
2	True	
3	True	

 Test your understanding 2

The answer is **D**.

The duty of confidentiality can be overridden if the client gives authority or if there is a legal, regulatory or professional duty to disclose.

 Test your understanding 3

The answer is **C**.

 Test your understanding 4

Residence status

1   Dieter has been in the UK for 222 days in the tax year 2018/19, which is more than 183 days.

Accordingly, he will automatically be treated as UK resident in the tax year 2018/19.

2   Simone has not been resident in the UK in any of the three previous tax years, and has been in the UK for less than 46 days.

Accordingly, she will automatically be treated as **not UK resident** in the tax year 2018/19.

3   Fred spent 42 days in the UK in the tax year 2018/19.

–   He has spent too many days in the UK to be automatically not resident (i.e. > 16 days as previously resident in UK).

–   He is not automatically resident as he has not been in the UK for sufficient days, has an overseas home and has not had full-time work in the UK during the tax year 2018/19.

Fred has been UK resident and is now leaving the UK.

He was in the UK in the tax year 2018/19 for between 16 and 45 days and will be UK resident if he meets at least four of the UK ties tests.

Fred meets the:

–   close family tie

–   accommodation tie (made use of a UK house)

–   days in UK tie (spent more than 90 days in UK in both of previous two tax years), and

–   country tie (spent more time in UK than any other country).

He is therefore UK resident in the tax year 2018/19.

🔍 Test your understanding 5

Domicile status

1   Sunita has a domicile of origin in the UK. She does not appear to have made a domicile of choice and therefore is still domiciled in the UK. She is not deemed domiciled in the UK under condition A, as she was not born in the UK and is not resident in the UK.

2   Francoise was born in the UK and had a domicile of origin in the UK.

He will have acquired a domicile of dependence in France when his father moved there, as he was under 16.

Although he is still domiciled in France, he was UK resident in 2018/19, was born in the UK and had a domicile of origin in the UK, therefore he is treated as deemed domiciled in the UK under condition A.

3   Petra has been resident in the UK from 2004/05 through to 2017/18 – that is 14 of the last 20 tax years. She is not deemed domiciled in 2018/19 but will become so in the following tax year.

Test your understanding 6

Professional conduct in relation to taxation – part 1

The answers are in the following paragraphs of the AAT guidelines 'Personal conduct in relation to taxation'.

1   3.3 – The taxpayer has primary responsibility to submit correct and complete returns to the best of her knowledge and belief.

2   5.1 – The term 'irregularity' is intended to include all errors whether the error is made by the client, the member, HMRC or any other party involved in a client's tax affairs.

3   6.31 – A member who receives a request for data, some of which she believes may be subject to privilege, should take independent legal advice on the position, unless expert in this area.

4   2.2 – To not allow bias, conflict of interest or undue influence of others to override professional or business judgements.

5   3.14 – A member should ensure that her client is adequately aware of the issues involved and their potential implications.

Test your understanding 7

Professional conduct in relation to taxation – part 2

The answers are in the following paragraphs of the AAT guidelines 'Personal conduct in relation to taxation'.

1   3.3 – The return may include reasonable estimates where necessary.

2   6.8 – Disclosure in response to informal requests not made under any statutory power to demand data can only be made with the client's permission.

3   4.6 – Clearly a member must never be knowingly involved in tax evasion, although, of course, it is appropriate to act for a client who is rectifying their affairs.

4   4.13 – Ultimately it is the client's decision as to what planning is appropriate having received advice and taking into account their own broader commercial objectives and ethical stance.

5   3.10 – Materiality does not extend beyond the accounting profits and cannot be applied when completing tax returns.

Test your understanding 8

Professional conduct in relation to taxation – part 3

The answers are in the following paragraphs of the AAT guidelines 'Personal conduct in relation to taxation'.

1   2.2 – When there is a legal or professional right or duty to disclose.

2   4.14 – The member should warn the client of the potential risks of proceeding without full advice and ensure that the restriction in the scope of the member's advice is recorded in writing.

3   5.2 – The client should be informed as soon as the member has knowledge of the possible irregularities.

4   3.4 – The member is responsible to the client for the accuracy of the return based on the information provided.

5   2.2 – To be straightforward and honest in all professional and business relationships.

 Test your understanding 9

Professional conduct in relation to taxation – part 4

The answers are in the following paragraphs of the AAT guidelines 'Personal conduct in relation to taxation'.

1   4.7 – Despite attempts by courts over the years to elucidate tax 'avoidance' and to distinguish this from acceptable tax planning or mitigation, there is no widely accepted definition.

2   5.8 – In any situation where a member has concerns about her own position, she should take specialist legal advice.

3   3.8 – Whether an amount is to be regarded as material depends upon the facts and circumstances of each case.

4   6.4 – Where a member no longer acts for a client, the member remains subject to the duty of confidentiality.

5   3.21 – It is essential that the member advises the client to review her tax return before it is submitted.

Test your understanding 10

Barque Ltd

In order to comply with the fundamental principles set out in 'Professional conduct in relation to taxation' we must:

— be straightforward and honest in our professional and business relationships; and

— comply with relevant laws and regulations and avoid any action that discredits the profession.

It is our firm's responsibility to provide the services set out in our engagement letter competently and with due care. It may be that, due to the terms of the letter, we owe a duty of care to Barque Ltd in respect of this matter. In such a situation we would have to state that we are unwilling to assist them and suggest that the company seeks alternative advice.

We can point out the potential risks and rewards of adopting a strategy which, in our opinion, is unlikely to be successful but it is up to Barque Ltd to decide on their tax strategy. If Barque Ltd decides to go ahead despite our advice, we should ensure that we have documented the restricted advice which we have given.

We should also ensure that we document all of our discussions on this matter so that we have a record to which we can refer in the future if necessary.

We should be aware that the involvement of the firm in aggressive tax planning could have a negative effect on the public's perception of the profession.

Finally, if we are of the opinion that the strategy which Barque Ltd intends to adopt amounts to tax evasion we should explain the implications of this to the company and, of course, have no involvement whatsoever in the proposals.

Test your understanding 11

Qual systems Ltd

In order to comply with the fundamental principles set out in 'Professional conduct in relation to taxation' we must:

–   be straightforward and honest in our professional and business relationships

–   respect the confidentiality of information acquired as a result of professional and business relationships and, therefore, not disclose any such information to third parties without proper and specific authority, unless there is a legal or professional right or duty to disclose; and

–   comply with relevant laws and regulations and avoid any action that discredits the profession.

The duty to respect the confidentiality of information still applies in relation to Qual Systems Ltd even though it is no longer a client.

A telephone call is an informal request for information as opposed to one that is statutory. Accordingly, we need permission from Qual Systems before we can provide the information requested. In addition, it may be advisable to ask HM Revenue and Customs to put the request in writing.

We should point out to Qual Systems Ltd that, although there is no obligation to comply with the request, it may be in their best interest to do so. In connection with this, we should advise the company of the possible consequences of refusing to provide the information, for example it may be superseded by a more onerous statutory request.

Appendix

Professional conduct in relation to taxation

Extracts relevant for Personal Tax (PLTX) unit AQ2016

Introduction

This document comprises data that you may need to consult during your Personal Tax computer-based assessment. The material can be consulted during the sample and live assessments through pop-up windows. It is made available here so you can familiarise yourself with the content before the test.

Do not take a print of this document into the exam room with you. Unless you need a printed version as part of reasonable adjustments for particular needs, in which case you must discuss this with your tutor at least six weeks before the assessment date.

This document may be changed to reflect periodical updates in the computer-based assessment, so please check you have the most recent version while studying. This version is for use in AAT assessments 1 January – 31 December 2019.

We are grateful to the Association of Accounting Technicians for permission to reproduce this reference material. The page numbering shown below has been updated to refer to the pages where the content can be found within the Kaplan text.

Contents

1 Interpretation and abbreviations

Context

Tax advisers operate in a complex business and financial environment. The increasing public focus on the role of taxation in wider society means a greater interest in the actions of tax advisers and their clients.

This guidance, written by the professional bodies for their members working in tax, sets out the hallmarks of a good tax adviser, and in particular the fundamental principles of behaviour that members are expected to follow.

Interpretation

1.1   In this guidance:

- 'Client' includes, where the context requires, 'former client'.

- 'Member' (and 'members') includes 'firm' or 'practice' and the staff thereof.

- For simplicity, 'she' and 'her' are used throughout but should be taken to include 'he' and 'his'.

- Words in the singular include the plural and words in the plural include the singular.

Abbreviations

1.2   The following abbreviations have been used:

CCAB	Consultative Committee of Accountancy Bodies
DOTAS	Disclosure of Tax Avoidance Schemes
GAAP	Generally Accepted Accounting Principles
GAAR	General Anti-Abuse Rule in Finance Act 2013
HMRC	Her Majesty's Revenue and Customs
MLRO	Money Laundering Reporting Officer
NCA	National Crime Agency (previously the Serious Organised Crime Agency, SOCA)
POTAS	Promoters of Tax Avoidance Schemes
SRN	Scheme Reference Number

2   Fundamental principles

Overview of the fundamental principles

2.1   Ethical behaviour in the tax profession is critical. The work carried out by a member needs to be trusted by society at large as well as by clients and other stakeholders. What a member does reflects not just on themselves but on the profession as a whole.

2.2   A member must comply with the following fundamental principles:

Integrity

To be straightforward and honest in all professional and business relationships.

Objectivity

To not allow bias, conflict of interest or undue influence of others to override professional or business judgements.

Professional competence and due care

To maintain professional knowledge and skill at the level required to ensure that a client or employer receives competent professional service based on current developments in practice, legislation and techniques and act diligently and in accordance with applicable technical and professional standards.

Confidentiality

To respect the confidentiality of information acquired as a result of professional and business relationships and, therefore, not disclose any such information to third parties without proper and specific authority, unless there is a legal or professional right or duty to disclose, nor use the information for the personal advantage of the member or third parties.

Professional behaviour

To comply with relevant laws and regulations and avoid any action that discredits the profession.

Each of these fundamental principles is discussed in more detail in the context of taxation services.

3 Tax returns

Definition of tax return (return)

3.1 For the purposes of this Chapter, the term 'return' includes any document or online submission of data that is prepared on behalf of the client for the purposes of disclosing to any taxing authority details that are to be used in the calculation of tax due by a client or a refund of tax due to the client or for other official purposes and, for example, includes:

- Self-assessment returns for income or corporation tax

- VAT and Customs returns

- PAYE returns

- Inheritance tax returns

- Returns or claims in respect of any other tax or duties where paid to the UK Government or any authority, such as a devolved government.

3.2 A letter giving details in respect of a return or as an amendment to a return including, for example, any voluntary disclosure of an error should be dealt with as if it was a return.

Taxpayer's responsibility

3.3 The taxpayer has primary responsibility to submit correct and complete returns to the best of her knowledge and belief. The return may include reasonable estimates where necessary. It follows that the final decision as to whether to disclose any issue is that of the client.

Member's responsibility

3.4 A member who prepares a return on behalf of a client is responsible to the client for the accuracy of the return based on the information provided.

3.5 In dealing with HMRC in relation to a client's tax affairs a member must bear in mind her duty of confidentiality to the client and that she is acting as the agent of her client. She has a duty to act in the best interests of her client.

3.6 A member must act in good faith in dealings with HMRC in accordance with the fundamental principle of integrity. In particular the member must take reasonable care and exercise appropriate professional scepticism when making statements or asserting facts on behalf of a client. Where acting as a tax agent, a member is not required to audit the figures in the books and records provided or verify information provided by a client or by a third party. A member should take care not to be associated with the presentation of facts she knows or believes to be incorrect or misleading nor to assert tax positions in a tax return which she considers have no sustainable basis.

3.7 When a member is communicating with HMRC, she should consider whether she needs to make it clear to what extent she is relying on information which has been supplied by the client or a third party.

Materiality

3.8 Whether an amount is to be regarded as material depends upon the facts and circumstances of each case.

3.9 The profits of a trade, profession, vocation or property business must be computed in accordance with GAAP subject to any adjustment required or authorised by law in computing profits for those purposes. This permits a trade, profession, vocation or property business to disregard non-material adjustments in computing its accounting profits. However, it should be noted that for certain small businesses an election may be made to use the cash basis instead.

3.10 The application of GAAP, and therefore materiality, does not extend beyond the accounting profits. Thus the accounting concept of materiality cannot be applied when completing tax returns (direct and indirect), for example when:

- computing adjustments required to accounting figures so as to arrive at taxable profits

- allocating income, expenses and outgoings across the relevant boxes on a self-assessment tax return

- collating the aggregate figures from all shareholdings and bank accounts for disclosure on tax returns.

Disclosure

3.11 If a client is unwilling to include in a tax return the minimum information required by law, the member should follow the guidance in Chapter 5 Irregularities. 3.12 – 3.18 give guidance on some of the more common areas of uncertainty over disclosure.

3.12 In general, it is likely to be in a client's own interests to ensure that factors relevant to her tax liability are adequately disclosed to HMRC because:

- her relationship with HMRC is more likely to be on a satisfactory footing if she can demonstrate good faith in her dealings with them; and

- she will reduce the risk of a discovery or further assessment and may reduce exposure to interest and penalties.

3.13 It may be advisable to consider fuller disclosure than is strictly necessary. The factors involved in making this decision include:

- the terms of the applicable law

- the view taken by the member

- the extent of any doubt that exists

- the manner in which disclosure is to be made; and

- the size and gravity of the item in question.

3.14 When advocating fuller disclosure than is strictly necessary a member should ensure that her client is adequately aware of the issues involved and their potential implications. Fuller disclosure should not be made unless the client consents to the level of disclosure.

3.15 Cases will arise where there is doubt as to the correct treatment of an item of income or expenditure, or the computation of a gain or allowance. In such cases a member ought to consider carefully what disclosure, if any, might be necessary. For example, additional disclosure should be considered where:

- a return relies on a valuation

- there is inherent doubt as to the correct treatment of an item, for example, expenditure on repairs which might be regarded as capital in whole or part, or the VAT liability of a particular transaction; or

- HMRC has published its interpretation or has indicated its practice on a point, but the client proposes to adopt a different view, whether or not supported by Counsel's opinion. The member should refer to the guidance on the Veltema case and 3.19.

3.16 A member who is uncertain whether her client should disclose a particular item or of its treatment should consider taking further advice before reaching a decision. She should use her best endeavours to ensure that the client understands the issues, implications and the proposed course of action. Such a decision may have to be justified at a later date, so the member's files should contain sufficient evidence to support the position taken, including contemporaneous notes of discussions with the client and/or with other advisers, copies of any second opinion obtained and the client's final decision. A failure to take reasonable care may result in HMRC imposing a penalty if an error is identified after an enquiry.

3.17 The 2012 case of Charlton clarified the law on discovery in relation to tax schemes disclosed to HMRC under DOTAS. The Upper Tribunal made clear that where the taxpayer has:

(i) disclosed details of a significant allowable loss claim

(ii) declared relatively modest income/gains; and/or

(iii) included the SRN issued by HMRC on the appropriate self-assessment tax return,

an HMRC officer of reasonable knowledge and skill would be expected to infer that the taxpayer had entered into a tax avoidance scheme (and that fuller details of such scheme would be contained in the relevant AAG1 Form). As a result, HMRC would be precluded, in most cases, from raising a discovery assessment in a situation where the client implemented the disclosed scheme and HMRC failed to open an enquiry within the required time.

3.18 It is essential where a member is involved in the preparation of a self-assessment tax return which includes a scheme disclosed under DOTAS that the member takes care to ensure:

- that the tax return provides sufficient details of any transactions entered into (in case the AAG1 Form is incomplete)

- that the SRN is recorded properly in the appropriate box included for this purpose on a self-assessment tax return; and

- the SRN is shown for the self-assessment return for each year in which the scheme is expected to give the client a tax advantage.

Supporting documents

3.19 For the most part, HMRC does not consider that it is necessary for a taxpayer to provide supporting documentation in order to satisfy the taxpayer's overriding need to make a correct return. HMRC's view is that, where it is necessary for that purpose, explanatory information should be entered in the 'white space' provided on the return. However, HMRC does recognise that the taxpayer may wish to supply further details of a particular computation or transaction in order to minimise the risk of a discovery assessment being raised at a later time.

3.20 Further HMRC guidance says that sending attachments with a tax return is intended for those cases where the taxpayer 'feels it is crucial to provide additional information to support the return but for some reason cannot utilise the white space'.

Approval of tax returns

3.21 It is essential that the member advises the client to review her tax return before it is submitted.

3.22 The member should draw the client's attention to the responsibility which the client is taking in approving the return as correct and complete. Attention should be drawn to any judgemental areas or positions reflected in the return to ensure that the client is aware of these and their implications before she approves the return.

3.23 A member should obtain evidence of the client's approval of the return in electronic or non-electronic form.

4 Tax advice

Introduction

4.1 Giving tax advice covers a variety of activities. It can involve advising a client on a choice afforded to her by legislation, for example, whether to establish a business as a sole trader, partnership or company. It could be advising on the tax implications of buying or selling an asset or business, or advising on succession planning.

4.2 For the most part clients are seeking advice on how to structure their affairs, either personal or commercial, in a way that is tax efficient and ensures that they comply with their legal and regulatory requirements. Transactions based on advice which are centred around non-tax objectives are less likely to attract scrutiny or criticism from stakeholders and are much more likely to withstand challenge by HMRC.

4.3 Some tax strategies have been the subject of heated public debate, raising ethical challenges. Involvement in certain arrangements could subject the client and the member to significantly greater compliance requirements, scrutiny or investigation as well as criticism from the media, government and other stakeholders and difficulties in obtaining professional indemnity insurance cover.

4.4 The definition of 'avoidance' is an evolving area that can depend on the tax legislation, the intention of Parliament, interpretations in case law and the varying perceptions of different stakeholders and is discussed further below.

4.5 A member should consider the contents of this Chapter carefully when giving tax advice and the potential negative impact of her actions on the public perception of the integrity of the tax profession more generally.

4.6 Clearly a member must never be knowingly involved in tax evasion, although, of course, it is appropriate to act for a client who is rectifying their affairs.

Tax planning vs tax avoidance?

4.7 Despite attempts by courts over the years to elucidate tax 'avoidance' and to distinguish this from acceptable tax planning or mitigation, there is no widely accepted definition.

4.8 Publicly, the term 'avoidance' is used in the context of a wide range of activities, be it multinational structuring or entering contrived tax-motivated schemes. The application of one word to a range of activities and behaviours oversimplifies the concept and has led to confusion.

4.9 In a 2012 paper on tax avoidance, the Oxford University Centre for Business Taxation states that transactions generally do not fall into clear categories of tax avoidance, mitigation or planning. Similarly, it is often not clear whether something is acceptable or unacceptable. Instead the paper concludes that there is:

'a continuum from transactions that would not be effective to save tax under the law as it stands at present to tax planning that would be accepted by revenue authorities and courts without question.'

Member's responsibility in giving tax planning advice

4.10 A member is required to act with professional competence and due care within the scope of her engagement letter.

4.11 A member should understand her client's expectations around tax advice or tax planning, and ensure that engagement letters reflect the member's role and responsibilities, including limitations in or amendments to that role. The importance of this has been highlighted by the Mehjoo case.

4.12 A member does not have to advise on or recommend tax planning which she does not consider to be appropriate or otherwise does not align with her own business principles and ethics. However, in this situation the member may need to ensure that the advice she does not wish to give is outside the scope of her engagement. If the member may owe a legal duty of care to the client to advise in this area, the member should ensure that she complies with this by, for example, advising the client that there are opportunities that the client could undertake, even though the member is unwilling to assist, and recommending that the client seeks alternative advice. Any such discussions should be well documented by the member.

4.13 Ultimately it is the client's decision as to what planning is appropriate having received advice and taking into account their own broader commercial objectives and ethical stance. However, the member should ensure that the client is made aware of the risks and rewards of any planning, including that there may be adverse reputational consequences. It is advisable to ensure that the basis for recommended tax planning is clearly identified in documentation.

4.14 Occasionally a client may advise a member that she intends to proceed with a tax planning arrangement without taking full advice from him on the relevant issues or despite the advice the member has given. In such cases the member should warn the client of the potential risks of proceeding without full advice and ensure that the restriction in the scope of the member's advice is recorded in writing.

4.15 Where a client wishes to pursue a claim for a tax advantage which the member feels has no sustainable basis the member should refer to Chapter 5 Irregularities for further guidance.

4.16 If Counsel's opinion is sought on the planning the member should consider including the question as to whether, in Counsel's view, the GAAR could apply to the transaction.

4.17 It should be noted that any legal opinion provided, for example by Counsel, will be based on the assumptions stated in the instructions for the opinion and on execution of the arrangement exactly as stated. HMRC and the courts will not be constrained by these assumptions.

The different roles of a Tax Adviser

4.18 A member may be involved in tax planning arrangements in the following ways:

- Advising on a planning arrangement.

- Introducing another adviser's planning arrangement.

- Providing a second opinion on a third party's planning arrangement.

- Compliance services in relation to a return which includes a planning arrangement. A member should always make a record of any advice given.

5 Irregularities

Introduction

5.1 For the purposes of this Chapter, the term 'irregularity' is intended to include all errors whether the error is made by the client, the member, HMRC or any other party involved in a client's tax affairs.

5.2 In the course of a member's relationship with the client, the member may become aware of possible irregularities in the client's tax affairs. Unless already aware of the possible irregularities in question, the client should be informed as soon as the member has knowledge of them.

5.3 Where the irregularity has resulted in the client paying too much tax the member should advise the client about making a repayment claim and have regard to any relevant time limits. With the exception of this paragraph, the rest of this Chapter deals solely with situations where sums may be due to HMRC.

5.4 On occasion, it may be apparent that an error made by HMRC has meant that the client has not paid tax actually due or she has been incorrectly repaid tax. Correcting such mistakes may cause expense to a member and thereby to her clients. A member should bear in mind that, in some circumstances, clients or agents may be able to claim for additional professional costs incurred and compensation from HMRC.

5.5 A member must act correctly from the outset. A member should keep sufficient appropriate records of discussions and advice and when dealing with irregularities the member should:

- Give the client appropriate advice

- If necessary, so long as she continues to act for the client, seek to persuade the client to behave correctly

- Take care not to appear to be assisting a client to plan or commit any criminal offence or to conceal any offence which has been committed; and

- In appropriate situations, or where in doubt, discuss the client's situation with a colleague or an independent third party.

5.6 Once aware of a possible irregularity, a member must bear in mind the legislation on money laundering and the obligations and duties which this places upon him.

5.7 A member should also consider whether the irregularity could give rise to a circumstance requiring notification to her professional indemnity insurers.

5.8 In any situation where a member has concerns about her own position, she should take specialist legal advice. This might arise, for example, where a client appears to have used the member to assist in the commission of a criminal offence in such a way that doubt could arise as to whether the member had acted honestly and in good faith.

5.9 The irregularity steps flowchart (5.10) summarises the recommended steps a member should take where a possible irregularity arises.

5.10 Steps to take if there is a possible irregularity

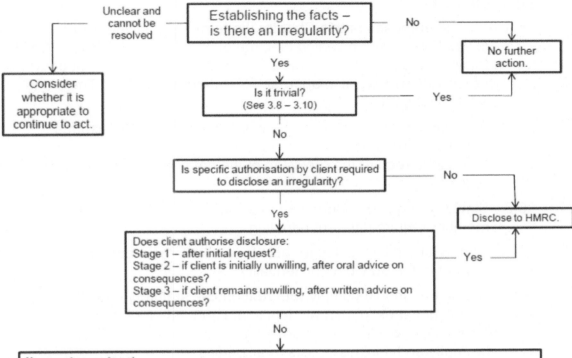

You must cease to act
- Advise client in writing that you no longer act for them in respect of any tax matters and, if relevant, other client matters.
- Notify HMRC that you have ceased to act, if relevant.
- Consider if you need to advise HMRC that any accounts/statements carrying a report signed by you can no longer be relied upon.
- Consider whether a report should be made to MLRO/NCA.
- Carefully consider your response to any professional enquiry letter.

At all times consider your obligations under anti-money laundering legislation and whether you need to submit a Suspicious Activity Report.

6 Access to data by HMRC

Introduction

6.1 For the purposes of this Chapter the term 'data' includes documents in whatever form (including electronic) and other information. While this guidance relates to HMRC requests, other government bodies or organisations may also approach the member for data. The same principles apply.

6.2 A distinction must be drawn between a request for data made informally and those requests for data which are made in exercise of a power to require the provision of the data requested ('statutory requests').

6.3 Similarly, requests addressed to a client and those addressed to a member require different handling.

6.4 Where a member no longer acts for a client, the member remains subject to the duty of confidentiality.

6.5 A member should comply with reasonable statutory requests and should not seek to frustrate legitimate requests for information. Adopting a constructive approach may help to resolve issues promptly and minimise costs to all parties.

6.6 Whilst a member should be aware of HMRC's powers in relation to the access, inspection and removal of data, given the complexity of the law relating to information powers, it may be appropriate to take specialist advice.

6.7 Revenue Scotland will have separate powers under the Revenue Scotland and Tax Powers Act 2014.

Informal requests addressed to the member

6.8 Disclosure in response to informal requests not made under any statutory power to demand data can only be made with the client's permission.

6.9 Sometimes the client will have authorised routine disclosure of relevant data, for example, through the engagement letter. However, if there is any doubt about whether the client has authorised disclosure or about the accuracy of details, the member should ask the client to approve what is to be disclosed.

6.10 Where an oral enquiry is made by HMRC, a member should consider asking for it to be put in writing so that a response may be agreed with the client.

6.11 Although there is no obligation to comply with an informal request in whole or in part, a member should advise the client whether it is in the client's best interests to disclose such data.

6.12 Informal requests may be forerunners to statutory requests compelling the disclosure of data. Consequently, it may be sensible to comply with such requests or to seek to persuade HMRC that a more limited request is appropriate. The member should advise the client as to the reasonableness of the informal request and likely consequences of not providing the data, so that the client can decide on her preferred course of action.

Informal requests addressed to the client

6.13 From time to time HMRC chooses to communicate directly with clients rather than with the appointed agent.

6.14 HMRC recognises the significant value which tax agents bring to both their clients and to the operation of the tax system. However, HMRC has also made it clear that on occasions it may deal with the taxpayer as well as, or instead of, the agent.

6.15 Examples of where HMRC may contact a member's client directly include:

- where HMRC is using 'nudge' techniques to encourage taxpayers or claimants to re-check their financial records or to change behaviour

- where HMRC has become aware of particular assets, such as offshore investments, and the taxpayer is encouraged to consider whether a further tax disclosure is required

- where the taxpayer has engaged in what HMRC considers to be a tax avoidance scheme, as HMRC considers that this will better ensure that the client fully understands HMRC's view.

6.16 HMRC has given reassurances that it is working to ensure that initial contact on compliance checks will normally be via the agent and only if the agent does not reply within an appropriate timescale will the contact be direct to the client.

6.17 When the member assists a client in dealing with such requests from HMRC, the member should apply the principles in 6.8 – 6.12.

Statutory requests addressed to the client

6.18 In advising the client a member should consider whether the notice is valid, how to comply with the request and the consequences of non-compliance. Specialist advice may be needed, for example on such issues as whether the notice has been issued in accordance with the relevant tax legislation, whether the data requested is validly included in the notice, legal professional privilege and human rights.

6.19 Even if the notice is not valid, in many cases the client may conclude that the practical answer is to comply. If the notice is legally effective the client is legally obliged to comply with the request.

6.20 The member should also advise the client about any relevant right of appeal against the statutory request if appropriate and of the consequences of a failure to comply.

Statutory requests addressed to the member

6.21 The same principles apply to statutory requests to the member as statutory requests to clients.

6.22 If a statutory request is valid it overrides the member's duty of confidentiality to her client.

6.23 In cases where the member is not legally precluded by the terms of the notice from communicating with the client, the member should advise the client of the notice and keep the client informed of progress and developments.

6.24 The member remains under a duty to preserve the confidentiality of her client, so care must be taken to ensure that in complying with any notice the member does not provide information or data outside the scope of the notice.

6.25 If a member is faced with a situation in which HMRC is seeking to enforce disclosure by the removal of data, the member should consider seeking immediate advice from a specialist adviser or other practitioner with relevant specialist knowledge, before permitting such removal, to ensure that this is the legally correct course of action.

6.26 Where a Schedule 36 notice is in point a member should note that it does not allow HMRC to inspect business premises occupied by a member in her capacity as an adviser. Specialist advice should be sought in any situation where HMRC asserts otherwise.

Privileged data

6.27 Legal privilege arises under common law and may only be overridden if this is expressly or necessarily implicitly set out in legislation. It protects a party's right to communicate in confidence with a legal adviser. The privilege belongs to the client and not to the member. If a document is privileged:

- The client cannot be required to make disclosure of that document to HMRC and a member should be careful to ensure that her reasons for advising a client nevertheless to make such a disclosure are recorded in writing.

- It must not be disclosed by any other party, including the member, without the client's express permission.

6.28 There are two types of legal privilege under common law, legal advice privilege covering documents passing between a client and her legal adviser prepared for the purposes of obtaining or giving legal advice and litigation privilege for data created for the dominant purpose of litigation. Litigation privilege may arise where litigation has not begun, but is merely contemplated and may apply to data prepared by non-lawyer advisers (including tax advisers) if brought into existence for the purposes of the litigation.

6.29 Communications from a tax adviser who is not a practising lawyer will not attract legal advice privilege but other similar protections exist under statute law, including:

- a privilege reporting exemption which applies to the reporting of money laundering in certain circumstances.

- a privilege under Schedule 36 whereby a tax adviser does not have to provide data that is her property and which constitute communications between the adviser and either her client or another tax adviser of the client. Information about such communications is similarly privileged. However, care should be taken as not all data may be privileged.

6.30 Whether data is or is not privileged and protected from the need to disclose is a complex issue, which will turn on the facts of the particular situation.

6.31 A member who receives a request for data, some of which she believes may be subject to privilege, should take independent legal advice on the position, unless expert in this area.

Principles of income tax

2

Introduction

In the assessment you will have to calculate the taxable income of an individual and the individual's income tax payable.

In this chapter we look at the basic pro forma income tax computation with a view to building this up over the next few chapters.

ASSESSMENT CRITERIA
Calculate income tax, combining all income into one schedule (3.3)

CONTENTS
1   Sources of income
2   Pro forma income tax computation

1 Sources of income

1.1 Main sources

Individuals essentially obtain income from two main sources.

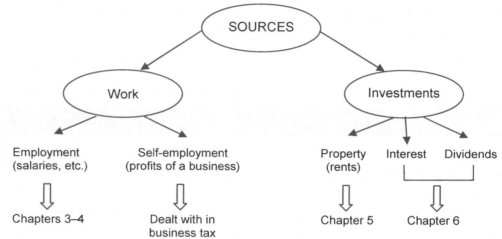

1.2 Classification of income

Income can either be classified as:

*   **taxable income** – which is shown on the income tax computation (section 2 below), or

*   **exempt income** – which is not shown on the income tax computation (1.5 below).

1.3 Taxable income

Each type of taxable income has a slightly different tax treatment.

The types of taxable income, which are each considered in detail in the following chapters, are:

Taxable income	Includes
Employment income	Salaries, wages, bonuses, benefits
Property income	Rents receivable less expenses of renting
Interest	Interest received from, for example, building societies, banks, etc.
Dividends	Dividends received from UK companies

The computation of income from self-employment is not considered in this study text as it is outside the scope of Personal Tax (it is covered in Business Tax).

Income from self-employment does, however, form part of an individual's taxable income. In an assessment question you will be told the amount of taxable self-employment income to include if necessary.

1.4 Deduction of tax at source

Income is always shown 'gross' in the income tax computation.

However, sometimes individuals receive income 'net' of tax. This means that the person paying the income has deducted tax before making the payment, and has paid the tax to HM Revenue and Customs (HMRC) on the individual's behalf.

These sources of income need to be 'grossed up' and the gross amount included in the income tax computation.

The common source of income received net of tax is salary from employment.

 Example

Amy's salary is £3,000 per month. The amount credited to her bank account each month, after deduction of PAYE, is £2,500, such that Amy receives £30,000 (£2,500 × 12) each year.

Amy's income tax computation must include her gross salary for the year of £36,000 (£3,000 × 12).

1.5 Exempt income

Exempt income, as stated earlier, does **not** go in the income tax computation.

Exempt income includes the following.

- Interest on NS&I Savings Certificates.

- Interest on Save As You Earn (SAYE) sharesave accounts.

- Interest on delayed income tax repayments.

- Interest, dividends and capital gains arising in respect of ISAs (individual savings accounts).

- Damages for personal injury or death.

- Scholarships and educational grants.

- Prizes, lottery winnings and gambling winnings.

- Statutory redundancy pay.

- Some social security benefits, including housing benefit, universal credit, working tax credit and child tax credit. Child benefit is also exempt but it triggers a tax charge for high income individuals. Calculation of this charge is not in the syllabus.

This is not a complete listing of exempt income, but does cover the main examples that appear in assessments.

2 Pro forma income tax computation

2.1 The main tax rates

For 2018/19 an individual must pay income tax on total taxable income at the basic, higher and additional rates.

Total taxable income is found by adding up the amounts of taxable income from all the different sources and deducting any available reliefs and allowances.

The basic rate of 20% is charged on the first £34,500 of taxable income.

The higher rate of 40% is charged on taxable income between £34,500 and £150,000.

The additional rate of 45% is charged on taxable income in excess of £150,000.

These tax rates are available for you to refer to in the assessment.

Taxable income in 2018/19

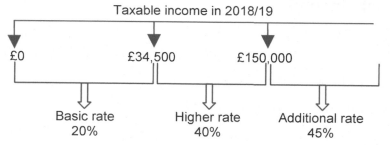

Special tax rates may apply to savings income and dividend income, as explained in the chapter on investment income, but other income is taxed at the above rates.

Example

An individual has taxable earned income of £150,400.

Calculate his income tax liability for 2018/19.

Solution

£		£ pp
34,500	× 20%	6,900.00
115,500	× 40%	46,200.00
400	× 45%	180.00
150,400		53,280.00

2.2 Pro forma income tax computation – overview

The following is an overview of the construction of a personal income tax computation.

It is essential to focus your attention on the key headings within the pro forma. They will be explained in more detail in the following chapters.

A Person

Income tax computation – 2018/19

	£
Earned income	X
Investment income	X
	—
Total income	X
Less: Reliefs	(X)
	—
Net income	X
Less: Personal allowance	(X)
	—
Taxable income	X
	—
Income tax liability	X
Less: Tax deducted at source	(X)
	—
Income tax payable	X
	—

A full pro forma is included the chapter on calculating income tax payable.

Test your understanding 1

Mark the following statements as true or false.

		True	False
1	Interest from a building society account is exempt from tax.		
2	Income from an ISA account is taxable.		
3	Income from employment is excluded from the income tax computation because it has been taxed under PAYE.		
4	The basic rate of income tax is 40%.		

3 Test your understanding

 Test your understanding 2

Ben has taxable earned income of £39,060.

What is his income tax liability for 2018/19?

Test your understanding 3

Mark the following statements as true or false.

		True	False
1	Income tax is payable on lottery winnings.		
2	Interest received in respect of a repayment of income tax from HM Revenue and Customs is taxable.		
3	Statutory redundancy pay of £5,000 is exempt from income tax.		
4	There are two rates of income tax on earned income – 20% and 45%.		

4 Summary

The chapter has prepared the foundations to gradually build up a full income tax computation by looking at:

- taxable income
- exempt income
- the pro forma income tax computation.

Test your understanding answers

Test your understanding 1

1 **False** – Interest from a building society account is taxable.

2 **False** – Income from an ISA is exempt.

3 **False** – The gross amount of the employment income should be included in the income tax computation.

4 **False** – The basic rate of income tax is 20%; 40% is the higher rate.

Test your understanding 2

The correct answer is **£8,724**

	£		£
34,500 × 20%			6,900
4,560 × 40%			1,824
	39,060		8,724

Test your understanding 3

1 **False** – Lottery winnings are exempt.

2 **False** – Interest in respect of a tax repayment is exempt.

3 **True** – Statutory redundancy pay is exempt from income tax.

4 **False** – There are three rates of income tax on earned income; 20%, 40% and 45%.

Introduction to employment income

Introduction

The assessment will test the different elements of an individual's employment income.

This will include some or all of the following:

	£
Cash income	X
Benefits (Chapter 4)	X
Less: Allowable expenses	(X)
Employment income	X

We will first cover the taxation of cash income and the deduction of expenses. We will then cover benefits in Chapter 4.

ASSESSMENT CRITERIA	CONTENTS
Calculate employment income, including salaries, wages, commissions and bonuses (2.1) Identify and calculate allowable and exempt expenses (2.1)	1 Employment status 2 Earnings 3 Allowable expenses and deductions 4 The PAYE system

1 Employment status

1.1 Introduction

An individual who works may be either an employee or self-employed (including business partners).

It is important to distinguish between the two because an employee is taxable on his employment income whilst a self-employed individual is taxable on his trading profits. The rules for the two types of income are different.

This text is concerned only with the calculation of employment income; the calculation of trading income is dealt with in the business tax paper.

1.2 Contract of service

In many instances it will be a straightforward matter to decide whether an individual is an employee or is self-employed. If it is not clear, there are various matters to take into account.

HM Revenue and Customs (HMRC) may be asked to give a status ruling to ensure that there is no doubt. The HMRC online Employment Status Indicator can also be used to determine the status of an individual.

The basic distinction is that an employee has a **contract of service**, whereas a self-employed person will have a **contract for services**.

Some of the features of a contract of service are:

- The employer is under an obligation to offer work and the employee is under an obligation to carry it out.

- The employer will control how the work is carried out.

- The employee will be committed to work a specified number of hours at fixed times and places.

- The employee must do the work himself; he cannot arrange for someone else to do it.

- The employee does not take any financial risk.

- An employee does not usually have to provide their own equipment.

- Employees are entitled to paid holidays and sickness benefits.

Test your understanding 1

For each statement, tick either employment or self-employment:

	Employment	Self-employment
Contract of service is for:		
Contract for services is for:		
A high level of control by another over the work performed would indicate what type of relationship?		

2 Earnings

2.1 Types of income

Employment income covers all earnings received from an employment. Such income includes salaries, wages, bonuses, commissions, directors' fees, tips, certain expense allowances and reimbursed expenses, and benefits.

Benefits are dealt with in Chapter 4.

Any pension income resulting from an employment is also taxable non-savings income.

2.2 Basis of assessment

The expression 'basis of assessment' means which income should we tax in which tax year.

The basis of assessment for employment income is the **receipts basis**.

This means that income is taxed in the tax year in which an employee receives it or becomes entitled to the payment, if earlier.

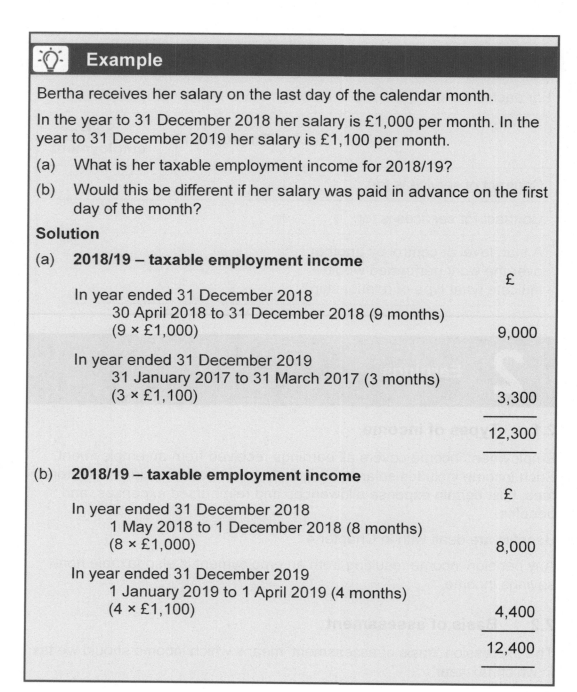

Example

Bertha receives her salary on the last day of the calendar month.

In the year to 31 December 2018 her salary is £1,000 per month. In the year to 31 December 2019 her salary is £1,100 per month.

(a) What is her taxable employment income for 2018/19?

(b) Would this be different if her salary was paid in advance on the first day of the month?

Solution

(a) **2018/19 – taxable employment income**

		£
In year ended 31 December 2018		
30 April 2018 to 31 December 2018 (9 months)		
(9 × £1,000)		9,000
In year ended 31 December 2019		
31 January 2017 to 31 March 2017 (3 months)		
(3 × £1,100)		3,300
		12,300

(b) **2018/19 – taxable employment income**

		£
In year ended 31 December 2018		
1 May 2018 to 1 December 2018 (8 months)		
(8 × £1,000)		8,000
In year ended 31 December 2019		
1 January 2019 to 1 April 2019 (4 months)		
(4 × £1,100)		4,400
		12,400

2.3   Expenses

Broadly speaking, expense allowances and reimbursed expenses are taxable income.

A deduction is available for allowable expenses incurred by the employee as set out in section 3 below. Where allowable expenses are incurred by the employee and reimbursed by the employer, the reimbursed income is exempt, as set out in section 3.4.

2.4 Bonuses

One of the main areas that can cause problems is bonuses.

Many individuals receive bonuses (for example sales representatives). The bonus may be based on the employer's accounting period (e.g. sales made in that period). However, the employee may not be entitled to payment until after the end of the period.

Remember that employees are taxed based on the receipts basis which is deemed to be the earlier of:

- Date of receipt
- Date employee became entitled to receipt.

There are special rules for directors, earnings are treated as received on the earlier of:

- Date of receipt
- Date director became entitled to receipt
- The date the amount is credited to the accounting records of the company
- The last day of the company's period of account (if the amount has been determined before then)
- The date the amount is determined (if determined after the end of the company's period of account).

 Example

Gordon is a salesman working for Jones Ltd. He is entitled to a bonus each year based on the sales he has made in the company's accounting period ended 31 December.

His recent bonuses have been as follows:

For the year ended	Date of payment/entitlement	£
31 December 2016	10 April 2017	8,000
31 December 2017	8 April 2018	10,000
31 December 2018	4 April 2019	9,500
31 December 2019	8 April 2020	7,500

What is the amount of taxable bonus in 2018/19?

Solution

The taxable amount is the amount received by Gordon in 2018/19.

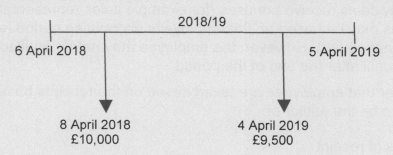

2018/19

6 April 2018   5 April 2019

8 April 2018   4 April 2019
£10,000   £9,500

Hence the total taxable bonus in 2018/19 is £19,500.

Note that no bonus will be taxable in 2019/20.

3   Allowable expenses and deductions

3.1   Principle of allowable expenses

Allowable expenses are those that can be deducted from earnings to arrive at the taxable employment income.

3.2   Wholly, exclusively and necessarily

The general rule for an expense to be deducted from earnings is that it must be incurred 'wholly, exclusively and necessarily' in the performance of the duties of employment.

If in doubt about an expense in the assessment, return to this rule to seek guidance.

The expense **cannot** be deducted **just** because it makes the job easier.

Example

A bank manager joined a golf club with a view to taking potential clients there. In his opinion it would make his job easier because in the relaxed atmosphere the potential clients would be more likely to put business his way.

Are the membership fees an allowable expense?

Solution

No.

The expense is not wholly, exclusively and necessarily incurred in the performance of the duties of employment.

NECESSARY – No, he could try to win business at his office. It is not necessary to play golf to be a bank manager!

EXCLUSIVELY – No, he could also go to the golf club in his own private time.

3.3 Other specific allowable expenses

Set out below are specific expenses that are allowable.

- **Costs of business travel and subsistence.**

  Business travel includes journeys made in the performance of an employee's duties. It does not include travel between home and the permanent workplace (i.e. ordinary commuting).

  However, special rules apply if an employee uses his own vehicle for business travel.

  Under the 'Approved Mileage Allowance Payments' (AMAP) system, only amounts paid in excess of the approved rates are taxable.

  If the amounts paid are lower, the employee can claim the shortfall as an allowable expense.

  The approved rates are:

  Cars

First 10,000 business miles per tax year	45p per mile
Additional mileage	25p per mile
Additional passengers (per passenger)	5p per mile
Motor cycles	24p per mile
Bicycles	20p per mile

  These figures are available for you to refer to in the assessment.

> **Example**
>
> John has travelled 12,000 business miles in 2018/19 in his own car. His employer pays 42p per mile.
>
> (a) How much of the mileage allowance is taxable?
>
> (b) How would your answer differ if John's employer paid 38p per mile?
>
> **Solution**
>
> (a) Taxable mileage allowance
>
> | | £ | £ |
> |---|---|---|
> | Income (12,000 × 42p) | | 5,040 |
> | Less: Allowable expense | | |
> | 10,000 × 45p | 4,500 | |
> | 2,000 × 25p | 500 | |
> | | ——— | (5,000) |
> | Taxable amount | | 40 |
>
> (b) If John's employer paid 38p per mile, the total amount received by John would be 12,000 × 38p = £4,560.
>
> John could deduct the shortfall of £440 (£5,000 – £4,560) as an allowable expense.

- **Professional subscriptions.**

  Professional subscriptions (e.g. annual subscriptions to AAT, subscriptions to trade associations, etc.) are allowable expenses. Compare this to golf club subscriptions mentioned earlier.

- **Amounts donated under the payroll deduction scheme.**

  Under this scheme employees can have sums deducted from their salary on a weekly/monthly basis by their employer and paid directly to charity. This is also referred to as payroll giving or Give As You Earn.

- **Contributions to company pension schemes.**

  Where an individual contributes to the employer's own company pension scheme (also known as an 'occupational pension scheme'), the amount contributed is deducted directly from wages/salaries.

  The amount deducted is an allowable expense (see more on pensions in Chapter 8).

  Contributions to the pension scheme by the employer are an exempt benefit (see Chapter 4).

- **Entertaining.**

  Where an employee incurs entertaining costs, (e.g. for entertaining clients), he will usually reclaim the costs from the employer. This reimbursement of allowable expenses is not taxable income (see section 3.4 below).

  Alternatively, he may have a regular specific 'entertaining allowance' which is always spent in its entirety on entertaining, e.g. £100 per month. Again, there will be no taxable income.

  However, if the employee pays for entertaining costs out of a general round sum allowance, the employee cannot claim a deduction for the entertaining expenses that he has incurred. Any part of the round sum allowance used to pay for other, tax deductible, expenses, such as business travel, will be exempt.

3.4 Reimbursement of employee's expenses by employer

Where an employer pays expenses on behalf of an employee or reimburses expenses to an employee the amounts concerned are taxable income for the employee unless the following exemption is available.

The exemption is available where the employee would be able to claim a tax deduction for the business related expenses under the rules set out above e.g. business travel, professional subscriptions, expenses which fall within the wholly, exclusively and necessarily provisions.

There is no need to report such exempt expenses to HMRC.

Where an expense is partly allowable and partly disallowable, then the exemption can be applied to the allowable part. For example, where an employee's home telephone bill is fully reimbursed, the exemption can be applied to the business calls, but not to the private calls and the line rental.

Reimbursed expenses which are not exempt must be reported to HMRC using a form P11D and included on the employee's tax return.

3.5 Flat rate payments

An employer can apply to HMRC for approval to reimburse tax free expenses at a flat rate or use HMRC tax-free benchmark rates (e.g. £5 subsistence allowance whilst travelling on company business, see Chapter 4).

The employer must have a system in place to check that the employee is actually incurring the expenses covered by the flat rate allowance.

3.6 Pro forma employment income computation – 2018/19

	£
Salary/fees/commission/bonus etc.	X
Non- exempt expense allowances and reimbursed expenses	X
Benefits (see Chapter 4)	X
	X
Less: Professional subscriptions	(X)
Donations under payroll giving schemes	(X)
Occupational pension scheme contributions	(X)
Entertaining expenses (where reimbursed or paid from a specific entertaining allowance)	(X)
Expenses incurred wholly, exclusively and necessarily in the performance of duties	(X)
Taxable employment income	X

Test your understanding 2

Underwood

Underwood is employed as an insurance salesman at a monthly salary of £1,450.

In addition to his basic salary he receives a bonus which is paid in May each year and which is related to the sales achieved by Underwood in the year to the previous 31 October.

His bonuses are as follows:

Bonus for year to	Paid during	£
31 October 2016	May 2017	1,920
31 October 2017	May 2018	1,260
31 October 2018	May 2019	2,700

Underwood made the following payments in respect of his employment in 2018/19.

	£
Contribution to occupational pension scheme	342
Subscription to Chartered Insurance Institute	100
Payroll giving scheme (in favour of Oxfam)	200
Gym membership – often meets clients at the gym	150

Using the following pro forma calculate Underwood's taxable employment income for 2018/19.

	£
Salary	
Bonus	
	————
Less: Allowable expenses	
	————
Taxable employment income	
	————

4 The PAYE system

4.1 Principle of the PAYE system

The PAYE system collects income tax at source from the earnings of employees. Employers deduct the income tax liabilities of their employees before paying them their salaries. The tax deducted is then paid to HMRC.

The aim of the PAYE system is to remove the requirement to submit a tax return from as many people as possible (i.e. all of their tax is deducted at source by their employer and paid to HMRC on their behalf).

The PAYE system will not be examined in the Personal Tax assessment.

Test your understanding 3

Mark each of the following statements as true or false.

		True	False
1	Sally is paid her bonus for the year ended 31 December 2017 in May 2018. Her bonus will be taxed partly in 2017/18 and partly in 2018/19.		
2	If Chen Li is paid 50p a mile by his employer for business mileage, there will be no tax consequences.		
3	Gail is employed as an electrician. Her subscription for the Financial Times is an allowable employment expense.		

5 Test your understanding

 Test your understanding 4

Egbert is the sales director of Pinafores Limited.

The company paid the following expenses in relation to Egbert in the year ended 5 April 2019:

	£
Sums reimbursed to Egbert:	
Business entertainment	46
Travelling and subsistence (all business related) – fares, hotels, meals etc.	938
General expenses allowance paid to Egbert	500

Egbert advises you that 35% of the general expenses allowance was used in entertaining customers and the balance was spent on business travelling.

Required:

How will each of these amounts be treated when calculating Egbert's income tax liability for 2018/19?

Test your understanding 5

Alan is the finance director of a large company and incurred the following costs during 2018/19.

Which one is deductible from his employment income?

A   Subscription to the local health club where he often meets clients

B   Travel between the two offices of his employer

C   Tips to taxi drivers if he chooses to take taxis home from work

D   Cost of two new suits bought to impress clients

 Test your understanding 6

Charles Thackery has the following income for 2018/19:

		£
(a)	Salary as a sales representative paid on the last day of the month:	
	year ending 31 December 2018	16,000
	year ending 31 December 2019	18,000
(b)	Bonus based on the company profits for the accounting year to:	
	30 September 2018 (paid 1 December 2018)	600
	30 September 2019 (paid 1 December 2019)	900
(c)	Mileage allowance paid (8,000 miles @ 50p)	4,000
	The allowance was only paid for business mileage.	

Based on the information above, answer the following questions:

1   What is the taxable salary for 2018/19?

2   What is the taxable bonus for 2018/19?

3   What is the taxable/allowable mileage allowance for 2018/19?

Test your understanding 7

Bartholomew has been employed by Telnet TV Ltd in central London for several years as a television producer.

The following information is available for the year 2018/19:

(1)   His annual salary is £52,000.

(2)   On 31 May 2018 he received a bonus of £7,644 in respect of the company's year ended 31 March 2018.

   The bonus for the company's year ended 31 March 2019, paid on 31 May 2019, was £10,400.

(3)   Telnet TV Ltd has a registered occupational pension scheme to which it contributes 10% of employees' basic salary. Bartholomew is required to contribute 5% of his basic salary.

Required:

Calculate the amount of employment income taxable on Bartholomew for 2018/19 using the following pro forma.

	£
Salary	
Bonus	
	___
Less: Pension contributions	
	___
Taxable employment income	
	___

 Test your understanding 8

Mel earns a salary of £45,000 per year as a copywriter for Columbus Ltd. Columbus Ltd prepares accounts to 31 March each year.

For the last two years, Mel has earned bonuses from her employer as follows:

	Paid	£
Year ended 31 March 2018	1 June 2018	8,000
Year ended 31 March 2019	1 June 2019	11,000

In addition, Mel incurred expenses in travelling to client's offices of £2,000 in 2018/19, which were not reimbursed by her employer.

What is Mel's taxable employment income for 2018/19?

6 Summary

The important aspects of this chapter are:

- **Basis of assessment** – when employment income is taxed.

  Bonuses are often tested here. Remember that all employment income, including bonuses, is taxable on the earlier of the date of receipt or entitlement to receipt.

- **Allowable expenses** – these are often included in an assessment.

Remember that for the expense to be allowable it must be incurred 'wholly, exclusively and necessarily' in the performance of the duties of the employment.

Test your understanding answers

 ### Test your understanding 1

Contract of service is for employment.

Contract for services is for self-employment.

A high level of control would indicate employment.

 ### Test your understanding 2

Underwood

Underwood's taxable employment income for 2018/19 is as follows:

	£	£
Basic salary (£1,450 × 12)		17,400
Bonus paid in May 2018		1,260
		18,660
Less: Allowable expenses		
Pension scheme	342	
Subscription	100	
Payroll giving scheme	200	
		(642)
Taxable employment income		18,018

 ### Test your understanding 3

1 **False** – The bonus will be taxed in 2018/19.

2 **False** – A mileage allowance of 50p per mile would result in an excess amount taxable on Chen Li.

3 **False** – It is not wholly, exclusively and necessarily incurred.

Test your understanding 4

Egbert

Treatment of expenses – 2018/19

Amounts paid to or on behalf of Egbert in respect of expenses are taxable and should be included in his employment income unless they are also allowable deductions from employment income.

Business entertainment expenses are allowable deductions from employment income unless they are paid out of a general expense allowance.

Business related travel and subsistence expenses are also allowable deductions from employment income.

Accordingly, all of the amounts are exempt income apart from the 35% of the general expenses allowance spent on entertaining.

Egbert will have taxable employment income of £175 (£500 × 35%).

Test your understanding 5

Only **B** is deductible.

Test your understanding 6

1   The answer is £16,500 (9/12 × £16,000 + 3/12 × £18,000)

2   The answer is £600 which is the bonus received in 2018/19

3   The answer is £400 taxable
    = 8,000 × (50p received – 45p allowed)

Test your understanding 7

Bartholomew

Taxable employment income – 2018/19

	£
Salary	52,000
Bonus (received) – May 2018	7,644
	59,644
Pension contributions (5% paid by employee) (employer's contribution is not taxable)	(2,600)
Taxable employment income	57,044

Test your understanding 8

The correct answer is £51,000.

	£
Salary	45,000
Bonus (received) – June 2018	8,000
	53,000
Less: Travelling expenses	(2,000)
Taxable employment income	51,000

Employment income – benefits

Introduction

In this chapter we look at the different types of benefits received by employees and how they are taxed.

This is an important area of the syllabus and is always likely to be tested in the assessment.

ASSESSMENT CRITERIA
Calculate taxable benefits (2.1)
Identify exempt benefits (2.1)
Change benefits to make them more tax efficient (3.5)

CONTENTS
1   General rules
2   Exempt benefits
3   Taxable benefits

1 General rules

1.1 Introduction

Taxable benefits are added to an employee's salary and bonus when calculating employment income (section 3 below).

Certain benefits are specifically exempt from income tax (section 2 below).

It is likely that benefits will be tested in every assessment.

1.2 General points

Before we consider the specific benefits, here are some general points which are likely to be tested frequently.

- If an employee makes a payment to his employer in respect of a benefit, the taxable amount is reduced by the payment.

	£
Value of benefit	X
Less: Contribution by employee towards the benefit	(X)
Taxable benefit	X

The only exception to this rule is that partial payments for private fuel cannot be deducted (covered later).

- An employee may be able to claim that a benefit (or part of it) was provided wholly, exclusively and necessarily for the purposes of the employment. Such benefits are not subject to income tax.

- For most benefits, **time apportion** the taxable amount if the benefit was only available for part of the tax year.

- This adjustment should be calculated in **months** and is likely to be a popular adjustment in assessment questions.

2 Exempt benefits

2.1 Types of exempt benefit

Information on the following exempt benefits is available for you to refer to in the assessment.

- Job related accommodation (see 3.3 below).

- Subsidised canteen provided it is available to all staff.

- Removal expenses up to £8,000 for a new employment or if an employee's job is relocated. This can include hotel costs whilst looking for somewhere to live, legal and estate agents' fees and any other costs related to the removal. There is a time limit such that if an employee needs to move in 2018/19 then expenses must be incurred or benefits provided by the end of 2019/20. If removal expenses exceed £8,000 then only the excess is taxable on the employee.

- Personal expenses (e.g. telephone calls home, newspapers, laundry) paid by the employer whilst the employee is required to stay away on business. The payment limits are up to £5 per night in the UK and £10 per night for overseas. The payments can be averaged over a single trip, e.g. an employee incurs costs of £14 for a three night trip, which is under £15 (5 × 3), therefore the whole amount is exempt, even if the employee spent more than £5 on one night. If the total payments for a trip exceed these limits then the **whole** amount is taxable, e.g. if an employer reimburses expenses of £22 for a four night trip then the whole £22 is taxable.

- Workplace nurseries (crèches) (provided by the employer). These can be at the workplace or in other premises that the employer manages and finances.

- Vouchers for childcare provided by an **approved** child carer subject to a maximum depending on the tax status of the employee:
  - Basic rate taxpayers — the first £55 per week
  - Higher rate taxpayers — the first £28 per week
  - Additional rate taxpayers — the first £25 per week

- From 6 April 2017 qualifying taxpayers can open a tax-free childcare account. For each £8 paid into the account, HMRC will contribute an additional £2 subject to a maximum of £2,000 a year per child (£4,000 for a disabled child.) The money can then be used to pay for approved childcare.

- Sport and recreational facilities available to all staff but not to the public generally. The facilities can also be used by former employees and employees' families.

- The provision of one mobile telephone per employee (including smartphones). Tablets and computers used to make telephone calls are not exempt because they use the internet to make the calls.

- Contributions by an employer towards the additional household costs incurred by an employee working from home instead of at the employer's premises of up to £4 per week/£18 per month. Only payments above the limit require supporting evidence.

- A long service award of £50 for each year of service provided service is at least 20 years. The award must not be in cash and the recipient must not have had an award within the previous 10 years.

- The funding of an annual party or similar event (e.g. Christmas office party or staff summer outing) up to £150 per attendee per tax year. If the event costs more than £150 per head none of the amount is exempt. If employees attend two events with total costs more than £150 then only one of the events (with a cost below £150) can be exempt. The more expensive of the two events should be chosen for the exemption.

- Awards in accordance with a staff suggestion scheme. These reward employees for suggestions that improve the employer's business and which are not made as part of the employee's normal job. Awards up to a maximum of £5,000 can be exempt.

- Non-cash gifts received from someone other than the employer and costing no more than £250 per donor per tax year. The gift must not be in recognition of particular services by the employee in the course of employment.

- The provision of an annual private medical and/or a health screening.

- Parking spaces at or near place of work – for cars, bicycles or motorcycles.

- Provision of eye care tests and/or corrective glasses for visual display units (VDU) use.

- Low-rate or interest free loans, provided the total loans to an employee do not exceed £10,000 at any time during the tax year (see section 3.7).

- An employee who attends a full time course can receive tax free pay of up to £15,480 per academic year.

The following benefits are also exempt from income tax, but no information in respect of these benefits is provided in the assessment.

- Contributions by an employer to a registered pension scheme.

- The expenses of work related training borne by the employer including associated costs such as books.

- Trivial benefits (except vouchers) with a cost to the employer of less than £50 per gift and which are not provided in recognition of services provided by the employee. This exemption applies to low value benefits given for non-work reasons, for example, birthday gifts.

- Retraining courses for employees made redundant to provide them with skills to get a new job or become self-employed.

- The occasional provision of a late night taxi where an employee is required to work later than usual.

- Private medical insurance for employees working overseas.

- The provision of bicycles or cycling safety equipment to enable employees to get to and from work, provided they are available to staff generally.

- Works buses used to transport employees to/from work and available to employees generally. Employers can also provide subsidies to local bus companies to assist them in running services to help employees travel to/from work. In return the employees receive free or reduced fares.

- Scholarships provided by an employer to a family member of an employee are **not** exempt if the payment is provided by reason of the employment – that is the payment would not have been made if the employee did not work for the employer. However, scholarships can be exempt if they meet the following conditions:

  - The scholarship would still have been awarded even if the employee had not worked for the employer.

  - The recipient is in full time education.

  - The payment is made from a trust fund or a special scheme.

  - No more than 25% of the fund is used to provide scholarships linked to employment.

3 Taxable benefits

3.1 General rule for taxable benefits

The general rule is that the taxable amount of a benefit is:

> Cost to the employer of providing the benefit
>
> less any amount contributed towards the cost by the employee

These rules apply where, for example, an employer pays for private health insurance, for membership of a sports club for an employee or the payment by an employer of an employee's liabilities (e.g. telephone bill).

This rule applies even if, thanks to the employer's buying power, the employer's cost is less than the price an employee would have to pay.

3.2 Specific rules

There are specific rules in respect of the following:

Type of benefit	Amount taxable
Cash vouchers	Cash receivable when cashed in
Non-cash vouchers (includes transport vouchers, cheque vouchers)	Cost of voucher to the employer
Credit cards	Whatever private expenses the employee charges to the card but does not reimburse (but not interest and annual fee)
Accommodation	Section 3.3 below
Company cars	Section 3.4 below
Fuel provided for company cars	Section 3.5 below
Vans	Section 3.6 below
Beneficial loans	Section 3.7 below
Use of assets	Section 3.8 below
Gifts of assets	Section 3.9 below

3.3   Accommodation

The taxable benefit amount depends on whether or not the accommodation is 'job related'.

Accommodation is 'job related':

(a)   if it is **necessary** for the proper performance of employment duties

(b)   if it is provided for the **better performance** of duties and it is **customary** to provide accommodation in such circumstances

(c)   if there is a **special security** threat and the accommodation is part of the arrangements to counter the threat.

'Job related' therefore includes accommodation provided for caretakers, hotel staff, clergy and certain members of the government.

A director can only claim exemption under (a) or (b) if:

*   he has no material interest in the company, and

*   he is a full time working director or the company is a non-profit making organisation.

The calculation of the taxable benefit is split into three parts.

3.3.1   Part 1 – Basic charge

The basic charge for being provided with accommodation is:

Not job related	Job related
Higher of (i) Annual value of the property (also known as gross rateable value or market rental value), which will be provided in the question, and (ii) rent paid by employer (where the property is rented rather than owned by the employer).	Exempt benefit

Example

Harry is provided with a flat to live in by his employer (it is not job related accommodation).

The flat has an annual value of £2,000 and the employer pays rent of £200 per month.

Harry contributes £50 per month towards the private use of the flat.

Required:

What is his taxable benefit in 2018/19?

Solution

	£	£
Basic charge		
Higher of (i) annual value; and	2,000	
(ii) rent paid by employer (12 × £200)	2,400	
	——	2,400
Less: Contribution by employee		
(as mentioned in 1.2 above) (12 × £50)		(600)
		——
Taxable benefit		1,800
		——

3.3.2   Part 2 – Expensive accommodation charge

If the accommodation provided is purchased by the company and cost more than £75,000, it is deemed to be 'expensive'.

The £75,000 figure is available for you to refer in the assessment.

An additional benefit may apply as follows:

Not job related	Job related
(Cost – £75,000) × Official rate of interest	Exempt benefit

The official rate of interest is set annually by HMRC and is 2.5% in the tax year 2018/19. The rate will be given to you in the assessment.

Cost includes any improvements made to the property before 6 April in the tax year for which the benefit is being calculated. So if the benefit is being calculated for 2018/19, then all improvement costs incurred up to 5 April 2018 must be included in the 'cost' figure.

Example

Jack was provided with a house to live in by his employer throughout 2018/19 (not job related). It cost his employer £150,000 in June 2013. An extension was added in May 2016 costing £50,000. The house has an annual value of £3,000.

Required:

What is the taxable benefit for 2018/19?

Solution

	£	£
Basic charge		
Higher of (i) annual value; and	3,000	
(ii) rent paid by employer (owned)	Nil	
	——	3,000
Expensive accommodation		
((£150,000 + £50,000) – £75,000) × 2.5%		3,125
		——
Taxable benefit		6,125

If the accommodation was purchased by the company more than 6 years before the employee moves in, then a different rule applies.

Cost is replaced by the market value of the property at the date the employee moves in, plus the cost of any improvements made after the employee moves in but before the 6 April in the tax year of calculation.

 Example

Sanjay was provided with a house to live in by his employer. It is not job related accommodation. The house cost £100,000 when the company bought it in December 2008.

Sanjay moved in during March 2016 when the property was worth £210,000. In July 2018 an extension was built on the house costing £32,000.

What is the 'expensive' accommodation charge in Sanjay's benefit calculation for 2018/19?

Solution

The answer:

(£210,000 – £75,000) × 2.5% = £3,375

Since the employer bought the house more than 6 years before Sanjay moved in, the cost is replaced by market value at March 2016.

The cost of the extension in July 2018 is ignored for 2018/19. It will be included in the 'expensive' accommodation benefit calculation for 2019/20 and thereafter.

3.3.3 Part 3 – Provision of services

Not job related	Job related
Use of furniture	
– 20% per annum of market value when first provided (usually cost)	The same as not job related
Household expenses	– but restricted to:
(e.g. heating, maintenance, decorating, but not capital improvements)	10% of **other** employment income
– cost to employer	– The restriction will be given to you in the assessment.

Example

Amy is a hotel manager and is provided with accommodation on the site of the hotel (job related). Her annual salary is £25,000. She has other benefits of £500 and makes payments into her employer's registered occupational pension scheme of £2,000 per annum.

The accommodation has an annual value of £1,500 and cost her employer £90,000 four years ago. The accommodation contains furniture which cost her employer £10,000 four years ago (when she first moved into the accommodation). The employer pays all of her household bills totalling £1,000.

Required:

Calculate the taxable accommodation benefit for 2018/19.

Solution

	£
Basic charge (exempt)	Nil
Expensive accommodation charge (exempt)	Nil
Provision of services – furniture (20% × £10,000)	2,000
– household bills	1,000
Total	3,000
Restricted to (10% × other employment income)	
(10% × £23,500) (W)	2,350

Working: Other employment income

	£
Salary	25,000
Other benefits	500
Less: Allowable expenses	(2,000)
	23,500

There are many places to go wrong in calculating an accommodation benefit.

Before starting to calculate consider all the factors that can impact it (e.g. does it cost more than £75,000, is it owned or rented by the employer, is it job related, and was it bought by the employer more than 6 years before the employee moved in?).

Test your understanding 1

Mr X

Mr X has a salary of £30,000 and lives in a furnished company flat that cost his employers £105,000 in June 2013.

The annual value of the flat is £2,400 and Mr X pays his employer rent of £100 a month. The accommodation is not job related. Furniture costing £6,500 was first provided in June 2013.

Required:

Which is the correct figure for Mr X's taxable benefit for 2018/19?

Test your understanding 2

Read the following statements which relate to the provision of accommodation for an employee which is not job related.

Mark each statement as true or false.

		True	False
1	Furniture provided by an employer for use by an employee is taxed at 20% per annum of the market value when first made available.		
2	Furniture provided by an employer for use by an employee is taxed on 20% of the cost to the employer in the year of purchase.		
3	The running costs of the accommodation which are paid for by the employer are taxed on the employee at 20% of their total cost.		
4	The running costs of the accommodation which are paid for by the employer are taxed on the employee at their total cost.		

3.4 Company cars

It is likely that this benefit will be tested in the assessment.

When a car is made available by an employer for **private** use, a taxable benefit arises as a result of the private use of the car.

The benefit is calculated as a percentage of the list price of the car when first registered.

$$\text{Benefit} = (\% \times \text{List price when new})$$

List price

The list price may be different from the price paid for the car by the employer. Take care to select the correct figure.

The cost of any extra accessories provided with the car must be added to the list price. In addition, the cost of any accessories acquired subsequently must also be added to the list price, but only if the accessory cost more than £100.

The list price can be reduced by any capital contribution made by the employee towards the purchase of the car, subject to a maximum deduction of £5,000. This maximum is not provided in the rates and allowances available in the assessment.

Determining the percentage

The usual minimum percentage is 20% and the maximum is 37%.

The percentage depends on the rate at which the car emits carbon dioxide (CO_2). This is usually recorded on the car's registration document (and is supplied in the assessment).

If the emission rate is 95 grams per kilometre travelled (for 2018/19), the percentage of 20% applies to petrol cars.

This is increased by 1% for every extra complete 5 grams emitted.

Diesel engine vehicles are surcharged an extra 4% to reflect the additional pollutants compared to petrol engines for the same carbon dioxide level of emission.

The additional 4% does not apply to diesel cars which are registered after 1 September 2017 and meet the RDE2 standards. You will be told in the assessment if the car meets these standards.

However, for both petrol and diesel cars the maximum percentage is 37%.

These figures are all available for you to refer to in the assessment apart from the maximum of 37%.

 Example

Louise is provided with a company car with a carbon dioxide emission rate of 107 g/km.

What percentage is to be applied assuming the car runs on:

(a)   petrol

(b)   diesel?

Solution

(a)   107 g/km petrol

Ignore the extra 2 g/km (always round down to the next 0 or 5).

∴ 105 g/km

95 g/km	20%
105 g/km = extra 10 g/km	
Therefore 10 × $^1/_5$	2%
Appropriate percentage	22%

(b)   107 g/km diesel

As above	22%
Diesel supplement	4%
Appropriate percentage	26%

Always look out for the type of fuel.

There are lower percentages for cars with low carbon dioxide emissions.

Emissions	*Petrol*	*Diesel*
0 g/km to 50 g/km	13%	17%
51 g/km to 75 g/km	16%	20%
76 g/km to 94 g/km	19%	23%

These percentages are also available for you to refer to in the assessment.

 Test your understanding 3

What percentage would be applied for petrol cars with the following CO_2 emissions?

1   84 g/km

2   72 g/km

3   138 g/km

4   228 g/km

Non-availability

Where a car is unavailable to the employee for 30 consecutive days or more during any part of the tax year, the benefit is reduced proportionately.

Temporary non-availability of less than 30 days is ignored.

Where a car is unavailable for part of the tax year, the benefit would be calculated on a daily basis. However, in the assessment you should prepare calculations to the nearest month unless you are told otherwise.

Running costs

Running expenses (for example servicing and insurance) are deemed to be included in the benefit figure and **do not** produce an additional benefit.

However, the provision of a **chauffeur** is counted as an additional benefit valued at the **private use portion** of the chauffeur's employment costs.

Contributions for private use

Employees are commonly required to make a monthly payment towards the cost of **private use**. Such contributions made by the employee are deducted from the taxable benefit.

Remember that where the employee contributes towards the **cost of purchasing** the car, the treatment is different; such a contribution reduces the list price used in calculating the benefit.

Cars used only for business

Where an employee is specifically forbidden from using his company car for private purposes and, as a matter of fact, does not so use it, there will be no taxable car benefit.

There is also no benefit where there is provision of a company car (and associated services) which is a 'pool' car.

A pool car is one which is not exclusively used by any one employee, and which is not available for travel from home to work, being garaged at company premises, and is only used for business travel.

Test your understanding 4

1   Sue is provided with petrol driven car by her employer that cost £15,400. The emission rate shown on the registration document is 157 grams of carbon dioxide per kilometre and the list price of the car when new was £16,000.

   During 2018/19 Sue drove 3,000 business miles and paid her employer £2,000 in respect of her private use of the car.

   Required:

   What is the benefit taxable on Sue for 2018/19?

   [   ]

2   Paul is provided with a diesel powered car by his employer that cost £34,000. The list price of the car when new was £39,000. Paul paid £3,000 towards the purchase of the car.

   During 2018/19 Paul drove 28,000 business miles. The emission rating of the car is 197 g/km.

   Required:

   What is the benefit taxable on Paul for 2018/19?

   [   ]

3.5 Fuel provided for private purposes

The provision of petrol or diesel in a company car for **private use** is the subject of a benefit charge which is in addition to the charge for the provision of the car itself.

The benefit is calculated as £23,400 multiplied by the same percentage used for calculating the car benefit.

The figure of £23,400 is available for you to refer to in the assessment.

The fuel benefit is £Nil if either:

*   the employee has to pay his employer for all fuel provided for private use; or

*   the fuel is only provided by the employer for business use.

There is no reduction in the fuel benefit if the employee only **partially** reimburses his employer for private fuel. This is a common source of error in questions.

Where the car is unavailable to the employee for 30 consecutive days or more during any part of the tax year, both the car and fuel benefit are reduced proportionately.

In these circumstances, the benefit would be calculated on a daily rather than a monthly basis. However, in the assessment you should work to the nearest month.

Temporary non-availability of less than 30 days is ignored.

If private use fuel is withdrawn during the year, the fuel benefit figure is reduced pro rata. However, this only applies if the withdrawal is permanent.

For example, if the car is provided throughout the year but the provision of private use fuel is only suspended between 1 November 2018 and 31 January 2019, a full year's charge will still apply.

 Example

From 1 November 2018 Joan's employer provided her with a car. The car had a list price of £15,000 and an emission rate of 129 g/km. Up to 5 April 2019 Joan drove 6,000 miles of which 4,500 were private. The company paid for all running expenses.

Between 1 November 2018 and 31 January 2019 the company paid for all petrol usage including private use. Joan made a contribution to her employer of £15 per month towards the provision of the petrol for her private use. From 1 February 2019 her employer only paid for business use petrol.

Required:

Calculate Joan's taxable benefits for 2018/19.

Solution

	£
Car benefit (£15,000 × 26% × $^5/_{12}$)	1,625
Fuel benefit (£23,400 × 26% × $^3/_{12}$)	1,521
	———
Taxable benefits	3,146
	———

The percentage is 26% = 20% + (125 – 95) × $^1/_5$.

The car was available for 5 months (1 November 2018 to 5 April 2019).

Fuel for private use was only available for 3 months (1 November 2018 to 31 January 2019). Fuel was permanently withdrawn from 1 February 2019.

The contribution towards the cost of private petrol does not reduce the fuel benefit, as the cost of the private petrol was not reimbursed in full.

3.6 Company vans

In the case of a company van with private use the taxable benefits are:

- £3,350 per annum for unrestricted private use of the van

- £633 per annum if private fuel is provided by the employer.

Where the van does not emit any carbon dioxide, the benefit is only 40% of the full benefit, i.e. £1,340 (£3,350 × 40%).

The above information is available for you to refer to in the assessment.

Taking the van home at night is not treated as private use.

Incidental private use, such as the occasional trip to the rubbish tip, is ignored. However, this would not extend to regular shopping trips.

These benefits are time apportioned if the van is unavailable to the employee for 30 consecutive days or more during any part of the tax year.

3.7 Beneficial loans

Where by reason of employment an employee or a relative is provided with an interest free or cheap loan, the benefit derived from such an arrangement is taxable.

There is no taxable benefit where:

- the total loans to an employee do not exceed £10,000 at any time during the tax year; or

- the loan is used by the employee to purchase equipment required for the purposes of his employment; or

- the loan is used by the employee to pay for expenditure incurred wholly, exclusively and necessarily in the performance of the duties of the employment.

The taxable benefit is calculated as follows:

	£
Loan outstanding × the official rate of interest (ORI)	X
Less: Interest actually paid by the employee	(X)
Taxable benefit	X

Although the interest actually paid by the employee should be deducted, in the assessment, this can also be calculated on an average basis.

The figure of £10,000 and the ORI are available for you to refer to in the assessment.

Where the loan is provided or repaid part way through the year, the benefit is calculated using either the average or the precise method.

- *Precise method*

  Interest is calculated on the balance of the loan on a daily basis.

- *Average method*

	£
½ × (Balance outstanding at beginning of year + Balance outstanding at the end of the year) × ORI	X
Less: Interest actually paid by the employee (Note)	(X)
Taxable benefit	X

Note – Strictly, the interest actually paid by the taxpayer should be deducted. However, historically the AAT have also calculated the interest paid on the average basis. This can be seen in the first example below.

Usually, the average method will be used for simplicity.

If the loan was provided or repaid during the tax year, the amount of the loan on those dates is used instead of the balance at the beginning or end of the tax year and the benefit is multiplied by the proportion of the year that the loan was available.

A taxable benefit arises in respect of any amount of loan written off by the employer, even if the loan was for less than £10,000.

Example

Bob was loaned £15,000 by his employer on 6 August 2017. He repaid £2,000 on 6 November 2018. His employer charged interest at 1%.

Required:

Calculate the amount taxable on Bob in 2018/19.

Solution

The taxable benefit using the average method is:

	£
½ × (£15,000 + £13,000) × 2.5%	350
Less interest paid: ½ × (£15,000 + £13,000) × 1%	(140)
Taxable benefit	210

An alternative way to calculate the above answer would be:

	£
½ × (£15,000 + £13,000) × (2.5% – 1%)	210

Note that the interest actually paid be Bob would have been:

(£15,000 × 1% × 7/12) + (£13,000 × 1% × 5/12) = £142.

However, in the assessment the interest paid should be calculated on the average basis and would therefore be £140 as shown above.

Example

Flora was loaned £15,000, interest free, by her employer on 6 August 2018 and repaid £2,000 on 6 September 2018.

Required:

Calculate the amount taxable on Flora in 2018/19.

Solution

The taxable benefit using the average method is:

	£
½ × (£15,000 + £13,000) × 8/12 × 2.5%	233
Less: Interest paid by employee	(Nil)
Taxable benefit	233

3.8 Use of assets

If an asset (for example, a television) is owned by the employer but the employee is allowed to use it privately, the taxable benefit is calculated as:

20% of the open market value when the asset was first made available (usually 20% of the cost).

This has been seen already as part of the accommodation benefit.

The figure of 20% is available for you to refer to in the assessment.

If the employer does not own the asset, but rents it, the benefit is the greater of 20% of the value of the asset and the rent paid by the employer.

3.9 Gifts of assets

If an asset which is **new** is gifted to the employee, the benefit will be the **cost to the company**.

If an asset has been **used** and is then subsequently gifted to an employee, the benefit is the **higher of**:

- market value (MV) at the date of the gift (less the amount paid by the employee), or

- original market value less benefit amounts assessed to date (less the amount paid by the employee)

- This rule does not apply for cars or bicycles, the gift of these assets will just be the market value (MV) at the date of the gift (less the amount paid by employee.

 Example

A suit costing £300 was purchased for Bill's use by his employer on 6 April 2017. One year later Bill purchased the suit for £20. Its market value at that time is estimated to be £30.

Required:

Calculate the amounts taxable on Bill.

Solution

The taxable benefits are computed as follows:

	£
2017/18 – Use of suit	
Annual value (20% × £300)	60
2018/19 – Purchase of suit	
Suit's current market value	30
Less: Price paid by employee	(20)
	——
	10
	——
	£
Suit's original market value	300
Less: Taxed in 2017/18 in respect of use	(60)
Less: Price paid by employee	(20)
	——
	220
	——

Thus the taxable benefit in 2018/19 is £220, being the greater of £10 and £220.

Test your understanding 5

June gives you the following information about her employment.

- She belongs to a private medical insurance scheme and her employer paid the required premium of £1,270 (including £650 for her family).

- June took meals in the fully subsidised staff canteen, the cost for the year being £335.

- June was paid a round sum expense allowance of £1,870, out of which she paid £800 on entertaining customers and £550 on business travel.

Required:

On what amount will June be taxed in respect of these items?

 Test your understanding 6

1   Raider is employed by Coliseum Ltd.

When at the company's premises Raider has use of a petrol driven car owned by the company for business journeys only. It had a list price of £62,000 and an emission rating of 208 g/km. It costs £4,800 a year to run and the chauffeur's salary is £17,500. It is garaged at the company's head office and is also used by all the directors.

Required:

What is Raider's taxable benefit in respect of this arrangement?

2   Raider is also provided with a two-year-old Rover car. Coliseum Ltd paid £16,100 for the car, which had a list price of £17,000. However, Raider prefers to use his own car, a Lotus, and therefore lets his wife use the Rover.

The company pays for all of the running costs of the Rover car, including petrol for private use.

The carbon dioxide emission rate of the Rover is 207 g/km. Raider's business mileage in his own car is 12,000 miles. Both cars run on petrol.

Required:

What is the total taxable employment income in respect of these two vehicles?

KAPLAN PUBLISHING

Test your understanding 7

Read the following statements and mark each one as true or false.

		True	False
1	Howie is loaned a new computer costing £1,000 by his employer on 6 April 2018. The taxable benefit for 2018/19 is £200.		
2	If the computer had been given to Howie on 6 April 2018 there would be no taxable benefit.		
3	Dale is a housemaster at a boarding school and is required to live on the premises. This is an example of job related accommodation.		
4	Ken drives a company van. He is required to take it home every night ready for work in the morning as he frequently drives from home straight to the customer's premises. He does not use it for any other private purposes. The taxable benefit is £3,350.		

3.10 Changing benefits to make them more tax efficient

It may be possible for an employee to choose a different benefit in order to reduce their taxable employment income. For example, choosing a car with lower CO_2 emissions will reduce the car and fuel benefit.

Alternatively they may be able to substitute a taxable benefit with one that is exempt, such as receiving childcare vouchers under the threshold to use with an approved childcare provider, rather than payments to an unapproved provider.

4 Test your understanding

Test your understanding 8

Ethelred is the finance director of Buttercup Ltd. The company provided him with benefits in the year ended 5 April 2019 as follows:

	£
Season travel ticket from home to office	292
Car owned by the company:	
Citroen CX 2000	
List price when new	13,800
First registered on 1 October 2015	
Emission rating: 112 g/km	
Private medical insurance	1,628

Ethelred advises you that during the year his car did 16,800 miles, of which 3,360 miles represented private use, and that the company paid £1,848 in respect of all of the petrol for the car.

Ethelred paid £800 towards the cost of purchasing the car.

He also paid £1,000 to Buttercup Ltd for his wife and family to be included on the private medical insurance.

Required:

1 What is the taxable benefit in respect of the season travel ticket?

2 What is the total taxable benefit in respect of the car?

3 What is the taxable benefit in respect of the private medical insurance?

Test your understanding 9

William Makepeace has the following employment income for 2018/19:

(a) William has the use of a company car throughout the year, all the costs being met by his employer.

The details for the year ended 5 April 2019 are:

	£
List price of car when new in 2016	8,000
Cost of car in 2016	7,800
Emission rating: 106 g/km	
Contribution made by William for:	
Private use of car	600
Private use petrol	480

The total mileage for the year was 20,000 miles of which 15,000 miles were for private motoring.

During the year, however, William had two accidents and the car was incapable of being used for 12 days in July 2018 and for all of November and December 2018, whilst repairs were being carried out.

No replacement car was provided during these periods.

(b) William had a loan of £50,000 from his employer throughout the year on which he paid interest of 0.5%. The loan had been used to purchase a yacht.

Required:

1 What is William's taxable car benefit for 2018/19?

2 What is William's fuel benefit for 2018/19?

3 What is William's loan benefit for 2018/19?

Test your understanding 10

Gordon is the managing director of a large manufacturing company. He receives the following benefits in addition to his salary.

School fees totalling £10,000 are paid direct to a school in respect of his two children.

He is provided with a petrol engine car (list price £25,000 when new in April 2014) with an emission rating of 205 g/km.

Gordon paid £1,300 towards the cost of purchasing the car. He also paid £150 per month towards the cost of his private use of the car. He is not provided with fuel for private use.

A car parking space is provided for him in a multi-storey car park near his office at a cost of £600 per annum.

He was provided with a laptop computer for personal use which cost £750 on 6 September 2018. Ownership of the laptop is retained by the company.

Required:

1   The school fees are not a taxable benefit. TRUE or FALSE?

2   What is Gordon's car benefit?

    A   £6,969

    B   £8,769

    C   £7,450

    D   £8,154

3   What is the benefit in respect of the car parking space?

    A   £600

    B   £Nil

4   What is the benefit in respect of the laptop computer?

    A   £150

    B   £87

    C   £75

    D   £62

Test your understanding 11

Gina is the sales director of a large manufacturing company. She receives the following benefits in addition to her salary.

The company supplied Gina with a mobile telephone which she used for making private and business calls. The phone cost £250.

Throughout 2018/19, the company provided Gina with a van, which Gina uses for both business and private purposes. The van is electric and does not emit any carbon dioxide.

The company paid £1,420 in January 2019 as the annual premium for private medical insurance cover for Gina and her family. She contributed £750 to her employer to include her husband in the scheme.

An interest free loan of £16,000 was made on 1 May 2018 to enable Gina to purchase a boat.

Required:

Show the total taxable benefit in respect of each of the above items for 2018/19.

 Test your understanding 12

Marianne was employed by Logistics Ltd at an annual salary of £52,000.

Throughout the year she was provided with a rent-free furnished flat which had an annual value of £1,500. Logistics Ltd paid £150,000 for the flat in 2017.

The furniture in the flat was paid for by Logistics Ltd in 2017 and had cost £20,000.

Logistics Ltd paid heating and lighting bills for the flat amounting to £3,000 during 2018/19.

Other benefits for 2018/19 amounted to £3,600.

Required:

Calculate the amount of employment income chargeable on Marianne for 2018/19 assuming:

(a) the occupation of the flat was job related

(b) the occupation of the flat was not job related.

Test your understanding 13

Merlin's annual salary from Shalot Limited is £50,000. He was relocated by Shalot Limited on 6 April 2018 and was reimbursed relevant relocation expenditure incurred of £10,000.

Shalot Limited provided Merlin with a loan of £30,000 on 6 April 2018 on which annual interest of 0.75% was payable.

Required:

What is the amount of employment income taxable on Merlin for 2018/19?

 Test your understanding 14

Joseph has been employed by Rock Radio in central London for several years as a producer.

On 1 January 2017 he was provided with a company flat which has an annual value of £5,000 and was let at an annual rent of £8,500 paid for by Rock Radio on a five year tenancy from the same date. The occupation of the flat was not 'job-related'.

The furniture in the flat had cost £40,000 when first provided by Rock Radio.

Rock Radio paid £7,000 for utility services, decorating and repairs for the flat.

Required:

What is the amount of Joseph's taxable accommodation benefit for 2018/19?

Test your understanding 15

Worf Limited provided Marina with the following benefits.

A loan of £32,300 on 6 April 2018 on which annual interest of 0.25% was payable.

A bicycle costing £400 and cycle safety equipment costing £100 was provided for Marina on 6 April 2018 and was to be used mainly for travel to and from work. All employees are entitled to this benefit.

Worf Limited provided group membership of a nearby gymnasium. The cost of Marina's membership was £350 per annum although the normal annual membership fee was £750.

Required:

1   What is the amount of the loan benefit taxable on Marina for 2018/19?

2   What is the total of the taxable benefits for the bicycle and cycle safety equipment and the gym membership?

 Test your understanding 16

Mr F Darcy is paid an annual salary of £36,000 and also bonuses based on his company's performance. The company's accounting year ends on 31 December each year and the bonuses are normally determined and paid on 31 May thereafter. In recent years bonuses have been:

Year to 31 December 2017   £8,000

Year to 31 December 2018   £4,000

Mr Darcy pays 7% of his basic salary to the company's registered occupational pension scheme.

Required:

Calculate Mr Darcy's employment income for 2018/19.

Test your understanding 17

On 6 July 2018, Kate was provided with a company loan of £25,000 on which she pays interest of 0.15% per annum.

Required:

What is the taxable benefit for 2018/19?

 Test your understanding 18

Would the following situations be treated as being job related, such that no accommodation benefit arises?

1	Accommodation provided for a caretaker of a school	YES/NO
2	Accommodation provided for a hotel worker	YES/NO
3	Accommodation provided for security reasons	YES/NO

 Test your understanding 19

Budget Ltd is an estate agent and provided the following benefits to a number of its employees during 2018/19.

Required:

Which of the following is NOT taxable employment income for 2018/19?

A   Medical insurance provided to a key member of staff

B   Free membership of the gym situated next door to the company headquarters

C   A second mobile phone provided to the chief executive of the company

D   Child care vouchers of £25 per week to the sales director, a higher rate taxpayer, who chose to redeem them with an approved child carer, rather than taking advantage of the on-site facilities

Test your understanding 20

Jacob was provided with a computer for private use on 1 October 2018. The market value of the computer when first provided was £4,300 and at 5 April 2019 the market value was £3,000.

Required:

What is the value of the benefit in respect of this computer for 2018/19?

 Test your understanding 21

Leo was provided with a house to live in by his employer. The employer rented the house from a local resident and paid rent of £32,000 per year. Leo paid rent of £12,000 per year to his employer. The property has an annual value of £9,750.

What is the taxable value of this benefit, assuming the accommodation is not job related?

5 Summary

You should be prepared for any/all of the taxable benefits to be tested.

Company cars

Employees are taxed on a percentage of the vehicle's list price.

The percentage used is dependent upon the level of CO_2 emissions normally ranging from 20% to 37% moving up in increments of 1% for every 5 g/km in excess of the base figure of 95 g/km.

There is also a 4% supplement for diesel engines (although the maximum percentage is still 37%).

Do not forget the lower rates for cars with low emissions.

The fuel benefit uses the same percentage as calculated for the car, applied to a figure of £23,400.

Accommodation

Employees are taxed in three areas in relation to non-job related accommodation provided by the employer:

- Basic charge:

  Annual value (always given in the assessment).

- Expensive accommodation charge:

  For accommodation costing more than £75,000, an additional benefit of ((Cost – £75,000) × 2.5% (ORI)) is also charged.

- Provision of services:

  - Use of furniture:

    Furniture is treated in the same way as an employee using an employer's assets (i.e. MV when provided × 20%).

  - Household expenses:

    Cost to employer.

Beneficial loan

Employees are taxed on the interest they would normally pay on a loan, when provided by an employer at below market rates of interest.

The calculation is: (Loan amount × 2.5% (ORI)) – interest paid

Exempt benefits

These are very likely to be tested.

Test your understanding answers

Test your understanding 1

The correct answer is £3,250.

	£
Basic charge – annual value (no rent paid by employer)	2,400
Expensive property charge	
(£105,000 – £75,000) = £30,000 × 2.5%	750
Use of furniture (20% × £6,500)	1,300
	4,450
Less: Contribution by employee (£100 × 12)	(1,200)
Taxable benefit	3,250

Test your understanding 2

1   **True**

2   **False** – Although often the MV when first made available is the same as the cost to the employer

3   **False**

4   **True**

Test your understanding 3

1   19% (Emissions between 76 g/km and 94 g/km)

2   16% (Emissions between 51 g/km and 75 g/km)

3   28% (20% + (135 – 95) × $^1/_5$)
    Round down emissions to 135 g/km

4   37% (20% + (225 – 95 g/km) × $^1/_5$ = 46%), but maximum is 37%
    Round down emissions to 225 g/km

Test your understanding 4

Sue and Paul

1   The correct answer is £3,120.

The amount of the benefit arising is as follows:

	£
£16,000 (the list price) × 32%	5,120
Less: Contribution	(2,000)
Benefit	3,120

The benefit is calculated at the rate of 32% being

20% + ((155 − 95) × $^1/_5$.)

2   The correct answer is £13,320.

The amount of the benefit arising is as follows:

(£39,000 − £3,000) × 37% = £13,320

The benefit is calculated at the maximum rate of 37%
(20% + (195 − 95) × $^1/_5$ + 4% (diesel) = 44%).

Note that the business mileage driven is of no relevance to the calculations.

Test your understanding 5

The correct answer is £2,590.

	£
Private medical insurance	1,270
Canteen	Exempt
Round sum expense allowance	1,870
Less: Business travel	(550)
Taxable amount	2,590

Test your understanding 6

1   There is no taxable benefit in respect of this arrangement because the car satisfies the conditions to be classified as a pool car.

2   The correct answer is £9,948.

The amount of the benefit arising is as follows:

	£
Car benefit (37% × £17,000)	6,290
Fuel benefit (37% × £23,400)	8,658
	14,948
Less: Mileage allowance claim for own car	(5,000)
	9,948

The benefit is calculated at the maximum rate of 37%
(20% + (205 − 95) × 1/5 = 42% so use maximum)

The business mileage claim is £5,000
((10,000 × 45p) + (2,000 × 25p))

Raider can claim relief for the business miles he does in his own car using the AMAP rates.

 Test your understanding 7

1   **True** – The benefit is (20% × £1,000).

2   **False** – The benefit would be £1,000, the market value of the asset.

3   **True**.

4   **False** – There is no benefit. Taking the van home at night is not treated as private use.

Test your understanding 8

Ethelred

		£
1	Season travel ticket	292
2	Motor car = 23% (W) × (£13,800 – £800)	2,990
	Petrol = 23% (W) × £23,400	5,382
		8,372
3	Private medical insurance (£1,628 – £1,000)	628

Working:

Appropriate percentage: 20% + (110 – 95) × ⅕ = 23%

Test your understanding 9

William Makepeace

		£	£
1	The correct answer is £867.		
	Car 22% × £8,000 × $\frac{10}{12}$	1,467	
	Less: Contribution	(600)	
			867
2	The correct answer is £4,070.		
	Fuel charge		
	£23,400 × 22% × $\frac{10}{12}$		4,290
3	The correct answer is £1,000.		
	Cheap loan £50,000 × (2.5% – 0.5%)		1,000

The car benefit percentage: 20% + (105 – 95) × $^1/_5$ = 22%.

The car and petrol benefits are pro-rated as the car was unavailable for use for more than 30 consecutive days during November and December 2018. No reduction is made for the 12 day period in July 2018.

No deduction is made for the contribution towards private use petrol as it did not cover the full cost.

📝 Test your understanding 10

Gordon

1   **False** – School fees are taxable on the cost to the employer.

		£	£
2	The correct answer is **A**.		
	Basic car benefit		
	((£25,000 – £1,300) × 37%) (W1)	8,769	
	Contribution towards private use		
	(£150 × 12)	(1,800)	
		———	6,969

3   The correct answer is **B** – Parking place is exempt

		£
4	The correct answer is **B**.	
	Provision of asset (computer)	
	(£750 × 20% × 7/12) (W2)	87
		———

Workings:

(W1) Appropriate percentage:

20% + (205 – 95) × ⅕ = 42% restricted to 37%.

(W2) The computer was only available from 6 September 2018 and therefore the benefit is time apportioned for 7 months.

Test your understanding 11

Gina

Benefits taxable as employment income – 2018/19

	£	£
Mobile telephone		
One phone per employee = exempt		Nil
Van		
(£3,350 × 40%)		1,340
Medical insurance cover		
Premium paid by employer	1,420	
Less: Contribution by Gina	(750)	
	———	670
Beneficial loan		
£16,000 × $\frac{11}{12}$ × 2.5% (Note)		367
		———
Total taxable benefits		2,377
		———

Note: The loan was only outstanding for 11 months during 2018/19. The average loan is £16,000 throughout the eleven month period. However the interest rate given in the question is an annual percentage and therefore needs to be time apportioned for the eleven month period of the loan.

Test your understanding 12

Marianne

Employment income – 2018/19

(a) Job-related accommodation

	£	£
Salary		52,000
Other benefits		3,600
		55,600
Living accommodation		Exempt
Other benefits in respect of accommodation		
Heating and lighting	3,000	
Furniture (£20,000 × 20%)	4,000	
	7,000	
Restricted to (10% × £55,600)		5,560
Employment income		61,160

(b) Not job-related accommodation

	£	£
Salary		52,000
Other benefits		3,600
		55,600
Living accommodation:		
Basic charge	1,500	
Expensive charge		
(£150,000 – £75,000) × 2.5%	1,875	
		3,375
Heating and lighting		3,000
Furniture (£20,000 × 20%)		4,000
Employment income		65,975

Test your understanding 13

The correct answer is £52,525.

	£
Salary	50,000
Relocation (W1)	2,000
Beneficial loan (W2)	525
Employment income	52,525

Workings:

(1) The first £8,000 of relocation expenses are tax-free provided they are reimbursed expenditure or paid direct to a third party (i.e. you cannot give an £8,000 round sum tax free to the employee).

(£10,000 – £8,000) = £2,000

(2) Beneficial loan:

£30,000 × (2.5% ORI less 0.75% paid) = £525

Test your understanding 14

The correct answer is £23,500.

	£
Accommodation	
(rent paid by employer higher than annual value)	8,500
Utility services, decorating and repairs	7,000
Use of furniture (£40,000 × 20%)	8,000
Taxable benefits	23,500

Test your understanding 15

1   The correct answer is £727.

£32,300 × (2.5% − 0.25%)	£727

2   The answer is £350.

The bicycle and cycle safety equipment are an exempt benefit provided available to employees generally.

Gym membership is taxable on the cost to the employer.	£350

Test your understanding 16

Mr Darcy

Employment income – 2018/19

	£
Salary	36,000
Bonus *(note)*	8,000
	44,000
Less: Pension contributions (7% × £36,000)	(2,520)
Employment income	41,480

Explanation of treatment

The bonus paid in May 2018 is taxable in 2018/19.

Test your understanding 17

The correct answer is £441.

£25,000 × (2.5% − 0.15%) × 9/12	£441

Test your understanding 18

1   Yes

2   Yes

3   Yes

Test your understanding 19

The answer is **D**.

Child care vouchers provided to a higher rate taxpayer of up to £28 per week are exempt provided they are spent with an approved child carer. The fact that the sales director chose an approved child carer rather than the on-site facilities is irrelevant for tax purposes.

The other items are all taxable.

Test your understanding 20

The correct answer is £430 (£4,300 × 20% × 6/12).

The computer was not made available until 1 October 2018 so the benefit must be time apportioned.

Test your understanding 21

The correct answer is £20,000 (£32,000 – £12,000).

The basic charge is the higher of the annual value or rent paid by the employer, which is £32,000, less the rent of £12,000 paid by Leo.

Property income

5

Introduction

This chapter explains how taxable property income is calculated and how losses can be relieved.

ASSESSMENT CRITERIA
Calculate profit and losses from residential furnished and unfurnished property (2.3)
Utilise losses on property (3.3)

CONTENTS
1   Property income
2   Allowable expenditure
3   Losses
4   Property allowance

1 Property income

1.1 Property letting

All income from letting property in the UK is added together.

It includes:

- rental income from land
- rental income from commercial property
- rental income from residential property.

1.2 Basis of assessment

It is critical to ensure that the correct amount of property income is taxed in a tax year. There are two possible ways to work out property income for a landlord.

(i) The default assumption is that a landlord will use the cash basis to work out their profit for the tax year. This is similar to what you saw with employment income and is illustrated below.

	£
Rental income received	X
Less: Allowable expenses paid (section 2)	(X)
Taxable property income	X

In the assessment, where there is more than one property being let out, you may be asked to calculate the profit on each property separately, or the total from all properties together.

(ii) Alternatively a landlord can elect to use the accruals basis. The accruals basis must be used if their gross annual rents exceed £150,000. The accruals basis means that we deal with income and expenses that **relate to the tax year**, not necessarily those paid and received in the year.

If a landlord wishes to elect to use the accruals basis they must do so within 12 months of 31 January following the relevant tax year – for the tax year 2018/19 the deadline is 31 January 2021.

You will be told in the assessment if a landlord has elected to use the accruals basis.

Any apportionment of income and expenses should be carried out to the nearest month.

	£
Net rental income receivable (less any non-recoverable amounts)	X
Less: Allowable expenses (section 2)	(X)
Taxable property income	X

The same basis (i.e. cash or accruals) must be used for all properties in a single property business.

 Example

In the tax year 2018/19, Mr Jenkins let out a property, beginning on 6 October 2018, at £2,000 per month.

Rent for the first 5 months was received on time. However, rent for the last month was not received until 20 April 2019.

What is the rental income taxable in 2018/19?

Solution

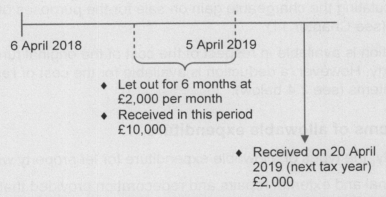

Under the cash basis we only consider the rents actually received from 6 October 2018 to the 5 April 2019. This would be £10,000 (5 × £2,000).

Under the accruals basis, we ignore the dates the amounts were received and instead tax what is due in the tax year.

The amounts relating to 2018/19 are the months from 6 October 2018 to 5 April 2019 which is six months and therefore the rental income would be £12,000 (6 × £2,000).

Mr Jenkins would need to elect for the accruals basis as his gross rents are under £150,000.

2 Allowable expenditure

2.1 'Wholly and exclusively'

Expenditure which may be deducted in computing the profit from property income is that which is incurred 'wholly and exclusively' for the purposes of letting.

Note: This rule is similar to that for allowable expenditure for employment income, but omits the 'necessarily' condition.

2.2 Capital expenditure

Knowledge of the treatment of capital expenditure for the cash basis is not assessed although it is very similar to the details below which refer primarily to the accruals basis.

The capital cost of the property is not an allowable deduction in calculating property income. Similarly, the cost of improving or enhancing the value of the property is not deductible.

These costs will normally be dealt with as part of the cost of the property when calculating the chargeable gain on sale for the purposes of capital gains tax (see Chapter 11).

No deduction is available in respect of the cost of the original furniture in the property. However, a deduction is available for the cost of **replacing** domestic items (see 2.4 below).

2.3 Items of allowable expenditure

Specifically, the types of allowable expenditure for let property will include:

(a) internal and external repairs and redecoration provided that they relate to the making good of current dilapidations. This would include the replacement of a broken boiler or the replacement of single glaze windows with double glazed ones.

Note that the cost of initial repairs necessary in order to make a property usable are not deductible (e.g. repairs to a roof which had been damaged prior to the purchase of the property).

(b) gardening

(c) cleaning

(d) agent's commission

(e) costs of collecting rents (legal costs), including unpaid rents

(f)   advertising for new tenants

(g)   insurance premiums against damage to the structure of the property

(h)   legal and accountancy costs for preparing claims, accounts and tax computations in respect of the property

(i)   maintenance of common parts of blocks, offices and flats

(j)   interest on loans taken out to buy or improve the property (tested regarding non-residential properties only)

(k)   council tax and water rates

(l)   irrecoverable rents

(m)   the cost of replacing domestic items (see 2.4 below).

A landlord can also claim a deduction for business mileage when using their own car using the approved mileage allowance payments (AMAP) rates as set out in Chapter 3.

The approved rates are:

Cars

First 10,000 business miles per tax year	45p per mile
Additional mileage	25p per mile
Motor cycles	24p per mile
Bicycles	20p per mile

These figures are available for you to refer to in the assessment.

 Example

Strudwick has one property, which he lets on a commercial basis.

The property is let for £2,000 per month paid in advance at the start of each month. The rent is increased to £2,500 from 1 January 2019.

During 2018/19 Strudwick has the following expenditure:

Mortgage interest paid	£5,000
Agent's commission paid	£750
Buildings insurance	
y/e 31 December 2018	£480
y/e 31 December 2019	£520

Strudwick always pays his insurance in advance on 1 January.

Calculate Strudwick's taxable property income for 2018/19 using the cash basis and the accruals basis.

Solution – cash basis

	£
Rentals (8 × £2,000) + (4 × £2,500)	26,000
Expenses: Mortgage interest	(5,000)
Agent's commission	(750)
Buildings insurance (1 January 2019)	(520)
Taxable property income	19,730

Under the cash basis Strudwick will make eight payments in 2018 from 1 May to 1 December. He will then make four payments in 2019 from 1 January to 1 April.

Solution – accruals basis

	£
Rentals (9 × £2,000) + (3 × £2,500)	25,500
Expenses: Mortgage interest	(5,000)
Agent's commission	(750)
Buildings insurance (9/12 × 480) + (3/12 × 520)	(490)
Taxable property income	19,260

Under the accruals basis Strudwick will ignore the cash payments and accrue nine months of insurance costs to 31 December 2018 and then three months to 31 March 2019. Although he receives £2,500 of rent on 1 April 2019 this relates to 2019/20 and so is not recognised in 2018/19.

📝 Test your understanding 1

Jane lets out two properties at an annual rental of £5,000 each. She incurs agent's fees of £1,200 on property 1 and £700 on property 2. She also incurs expenses of £6,000 repairing and redecorating property 2 during the year.

Required:

What is her taxable property income?

2.4   Replacement of domestic items

The cost of **replacing** domestic items in a residential property is an allowable deduction when calculating taxable property income. The cost of acquiring the original domestic items in the property is not allowable.

If the replacement item is substantially different from the original item the deduction is restricted to the cost which would have been incurred if the item had been replaced by a similar item.

The allowable deduction is reduced by any proceeds from the disposal of the original asset.

Domestic items are those items acquired for domestic use, e.g. furniture, furnishings, household appliances and kitchenware. However, 'fixtures' i.e. any plant and machinery that is fixed to a dwelling, including boilers and radiators are specifically excluded.

Although the replacement of fixtures and fittings such as boilers is specifically excluded from the replacement of domestic items rules, the replacement of such an item will generally be allowed as a repair to the property itself (see section 2.3 above). It is treated as if the fixture is a part of the house that has broken and is being repaired. Therefore, such a replacement will be an allowable deduction, although not under the replacement furniture relief rules.

Example

During 2018/19 Mr Lord let out a furnished property at a rent of £10,000 per year. The expenses incurred for the year are as follows:

	£
Repairs and maintenance (no capital items)	2,000
Council tax and water rates	500
Gardening and cleaning	250
Buildings insurance	300
New hall table	200
Replacement bed	800
Replacement chairs for kitchen	300

Mr Lord is raising the standard of the property's furnishings in order to be able to increase the rent charged. There was no table in the hall prior to the purchase. A bed of a similar standard to the old bed would have cost £450. Similarly, the new chairs cost £80 more than ones similar to those which were replaced.

The old chairs were sold for £40 but Mr Lord was unable to sell the bed.

What is Mr Lord's taxable property income for 2018/19?

Solution

	£	£
Rental income		10,000
Less: Allowable expenditure		
Repairs and maintenance	2,000	
Council tax and water rates	500	
Gardening and cleaning	250	
Buildings insurance	300	
Hall table (capital)	–	
Replacement of bed (note)	450	
Replacement of chairs (note)	180	
		(3,680)
Taxable property income		6,320

Note:

The allowable deduction in respect of the bed is restricted to £450, being the cost of a bed similar to the one replaced.

Similarly, the allowable deduction in respect of the chairs is £220 (£300 – £80) less the proceeds of £40 received in respect of the old chairs.

3 Losses

3.1 Treatment of a loss

A loss arises if allowable expenses are more than the rental income. For example in 2018/19:

	£
Rental income	10,000
Less: Allowable expenses	(10,500)
Loss	(500)

If this happens:

(i)   the tax computation will show property income = NIL.

Never show a negative figure in the tax computation; and

(ii)   the loss is carried forward and set off against the next available profit from property letting in future years (i.e. the £500 above is carried forward to the 2019/20 computation).

 Test your understanding 2

Are the following statements true or false?

1   Income from property is always taxed on a receipts basis.

2   The deduction allowed in respect of the replacement of a domestic item is restricted to the cost of an item similar to the one replaced.

3   Where the allowable expenses exceed the rental income, the loss arising can be deducted from the individual's other taxable income.

Test your understanding 3

Bernard Marks

Bernard Marks has presented you with a statement of income and expenditure on the three furnished properties that he lets out.

Property number	1	2	3
	£	£	£
Rental income received	3,000	3,500	2,500
Less: Expenses paid			
Agent's commission	(300)	(350)	(250)
Buildings insurance	(120)	(120)	(120)
Repairs and maintenance (Note)	(560)	(660)	(3,560)
Council tax	(400)	(450)	(380)
Accountancy fees	(50)	(50)	(50)
	———	———	———
Net income for year = £1,580	1,570	1,870	(1,860)
	———	———	———

Note

Repairs and maintenance is as follows:

	£	£	£
Gardening	260	260	260
General repairs (allowable)	300	400	800
Installation of central heating			2,500
Replacement furniture		340	
	560	1,000	3,560

The furniture in house 2 replaced furniture of a similar standard, which was sold for £35.

Required:

Calculate Bernard's taxable property income for 2018/19 assuming he elects for the accruals basis.

4 Property allowance

The property allowance is £1,000 and can be deducted from the gross rental income instead of deducting the allowable expenses. This would clearly be advantageous to a landlord who has a small amount of expenditure. For other landlords, with greater expenditure, deducting their actual expenditure from their rental receipts will give them a lower profit figure.

If property income is below £1,000 the allowance will apply automatically, giving the landlord assessable property income of £Nil. The taxpayer will not have to declare or pay tax on the income. If the taxpayer has actual expenditure in excess of their income they can elect to not use the allowance so as to generate a loss.

If property income is above £1,000 the landlord will deduct allowable expenses, unless they want to elect to use the property allowance, which can then be used in place of the actual expenditure. This would only be a preferable option if the actual expenditure was below £1,000.

The time limits for any elections with respect to the property allowance is within 12 months of 31 January following the relevant tax year – for the tax year 2018/19 the deadline is 31 January 2021.

Test your understanding 4

Four landlords have provided you with details of their income and expenditure for 2018/19 below.

Landlord	Bob £	Dave £	Jane £	Freddy £
Rental income received	500	600	3,800	6,500
Less: Expenses paid				
Agent's commission	(100)	(500)	(150)	(250)
Buildings insurance		(220)	(240)	(720)
Accountancy fees	(150)	(160)	(400)	(560)

Required:

Calculate their respective taxable property income for 2018/19 taking advantage of any elections that may be available.

5 Test your understanding

 Test your understanding 5

Alan owns a house which is let furnished throughout the year to 5 April 2019 at a rent of £650 per month, payable in advance.

Alan paid the following expenses during the year: water rates £300, council tax £850, property insurance £500, purchase of new cooker £665. The cooker replaced a similar item which was worn out.

What is Alan's taxable property income for 2018/19?

 Test your understanding 6

Rachman

On 1 December 2017, Rachman purchased a freehold block of flats for £200,000. All the flats were let unfurnished on monthly tenancies.

In the year to 5 April 2019, his receipts and payments were as follows:

	Year ended 5 April 2019 £
Receipts	
Rents collected (see (a))	26,280
Payments	
Repairs and maintenance (see (b))	1,480
Caretaker's wages	5,800
Insurance and incidentals (all allowable)	269
	7,549

(a) Rents

	£
Rents owing at beginning of period	240
Rents due	26,850
	27,090
Less: Rent owing at end of period	(810)
Cash received for rents	26,280

(b) Repairs and maintenance

	£
Garden maintenance	500
Lift maintenance	180
Normal decorations and incidental repairs	800
	1,480

Required:

Compute the taxable property income for 2018/19.

Test your understanding 7

James

In October 2017, James purchased a freehold flat for £150,000. The flat was let furnished for a monthly rent of £700 until 31 July 2018. Unfortunately' the tenant disappeared still owing the July rent.

The property was re-let from 1 October 2018 for a monthly rent of £750. Outgoings for the year to 5 April 2019 were:

	£
Agent's commission	1,163
Redecoration between tenants	1,745
Installation of central heating	1,980
Purchase of furniture (see (a))	800
Insurance and incidentals (all allowable)	547
Professional charges (see (b))	730
	———
	6,965
	———

(a)   James purchased a dining table and chairs at the request of the tenant who moved in on 1 October 2018.

(b)   Professional charges

Accountancy	420
Valuation for insurance purposes	310
	———
	730
	———

James has a significant property portfolio with gross rental income of over £200,000.

Required:

Compute the amount of the property income profit or loss for 2018/19.

Test your understanding 8

Arthur

Arthur has two shops which he lets.

Shop 1.

The annual rent was £3,000 on a lease which expired on 30 June 2018. Arthur took advantage of the shop being empty to carry out repairs and decorating. The shop was let to another tenant on a five-year lease at £4,000 per annum from 1 October 2018.

Shop 2.

The shop was purchased on 10 April 2018 and required treatment for dry-rot. Arthur also undertook some normal re-decorating work before the shop was let on 1 October 2018 on a seven-year lease at an annual rental of £6,000.

The rent for both shops was due in advance on the first day of each month.

The following expenditure was incurred in 2018/19:

	Shop 1 £		Shop 2 £	
Insurance	190		300	
Ground rent	10		40	
Repairs and decorating	3,900	(Note 1)	5,000	(Note 2)
Accountancy	50		50	
Advertising for tenant	100		100	

Notes:

(1) Includes £2,500 for re-roofing the shop following gale damage in February 2018. As the roof had been badly maintained the insurance company refused to pay for the repair work.

(2) Includes £3,000 for dry rot remedial treatment. The dry rot was present when the shop was bought in April 2018.

Required:

Using the following pro forma calculate the property income or loss made on each property for 2018/19 using the accruals basis.

	Shop 1 £	Shop 2 £
Income		
Expenses		
	——	——
Net profit/loss		
	——	——

6 Summary

Property income is an important aspect of preparing an income tax computation. The main issues to beware of are:

- Income and expenses   —   cash basis but can elect for the accruals basis.

- Capital items   —   disallow unless relate to revenue.

- Domestic items   —   cost of replacement is allowable.

- Losses   —   carry forward to the next tax year.

Test your understanding answers

Test your understanding 1

The correct answer is £2,100

	£
Rental income (£5,000 × 2)	10,000
Less: Expenses	
Agents fees (£1,200 + £700)	(1,900)
Repairs and redecoration	(6,000)
Taxable property income	2,100

Test your understanding 2

1   **False** – The accruals basis is used if the gross annual rents exceed £150,000 or if the landlord elects to use it.

2   **True**

3   **False** – The loss must be carried forward and set off against the next available profit from property letting in future years.

Test your understanding 3

Bernard Marks

Taxable property income – 2018/19

Property number	1	2	3	Total
	£	£	£	£
Rental income	3,000	3,500	2,500	9,000
Less: Allowable expenses				
Agent's commission	(300)	(350)	(250)	(900)
Building insurance	(120)	(120)	(120)	(360)
Repairs and maintenance	(560)	(660)	(1,060)*	(2,280)
Council tax	(400)	(450)	(380)	(1,230)
Accountancy fees	(50)	(50)	(50)	(150)
Furniture (£340 – £35)		(305)		(305)
Taxable property income	1,570	1,565	640	3,775

*The installation of central heating is capital and so is disallowed.

Test your understanding 4

Taxable property income – 2018/19

Landlord	Bob £	Dave £	Jane £	Freddy £
Without property allowance				
Rental income	500	600	3,800	6,500
Less: expenses paid				
Agent's commission	(100)	(500)	(150)	(900)
Building insurance		(220)	(240)	(360)
Accountancy fees	(150)	(160)	(400)	(150)
Profit/(Loss)	250	(280)	3,010	5,090
With property allowance				
Rental income	500	600	3,800	6,500
Less: Property allowance	(500)	(600)	(1,000)	(1,000)
Property income	0	0	2,800	5,500
Optimal position				
Taxable property income	0	(280)	2,800	5,090

Bob has rental income below £1,000 so will automatically receive the property allowance and will not have to declare any property income on his tax return.

Dave is also automatically entitled to the property allowance but would prefer to elect not to use it as this will give him a loss of £280 which he could set off against future property income.

Jane has rental income in excess of £1,000 and so will not get the property allowance automatically. However as her total expenses are below £1,000 at £790 (150 + 240 + 400) she will elect to use the property allowance to ensure her property income is as low as possible at £2,800 rather than £3,010 under the normal basis.

For Freddy the property allowance is also not applied automatically and he will not want to elect to use it as his total expenses of £1,410 are above £1,000 and thus he would be better off using the normal basis.

Test your understanding 5

The correct answer is £5,485.

Computation of taxable property income – 2018/19

	£	£
Rents (£650 × 12)		7,800
Less: Expenses (£300 + £850 + £500)	1,650	
Replacement cooker	665	
	———	(2,315)
		———
Taxable property income		5,485
		———

Note: The cooker replaced a similar domestic item and is therefore an allowable deduction.

Test your understanding 6

Rachman

Computation of taxable property income – 2018/19

	£	£
Rents received for 2018/19		26,280
Less: Garden maintenance	500	
Lift maintenance	180	
Normal decorations	800	
Caretaker's wages	5,800	
Insurance etc.	269	
	———	(7,549)
		———
Taxable property income		18,731
		———

✏️ Test your understanding 7

James

Computation of property income – 2018/19

	£	£
Rents		
(4 × £700) + (6 × £750) – £700 (Note 2)		6,600
Less: Agent's commission	1,163	
Normal redecorations	1,745	
Installation of central heating (Note 3)	–	
Purchase of furniture (Note 4)	–	
Insurance etc.	547	
Professional charges	730	
	———	(4,185)
Profit		2,415

Notes:

(1) As James' gross rental income exceeds £150,000 he will have to use the accruals basis to calculate his property income.

(2) Relief is available for irrecoverable rent.

(3) The cost of installing the central heating is not allowable as it represents an improvement rather than ongoing maintenance and is therefore capital in nature.

(4) The purchase of the dining furniture was not a replacement of domestic items and therefore the cost is not allowable.

Test your understanding 8

Arthur

Property income – 2018/19

	Shop 1 £	Shop 2 £
Income		
Rents accrued		
($\frac{3}{12} \times £3,000 + \frac{6}{12} \times £4,000$)	2,750	
($£6,000 \times \frac{6}{12}$)		3,000
	2,750	3,000
Expenses		
Less: Insurance	190	300
Ground rent	10	40
Repairs and decorating	3,900	2,000
Accountancy	50	50
Advertising for tenant	100	100
	4,250	2,490
Net profit/(loss)	(1,500)	510

Note: Repairs relating to conditions present when the building is purchased are not generally allowable as they represent capital expenditure (e.g. dry rot in Shop 2).

Investment income

Introduction

Investment income of some type will be part of the income tax computation of most individuals. It will feature in the assessment.

This chapter considers interest and dividends received. It explains how they are taxed and when they are not taxable.

ASSESSMENT CRITERIA
Identify and calculate taxable investment income (2.2)
Identify exempt investment income (2.2)
Maximise relevant exemptions and reliefs (3.5)
Change investment incomes to make them more tax efficient (3.5)
Make other changes that can minimise tax liabilities (3.5)

CONTENTS

1 Investment income
2 Savings income
3 Dividend income
4 Tax planning

1 Investment income

1.1 Types of investment income

Investment income can generally be separated into two categories.

1.2 Basis of assessment

All investment income is taxed on a **cash received basis**.

The period in respect of which the income has been paid is not relevant.

🔆 Example

Bank interest of £1,000 for the year to 30 June 2018 was received on 30 June 2018.

In which tax year is the income taxed?

Solution

The interest was received on 30 June 2018 which is in the tax year 2018/19. Hence, it is all taxed in 2018/19.

---

2 Savings income

2.1 Types of savings income

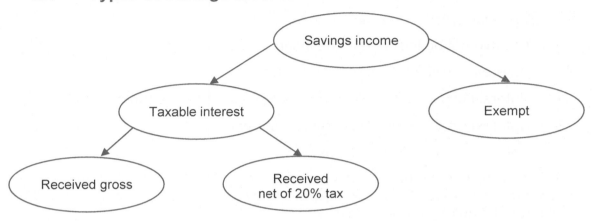

There are three possible treatments of savings income (interest).

- If received gross:

    Simply put the amount received in the tax computation.

- If received net of 20% tax:

    (i)   Gross up.

    $$\text{Taxable interest} = \text{Amount received} \times \frac{100}{80}$$

    (ii)   Put the gross amount in the tax computation.

- If exempt:

    Do not put in the tax computation, but make a note in your answer to state that it is exempt.

2.2 Interest received gross

Almost all interest is received gross, including interest in respect of:

- Bank accounts
- Building society accounts
- Quoted loan notes (debentures) of companies
- Gilts (for example, Treasury stock or Exchequer stock)
- NS&I accounts and bonds unless exempt (see below).

2.3　Interest received net of 20% tax

Interest received in respect of unquoted loan notes (debentures) of companies is received net of 20% tax.

2.4　Exempt interest

The following types of interest are exempt.

They should not be included in the income tax computation.

- Interest on NS&I Savings Certificates.
- Interest on Save As You Earn (SAYE) sharesave accounts.
- Interest on delayed repayments of income tax.
- Interest on ISAs (see 2.5 below).

These types of exempt interest were considered in Chapter 2, but are repeated here to reinforce that they are likely to be included amongst a list of other (taxable) interest received.

Interest on individual savings accounts (ISAs) is an example of exempt income which will almost certainly appear in the assessment.

2.5　Individual savings accounts (ISAs)

An investment of up to £20,000 per tax year can be made into an ISA by a UK individual aged at least 18 (or 16 in the case of a cash only ISA). ISAs are offered by many financial institutions who must comply with rules administered by HMRC.

The funds can be held as cash or invested in securities or stocks and shares.

- Interest arising on cash deposits is exempt from income tax.
- Dividends arising in respect of investments in shares are exempt from income tax.
- Gains arising on the sale of investments are exempt from capital gains tax.

The investment limit is available for you to refer to in the assessment.

2.6 Tax rates to apply to taxable savings income

The normal tax rates (as previously considered in Chapter 2) are:

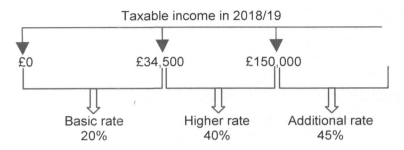

Taxable income in 2018/19

£0   £34,500   £150,000

Basic rate 20%   Higher rate 40%   Additional rate 45%

These are the rates of tax to apply to non-savings income (e.g. employment income and property income).

In addition, basic rate and higher rate taxpayers are entitled to a **savings allowance**.

The savings allowance is:

- Basic rate taxpayer   £1,000 of savings income
- Higher rate taxpayer   £500 of savings income
- Additional rate taxpayer   £Nil

The savings allowance operates like nil rate band, i.e. the amount of the allowance is taxable income, however the tax rate applied to the income covered by the allowance is 0%.

The normal rates of tax and savings allowances are available for you to refer to in the assessment.

 Test your understanding 1

Joseph has taxable non-savings income of £10,000 and taxable savings income of £9,000 for 2018/19. He has no other income.

What is Joseph's income tax liability in respect of his savings income for 2018/19?

Where an individual has non-savings and savings income, the non-savings income is taxed first and then the savings income, to work through the different rate bands.

Example

Patrick has taxable income in 2018/19 of:

(i)   £11,500

(ii)   £36,500

(iii)   £42,500

This includes £6,500 of savings income.

What is his income tax liability for the year?

Solution

(i)   £11,500 taxable income (£5,000 non-savings (N–S) and £6,500 savings (S).

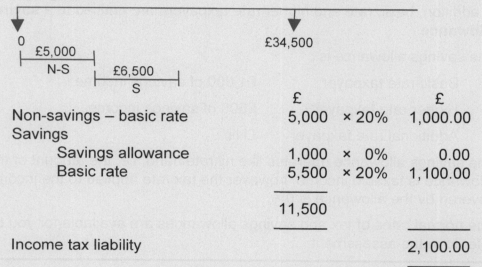

		£		£
Non-savings – basic rate		5,000	× 20%	1,000.00
Savings				
Savings allowance		1,000	× 0%	0.00
Basic rate		5,500	× 20%	1,100.00
		11,500		
Income tax liability				2,100.00

Note: As Patrick is a basic rate taxpayer the savings allowance is £1,000.

(ii) £36,500 taxable income (£30,000 non-savings and £6,500 savings).

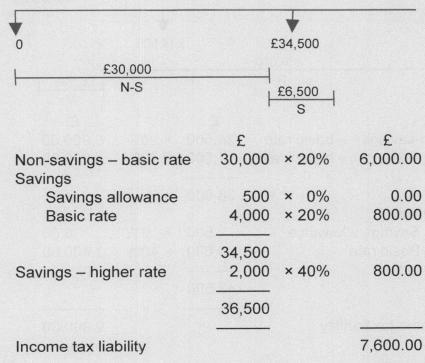

	£		£
Non-savings – basic rate	30,000	× 20%	6,000.00
Savings			
Savings allowance	500	× 0%	0.00
Basic rate	4,000	× 20%	800.00
	34,500		
Savings – higher rate	2,000	× 40%	800.00
	36,500		
Income tax liability			7,600.00

Notes: As Patrick is a higher rate taxpayer he is entitled to a savings allowance of £500. The savings allowance uses £500 of the basic rate band. Accordingly, only £4,000 of the savings income is taxed at 20%.

(iii) £42,500 taxable income (£36,000 non-savings and £6,500 savings).

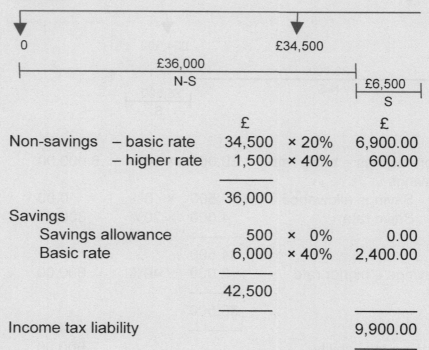

		£		£
Non-savings	– basic rate	34,500	× 20%	6,900.00
	– higher rate	1,500	× 40%	600.00
		36,000		
Savings				
Savings allowance		500	× 0%	0.00
Basic rate		6,000	× 40%	2,400.00
		42,500		
Income tax liability				9,900.00

Note: As Patrick is a higher rate taxpayer he is entitled to a savings allowance of £500.

3 Dividend income

3.1 Types of dividend income

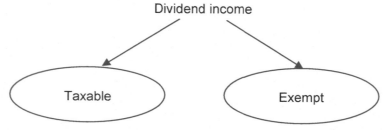

Dividend income is usually taxable (only dividends from ISA investments are exempt).

Dividends may be paid by:

* companies, or

* unit trusts and open-ended investment companies.

3.2 Tax rates

A dividend allowance applies to the first £2,000 of dividend income.

Unlike the savings allowance (which depends on the tax position of the individual) the dividend allowance **always applies** to the first £2,000 of dividend income.

The dividend allowance also operates as a nil rate band, in that up to £2,000 of dividend income is still taxable, but taxed at 0%. The dividend income taxed under the dividend allowance reduces the basic rate and higher rate bands when determining the rate of tax on the remaining dividend income.

Any remaining dividend income is taxed at the dividend rates set out below.

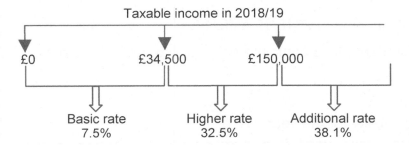

The tax rates in respect of dividends and the amount of the dividend allowance are available for you to refer to in the assessment.

Where an individual has a mixture of all different types of income, we work through the different rate bands in the order:

(i)   non-savings income

(ii)   savings income

(iii) dividend income.

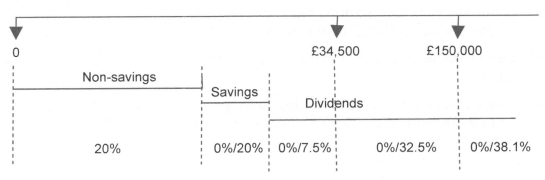

Test your understanding 2

Emily

Emily has taxable income in 2018/19 as follows:

£36,610 of which £2,000 is bank interest and £8,000 is dividend income.

Required:

Calculate her tax liability for the year.

 Test your understanding 3

Simon

Simon has taxable income in 2018/19 as follows:

£158,400 of which £26,300 is bank interest and £46,200 is dividend income.

Required:

Calculate his tax liability for the year.

4 Tax planning

4.1 ISAs

Interest income in respect of cash deposits in an ISA is exempt from income tax.

- Individuals whose savings income is not fully covered by the savings allowance should consider investing in an ISA.

Dividend income in respect of shares held in an ISA is exempt from income tax.

- Individuals with dividend income in excess of the dividend allowance of £2,000 should consider holding shares through an ISA.

4.2 Savings allowance and dividend allowance

Income is taxed at 0% in the following circumstances:

- Interest income which falls into the savings allowance.

- The first £2,000 of dividend income.

Individuals should consider adjusting the investments they hold in order to minimise their tax liability. For example, an individual with a considerable amount of savings income but no dividend income could invest some of his funds held on deposit in shares in order to generate tax-free dividends.

However, such decisions must be made with care as minimising the tax liability is not the only, or even the most important, consideration here. The individual must recognise that money invested in shares is not as secure as money on deposit in a bank due to the possibility that the value of the shares may fall.

4.3 Married couples and civil partnerships

Married couples and civil partners can arrange their income between them in order to minimise the total tax they pay as a couple.

If income generating assets are transferred from one spouse or civil partner to the other, the income will become taxable on the second person.

This tax planning can be used to maximise the use of each individual's:

- savings allowance

- dividend allowance

- lower tax bands

- personal allowance (see Chapter 7).

Test your understanding 4

Mark the following statements as true or false.

		True	False
1	Bernard is a higher rate taxpayer. In the tax year 2018/19, he received interest income of £270 and dividend income of £1,150. The rates of income tax which Bernard will pay on this investment income depends on how much non-savings income he has in the year.		
2	Anne's only income is an annual salary of £57,000 and dividend income of £2,700 each year. Anne would be better off if she were to sell shares which currently generate annual dividend income of £700 and deposit the proceeds in a bank account which would generate £600 of interest income each year.		
3	Mr Pickles earns an annual salary of £18,600 and has no other income. Mrs Pickles earns an annual salary of £73,000 and receives bank interest of £4,000 each year in respect of a bank deposit of £200,000. The total annual income tax liability of Mr and Mrs Pickles would be reduced if Mrs Pickles were to give £100,000 of her bank deposit to her husband.		

5 Test your understanding

 Test your understanding 5

Ralph

Ralph has taxable income in 2018/19 of £72,600.

This consists of non-savings income of £7,800, savings income of £14,700 and dividend income of £50,100.

Required:

Calculate Ralph's tax liability for the year.

6 Summary

Calculating an income tax liability is a fiddly task with many allowances and rates to deal with.

In order to be able to prepare an accurate computation in the assessment, you should practise as many questions as you can.

Make sure you understand any differences between your answer and the model solution so that you improve as you do each question.

Test your understanding answers

Test your understanding 1

The correct answer is £1,600.

	£		£
First	1,000	taxed at 0% savings allowance	0.00
Next	8,000	taxed at 20% basic rate	1,600.00
	9,000		
Income tax liability on savings income			1,600.00

Test your understanding 2

Emily

Step 1 – Analyse the income.

First separate the taxable income into non-savings income, savings income and dividend income. The easiest way to do this is to identify the dividend income then the savings income. The balance (if any) of the taxable income must then be non-savings.

In this case:

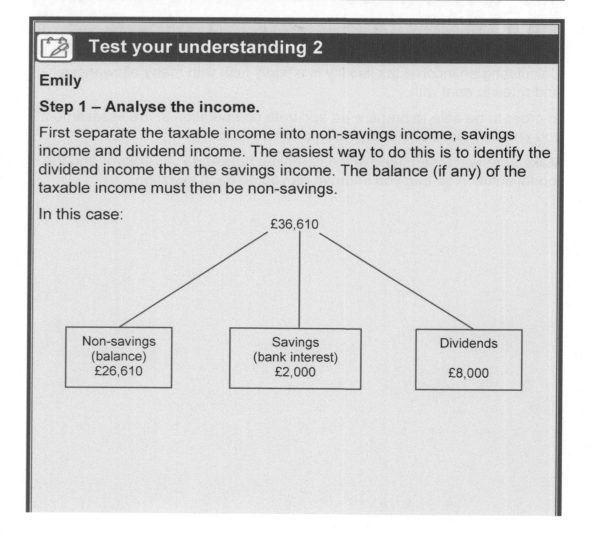

£36,610

| Non-savings (balance) £26,610 | Savings (bank interest) £2,000 | Dividends £8,000 |

Step 2 – Calculation of tax on non-savings income.

The tax liability can then be calculated, first on the non-savings income as follows:

£26,610 × 20%   £5,322.00

Step 3 – Calculation of tax on savings income.

The savings allowance is £500. This is because Emily's taxable income exceeds £34,500, such that she is a higher rate taxpayer.

There is £7,390 of the basic rate band left (£34,500 – £26,610 – £500).

This means that the remaining savings income of £1,500 (£2,000 – £500) all falls into the basic rate band, and will be taxed at 20%.

The tax on savings income is as follows:

	£
£500 × 0%	0.00
£1,500 × 20%	300.00
	300.00

Step 4 – Calculation of tax on dividend income.

The dividend allowance applies to the first £2,000 of the dividend income.

There is then £3,890 of the basic rate band remaining (£34,500 – £26,610 – £2,000 – £2,000).

This means that the next £3,890 of dividend income will be taxed at 7.5% with the balance of £2,110 (£8,000 – £2,000 – £3,890) at 32.5%.

Tax on dividend income is as follows:

	£
£2,000 × 0%	0.00
£3,890 × 7.5%	291.75
£2,110 × 32.5%	685.75
	977.50

Step 5 – In summary:

	£		£
Non-savings	26,610	× 20%	5,322.00
Savings			
Savings allowance	500	× 0%	0.00
Basic rate	1,500	× 20%	300.00
Dividends			
Dividend allowance	2,000	× 0%	0.00
Basic rate	3,890	× 7.5%	291.75
	——		
	34,500		
Dividends	2,110	× 32.5%	685.75
	——		
	36,610		
	——		
Income tax liability			6,599.50
			——

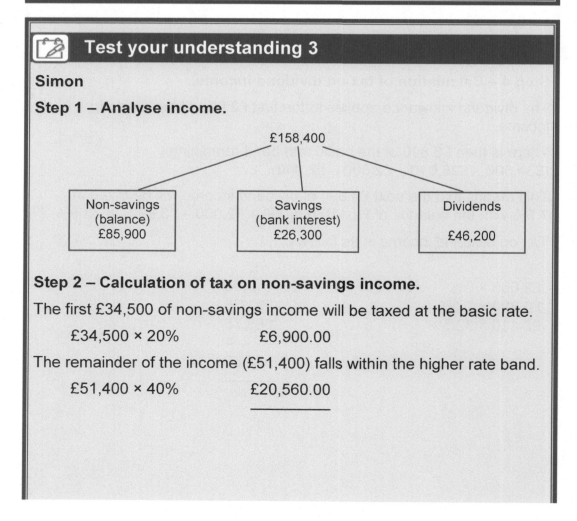

Test your understanding 3

Simon

Step 1 – Analyse income.

£158,400

| Non-savings (balance) £85,900 | Savings (bank interest) £26,300 | Dividends £46,200 |

Step 2 – Calculation of tax on non-savings income.

The first £34,500 of non-savings income will be taxed at the basic rate.

£34,500 × 20%   £6,900.00

The remainder of the income (£51,400) falls within the higher rate band.

£51,400 × 40%   £20,560.00

Step 3 – Calculation of tax on savings income.

The savings allowance is not available because Simon's taxable income exceeds £150,000, such that he is an additional rate taxpayer.

There is still £64,100 of the higher rate band left (£150,000 – £85,900).

This means that all £26,300 of savings income falls into the higher rate band, and will be taxed at 40%.

The tax on the savings income is as follows:

£26,300 × 40%	£10,520.00

Step 4 – Calculation of tax on dividend income.

The dividend allowance applies to the first £2,000 of the dividend income.

There is still £35,800 of the higher rate band left
(£150,000 – £85,900 – £26,300 – £2,000).

This means that £35,800 of dividend income will be taxed at 32.5% with the balance (£8,400) at 38.1%.

Tax on dividend income is as follows:

	£
£2,000 × 0%	0.00
£35,800 × 32.5%	11,635.00
£8,400 × 38.1%	3,200.40
	14,835.40

Step 5 – In summary:

	£		£
Non-savings	34,500	× 20%	6,900.00
Non-savings	51,400	× 40%	20,560.00
Savings	26,300	× 40%	10,520.00
Dividends	2,000	× 0%	0.00
Dividends	35,800	× 32.5%	11,635.00
	150,000		
Dividends	8,400	× 38.1%	3,200.40
	158,400		
Income tax liability			52,815.40

Test your understanding 4

1 **False** Bernard's savings income is less than his savings allowance of £500 (Bernard is a higher rate taxpayer) and his dividend income is less than the dividend allowance of £2,000. Accordingly, he will not pay any income tax in respect of his investment income regardless of how much other income he has.

2 **True** Anne's investment income would be £100 (£700 – £600) less if she were to adopt this strategy.

Anne is a higher rate taxpayer. Her income tax liability would reduce by £227.50 (£700 × 32.5%) if she were no longer to receive £700 of her dividend income.

Anne would then have £600 of savings income. She is entitled to a savings allowance of £500. Her income tax liability on the remaining £100 of savings income would be £40 (£100 × 40%).

In total, Anne's income tax liability would reduce by £187.50 (£227.50 – £40), which is more than the reduction in her investment income.

3 **True** Mrs Pickles' taxable savings income would be reduced by £2,000, such that her income tax liability would be reduced by £800 (£2,000 × 40%).

Mr Pickles would have taxable savings income of £2,000. He is a basic rate taxpayer and is therefore entitled to a savings allowance of £1,000. His income tax liability on the remaining £1,000 of savings income would be £200 (£1,000 × 20%).

Test your understanding 5

Ralph

Step 1 – Calculation of tax on non-savings income.

The non-savings income falls into the basic rate tax band.

£7,800 × 20%	£1,560.00
	————

Step 2 – Calculation of tax on savings income.

The savings allowance is £500. This is because Ralph's taxable income exceeds £34,500, such that he is a higher rate taxpayer.

There is then £26,200 of the basic rate band left (£34,500 – £7,800 – £500).

This means that the remaining savings income of £14,200 (£14,700 – £500) all falls into the basic rate band, and will be taxed at 20%.

The tax on savings income is as follows:

	£
£500 × 0%	0.00
£14,200 × 20%	2,840.00
	————
	2,840.00
	————

Step 3 – Calculation of tax on dividend income.

The dividend allowance applies to the first £2,000 of the dividend income.

There is then £10,000 of the basic rate band remaining (£34,500 – £7,800 – £14,700 – £2,000).

This means that the next £10,000 of dividend income will be taxed at 7.5% with the balance of £38,100 (£50,100 – £2,000 – £10,000) at 32.5%.

Tax on dividend income is as follows:

	£
£2,000 × 0%	0.00
£10,000 × 7.5%	750.00
£38,100× 32.5%	12,382.50
	13,132.50

Step 4 – In summary:

	£		£
Non-savings	7,800	× 20%	1,560.00
Savings			
Savings allowance	500	× 0%	0.00
Basic rate	14,200	× 20%	2,840.00
Dividends			
Dividend allowance	2,000	× 0%	0.00
Basic rate	10,000	× 7.5%	750.00
	34,500		
Dividends	38,100	× 32.5%	12,382.50
	72,600		
Income tax liability			17,532.50

Calculating income tax payable

7

Introduction

This chapter brings together all of the types of income considered in the earlier chapters. It then works towards calculating income tax payable.

This is an important chapter as calculation of taxable income and the income tax liability should always be tested.

ASSESSMENT CRITERIA	CONTENTS
Calculate personal allowances (3.1)	1 Pro forma income tax computation
Calculate restrictions on personal allowances (3.1)	2 Calculation of taxable income
Apply tax rates and bands (3.3)	3 Income from self-employment
Deduct income tax at source (3.3)	4 Reliefs
	5 Personal allowance (PA)
	6 Calculation of income tax payable
	7 Approach to computations in the assessment

1 Pro forma income tax computation

The income tax computation is completed in two stages:

(i)   calculation of taxable income

(ii)   calculation of income tax payable.

Each of these is looked at in turn in this chapter.

2 Calculation of taxable income

2.1 Overview of the calculation of taxable income

In Chapter 2 there was a pro forma income tax computation. It is repeated here with more detail added. This pro forma should be learned.

	£	£
A Person **Income tax computation – 2018/19**		
Earned income		
Employment income		X
Pension income		X
Income from self-employment		X
		X
Savings income		
Building society interest	X	
Bank interest	X	
Unquoted loan note interest (amount received × 100/80)	X	
Quoted loan note interest	X	
Treasury stock interest	X	
NS&I interest	X	
		X
Dividend income		X
Property income		X
Total income		X
Less: Reliefs		(X)
Net income		X
Less: Personal allowance (PA)		(X)
Taxable income		X

All the entries in the pro forma have been considered in detail in Chapters 3 to 6 with the exception of:

- income from self-employment

- reliefs, and

- personal allowance.

These are covered in sections 3 to 5 of this chapter.

2.2 Expanded pro forma income tax computation

The pro forma is expanded as set out below in order to assist in the calculation of the income tax liability.

As we have seen earlier, non-savings income is all income apart from savings income (interest) and dividends. Accordingly, it includes employment income, property income and income from self-employment. Non-savings income is sometimes referred to as 'other' income.

A Person

Income tax computation – 2018/19

	Total	Non-savings	Savings	Dividends
	£	£	£	£
Earned income	X	X		
Savings income	X		X	
Dividend income	X			X
Property income	X	X		
Total income	X	X	X	X
Less: Reliefs	(X)	(X)*		
Net income	X	X	X	X
Less: Personal allowance	(X)	(X)*		
Taxable income	X	X	X	X

* Reliefs and the personal allowance are deducted primarily from non-savings income. If the non-savings income is reduced to nil, any remaining deduction is then made from savings income and finally dividend income.

3 Income from self-employment

The computation of income from self-employment is covered in Business Tax, and is outside the scope of Personal Tax.

It does, however, form part of an individual's total income.

If a task in the assessment includes income from self-employment, you simply need to include the figure given to you for taxable trade profit in the income tax computation as earned income.

4 Reliefs

Relief is available for losses, certain types of expenditure incurred by the taxpayer and certain assets gifted to charity by the taxpayer.

The loss relief rules are not assessed in this unit but are covered in Business Tax.

4.1 Other reliefs

If an individual gives certain assets to charity, tax relief is available by deduction from total income.

The amount of the deduction is the value of the asset gifted.

The assets for which this treatment is available are:

(a) listed shares and securities
(i.e. where the company's name ends in 'plc')

(b) units in an authorised unit trust

(c) land and buildings which the charity agrees to accept.

There are other types of reliefs (e.g. certain 'qualifying interest payments'). These are unlikely to appear in the Personal Tax assessment.

5 Personal allowance (PA)

5.1 Availability

All individuals are entitled to a personal allowance of £11,850 for 2018/19.

This figure is available for you to refer to in the assessment.

The personal allowance is deducted from net income (i.e. total income less reliefs) in arriving at taxable income.

The personal allowance can only be relieved against income of the current tax year. Any unused amount cannot be carried forward or carried back, nor can it be offset against capital gains.

Example

Mavis has a salary of £23,000 in 2018/19 which is her only source of income.

Calculate her 2018/19 taxable income and tax liability.

Solution

	£
Total income	23,000
Less: Reliefs	(Nil)
Net income	23,000
Less: Personal allowance	(11,850)
Taxable income	11,150
Mavis' income tax liability is: (£11,150 × 20%)	£2,230.00

5.2 Restricted personal allowance

The personal allowance is restricted if an individual's net income exceeds £100,000.

The reduction is half of the amount by which the individual's net income exceeds £100,000. The allowance remaining is rounded up to the next whole pound.

Once an individual's net income exceeds £123,700 (£100,000 + (2 × £11,850)) they will not receive a personal allowance.

The personal allowance is never a negative number.

The income limit is available for you to refer to in the assessment.

Example

Dan has net income in 2018/19 of £111,475.

Calculate Dan's personal allowance for 2018/19.

Solution

	£
Personal allowance	11,850.00
Less: Restriction	
50% × (£111,475 – £100,000)	(5,737.50)
	6,112.50
Restricted allowance (rounded up)	6,113.00

Test your understanding 1

Leon

Leon has income for the 2018/19 tax year as follows:

	£
Employment income	95,000
Dividends received	15,000

Leon made a gift of quoted shares valued at £2,000 to a registered charity during the tax year 2018/19.

Required:

Compute Leon's taxable income for 2018/19.

---

6 Calculation of income tax payable

6.1 Tax rates

In Chapter 6 the different rates of income tax were considered in detail.

The rates are summarised below.

	Allowance	Basic rate band	Higher rate band	Additional rate band
Non-savings	N/A	20%	40%	45%
Savings*	£1,000 or	20%	40%	45%
	£500 or			
	Nil			
Dividends	£2,000	7.5%	32.5%	38.1%

Pence should be shown when calculating income tax; it is not correct to round calculations to the nearest pound.

However, in your assessment you must follow the instructions you are given for a particular task.

* There is a starting rate band of 0% that is sometimes available on savings income but this is not examinable.

6.2 Pro forma calculation of income tax payable

A Person

Income tax payable – 2018/19

	Total	Non-savings	Savings	Dividends
	£	£	£	£
Taxable income (from first part of pro forma)	X	A	B	C
Income tax				£.pp
Non-savings income A × 20%/40%/45%				X
Savings income B × 0%/20%/40%/45%				X
Dividend income C × 0%/7.5%/32.5%/38.1%				X
Income tax liability				X
Less: Tax deducted at source				(X)
Income tax payable				X

It is important to be able to distinguish between:

* income tax liability

    This is the total income tax due in respect of the taxpayer's income.

and

* income tax payable

    This is the total income tax still to be paid after taking off any tax deducted at source.

6.3 Tax deducted at source

The income tax **liability** is the total amount of income tax that an individual must pay to HM Revenue and Customs (HMRC) for a tax year.

Many individuals will have already paid some tax at source (known as tax credits).

* Salaries – have tax deducted under the PAYE system at all relevant rates (20%, 40% and 45%).

* Interest in respect of unquoted loan notes of companies has 20% tax deducted at source.

In these situations the payer (the employer or the company) pays the withheld tax to HMRC on behalf of the taxpayer.

These tax credits can reduce the tax liability leaving a smaller amount of tax still owed to HMRC (or possibly a tax repayment).

 Example

From the example in section 5.1, Mavis had PAYE deducted from her salary.

What is her income tax payable/repayable if the PAYE deducted was:

(a)   £2,080, or

(b)   £2,880?

Solution

	(a)	(b)
From section 5 solution		
Income tax liability	2,230.00	2,230.00
Less: Tax deducted at source		
PAYE	(2,080.00)	(2,880.00)
	————	————
Income tax payable	150.00	
	————	
Income tax repayable		(650.00)
		————

 Example

Stephanie was paid a gross salary in 2018/19 of £30,405. Her employer deducted income tax under PAYE of £5,060.

Stephanie also receives the following amounts of investment income in 2018/19.

	£
Dividends	18,300
Interest on unquoted loan notes	400
Bank interest	800

In June 2018 Stephanie donated shares in a quoted company worth £1,100 to a registered charity.

Calculate Stephanie's income tax payable for 2018/19.

Solution

Stephanie – Income tax computation – 2018/19

	Total	Non-savings	Savings	Dividends
	£	£	£	£
Employment income	30,405	30,405		
Interest on unquoted loan notes (£400 × 100/80)	500		500	
Bank interest	800		800	
Dividends	18,300			18,300
Total income	50,005	30,405	1,300	18,300
Less: Reliefs	(1,100)	(1,100)		
Net income	48,905	29,305	1,300	18,300
Less: PA	(11,850)	(11,850)		
Taxable income	37,055	17,455	1,300	18,300

Income tax

£			£
17,455	× 20%	(non-savings – basic rate)	3,491.00
500	× 0%	(savings allowance)	0.00
800	× 20%	(savings – basic rate)	160.00
2,000	× 0%	(dividends allowance)	0.00
13,745	× 7.5%	(dividends – basic rate)	1,030.87
34,500			
2,555	× 32.5%	(dividends – higher rate)	830.37
37,055			

		£
Income tax liability		5,512.24
Less: Tax deducted at source		
PAYE		(5,060.00)
Savings (£500 × 20%)		(100.00)
Income tax payable		352.24

Note: the savings allowance is £500 because Stephanie is a higher rate taxpayer.

Test your understanding 2

Stanley

The 2018/19 tax return of Stanley shows the following income for the year ended 5 April 2019:

	£
Gross salary from Dee Ltd	102,485
Dividends received	29,000
Interest received on unquoted loan notes	2,000
Building society interest received	1,000

Dee Ltd paid Stanley a performance related bonus. On 9 September 2017 he was paid his first bonus of £43,280 relating to the year ended 30 June 2017 and on 17 September 2018 he was paid £38,480 relating to the year ended 30 June 2018.

Stanley has travelled 11,500 business miles in his own car in 2018/19. Dee Ltd paid him 47p per mile.

During 2018/19 the PAYE paid was £57,800.

Required:

Compute Stanley's income tax payable for 2018/19.

Approach to this question

The first step is to draw up an income tax computation pro forma.

In this case, you will have to be careful when slotting in the figure for the bonus, as information is given for two tax years. You will also need to gross up any net amounts given (i.e. interest income from unquoted loan notes) by multiplying the net income by 100/80.

The income tax liability can then be calculated.

This question requires the calculation of tax payable, so you must then deduct from the tax liability tax paid under PAYE (pay as you earn) and also any tax suffered at source, (i.e. tax credits on savings income received net).

7 Approach to computations in the assessment

There will **normally** be at least one task in the assessment which requires you to prepare all or part of an income tax computation. However, the income tax computations in the assessment will not be as long as the example Stephanie or test your understanding 2 above. These are included to give you an overview and it is important that you practise full computations to increase your understanding of how income tax works.

A grid is provided in the assessment to assist you when preparing income tax computations. This will have between three and five columns:

- the left hand column is for descriptions

- the other columns are for numerical entry.

A five column grid will allow you to enter a full computation per the pro forma in this chapter. The example below shows a suggested approach.

Example

Arthur has a pension from his former employer of £17,600, a state pension of £5,200 and received dividends of £6,500 in 2018/19.

Required:

Calculate Arthur's income tax liability using the grid below.

Approach

Step 1

Use the paper provided in your assessment to draw up a standard income tax computation. This need not be particularly neat as it will be thrown away at the end of the assessment!

	Total	Non-savings	Dividends
	£	£	£
Employment pension	17,600	17,600	
State pension	5,200	5,200	
Dividends	6,500		6,500
Net income	29,300	22,800	6,500
Less: PA	(11,850)	(11,850)	
Taxable income	17,450	10,950	6,500

	£	
10,950 × 20%	(non-savings – basic rate)	2,190.00
2,000 × 0%	(dividends allowance)	0.00
4,500 × 7.5%	(dividends allowance – basic rate)	337.50
17,450		
Income tax liability		2,527.50

Step 2

Enter the figures into the assessment grid.

You cannot insert lines marking totals and subtotals. Remember to check you have enough space before you start – if not abbreviate.

	Total	Non-savings	Divis	
	£	£	£	
Employment pension	17,600	17,600		
State pension	5,200	5,200		
Dividends	6,500		6,500	
Total = Net income	29,300	22,800	6,500	
Less: PA	(11,850)	(11,850)		
Taxable income	17,450	10,950	6,500	
£10,950 × 20%	2,190.00			
£2,000 × 0%	0.00			
£4,500 × 7.5%	337.50			
Income tax liability	2,527.50			

This will be manually marked so you need to include your workings.

In some questions you may not have enough information to complete a full computation as the question may be more focused on calculating a restricted personal allowance.

In this case it is the figure of net income that you need without worrying about what type of income is included. If there is doubt as to the source of income, always assume it is 'non-savings income'.

It is possible that the space provided in the assessment will only have three columns. In that case, it will not be possible to separate out the income into different types in your on screen answer. It is still best to do this on paper first, however, when you input your answer you should show the workings in one of the first two columns and the total column on the right. Make sure that your workings make it clear where each figure has come from, for example, show a working of taxable non-savings income by deducting the personal allowance from the total non-savings income, or by deducting savings and dividend income from the total taxable income.

The following test your understanding shows both the five and the three column approach in the answer.

Test your understanding 3

Hossam

In the tax year 2018/19, Hossam has non-savings income of £50,000 together with bank interest of £2,250 and dividends of £4,000.

Required:

Calculate the income tax liability using the grid below.

8 Test your understanding

Test your understanding 4

Mary

Mary is employed as a sales representative at an annual salary of £37,900. She is provided with a company car by her employer which gave rise to a taxable benefit for 2018/19 of £5,700.

Mary is in an occupational pension scheme into which she pays 6% of her basic salary.

Mary received bank interest during 2018/19 of £6,500.

Required:

Calculate Mary's income tax liability for the year 2018/19 using this grid.

Note: You do not have enough columns here to set out a full columnar computation. You should still prepare a columnar computation in your workings. In your grid you can use the left hand columns for description and workings and simply enter your total column in the third column in the grid.

Test your understanding 5

Briony

Until 31 December 2018 Briony was employed by JJ Gyms Ltd as a fitness consultant. Her taxable employment income for 2018/19 was £39,295, from which PAYE of £6,700 was deducted.

On 1 January 2019 Briony commenced in self-employment running a music recording studio. Her taxable trade profit for 2018/19 is £15,415.

During 2018/19, Briony received rental income, after utilising the property allowance, from an investment property of £6,500 and dividend income of £6,710.

Required:

Calculate Briony's income tax payable for 2018/19.

 Test your understanding 6

Sally:

Sally has net income from employment and self-employment for 2018/19 of £47,965. She suffered PAYE on her employment income of £4,500.

Required:

What is Sally's income tax liability for 2018/19?

Test your understanding 7

Jon

Jon informs you of the following matters so that you can prepare his income tax computation.

- His salary for 2018/19 is £43,180 with tax deducted of £5,650.

- During June 2018 he cashed in his holding of NS&I Savings Certificates for £2,340. These had been purchased in 2013 for £2,000 and had earned 4% per annum compound for five years.

- Jon has been very lucky with his bets on the horses this year, winning £500 on the Derby (June 2018) but he tells you that most years he loses more than he wins.

- He received building society interest of £900 in the year to 5 April 2019.

- He received dividends of £3,100 in the year to 5 April 2019.

Required:

Calculate Jon's income tax payable for 2018/19.

Test your understanding 8

Marcel

Marcel's income for 2018/19 was as follows:

	£
Occupational pension (gross)	16,980
Interest on NS&I Savings Certificates	1,250
Dividends	6,200
Interest on British Government stocks	9,410
Bank interest	2,480

PAYE of £1,280 was deducted from the occupational pension.

Required:

Calculate the income tax payable by Marcel for 2018/19.

Test your understanding 9

Mr Black

Mr Black gives you the following information for 2018/19.

	£
Salary (PAYE deducted £6,420)	47,150
Dividends received	330
Bank interest received	728

Required:

What is the income tax payable by Mr Black for 2018/19?

 Test your understanding 10

Mark the following statements as true or false.

		True	False
1	The first £2,000 of dividend income is always taxed at 0%.		
2	The first £1,000 of savings income is always taxed at 0%.		
3	The tax credit in respect of PAYE can never be repaid but can be used to reduce the tax liability to nil.		
4	If a taxpayer has no taxable income for 2018/19 they can carry forward the benefit of their unused personal allowance to 2019/20.		

Test your understanding 11

Louis

Louis has provided you with the following information for 2018/19.

	£
Salary (PAYE deducted £44,250)	146,400
Dividends received	8,400
Bank interest received	7,000

Required:

Calculate the income tax payable by Louis for 2018/19.

9 Summary

This chapter has set out the two stages of the income tax computation:

(a) calculation of taxable income

(b) calculation of income tax payable.

It is worth noting that every individual is entitled to a personal allowance, but this will be reduced if their net income exceeds £100,000.

The key to preparing accurate income tax computations is to know the rules and then to practise.

Test your understanding answers

Test your understanding 1

Leon

Taxable income computation – 2018/19

	Total £
Employment income	95,000
Dividends received	15,000
Total income	110,000
Less: Reliefs – gift of quoted shares to charity	(2,000)
Net income	108,000
Less: PA (working)	(7,850)
Taxable income	100,150

Working:

	£
Personal allowance	11,850
Less: Restriction	
50% × (£108,000 – £100,000)	(4,000)
	7,850

Test your understanding 2

Stanley

Income tax computation – 2018/19

	Total £	Non-savings £	Savings £	Dividends £
Employment income				
– Salary	102,485			
– Bonus	38,480			
– Mileage (W)	530			
	141,495	141,495		
Interest on unquoted loan notes				
(£2,000 × 100/80)	2,500		2,500	
Building society interest	1,000		1,000	
Dividends	29,000			29,000
Total income	173,995	141,495	3,500	29,000
Less: PA (restricted)	(0)	(0)	(0)	(0)
Taxable income	173,995	141,495	3,500	29,000

Income tax

£			£
34,500	× 20%	(non-savings – basic rate)	6,900.00
106,995	× 40%	(non-savings – higher rate)	42,798.00
141,495			
3,500	× 40%	(savings – higher rate)	1,400.00
2,000	× 0%	(dividends allowance)	0.00
3,005	× 32.5%	(dividends – higher rate)	976.62
150,000			
23,995	× 38.1%	(dividends – additional rate)	9,142.09
173,995			

			£
Income tax liability			61,216.71
Less:	Tax deducted at source		
	Savings (£2,500 × 20%)		(500.00)
	PAYE		(57,800.00)
Income tax payable			2,916.71

Note: there is no savings allowance because Stanley is an additional rate taxpayer.

Working: Taxable mileage allowance

	£	£
Income (11,500 × 47p)		5,405
Less: Allowable expense		
10,000 × 45p	4,500	
1,500 × 25p	375	
	———	(4,875)
Taxable amount		530

📝 Test your understanding 3

Hossam – Five column approach

	Total	Non-savings	Savings	Divis
	£	£	£	£
Income	50,000	50,000		
Bank interest	2,250		2,250	
Dividends	4,000			4,000
Total = Net income	56,250	50,000	2,250	4,000
Less Personal allowance	(11,850)	(11,850)		
Taxable income	44,400	38,150	2,250	4,000
£34,500 × 20%	6,900.00			
£3,650 × 40%	1,460.00			
£500 × 0%	0.00			
£1,750 × 40%	700.00			
£2,000 × 0%	0.00			
£2,000 × 32.5%	650.00			
Income tax liability	9,710.00			

Note: the savings allowance is £500 because Hossam is a higher rate taxpayer.

Hossam – Three column approach

		Total
	£	£
Income		50,000
Bank interest		2,250
Dividends		4,000
Total = Net income		56,250
Less Personal allowance		(11,850)
Taxable income		44,400
Taxable non-savings income (£50,000 – £11,850)	38,150	
£34,500 × 20%		6,900.00
£3,650 × 40%		1,460.00
£500 × 0%		0.00
£1,750 × 40%		700.00
£4,000 × 0%		0.00
£2,000 × 32.5%		650.00
Income tax liability		9,710.00

📝 Test your understanding 4

Mary – income tax computation – 2018/19

		Total
		£
Salary and benefits (£37,900 + £5,700)		43,600
Less: 6% pension contribution (£37,900 × 6%)		(2,274)
Bank interest		6,500
Total = Net income		47,826
Less: Personal allowance		(11,850)
Taxable income		35,976
Non-savings (£35,976 – £6,500)	£29,476 × 20%	5,895.20
Savings (savings allowance)	£500 × 0%	0.00
Savings (£34,500 – £29,476 – £500)	£4,524 × 20%	904.80
Savings (£6,500 – £500 – £4,524)	£1,476 × 40%	590.40
Income tax liability		7,390.40

Note: the savings allowance is £500 because Mary is a higher rate taxpayer.

Workings:

(W1) Income tax computation – 2018/19

	Total	Non-savings	Savings
	£	£	£
Employment income (W2)	41,326	41,326	
Bank interest	2,500		6,500
Net income	43,826	41,326	6,500
Less: PA	(11,850)	(11,850)	
Taxable income	35,976	29,476	6,500

Income tax

£			£
29,476	× 20%	(non-savings – basic rate)	5,895.20
500	× 0%	(savings – allowance)	0.00
4,524	× 20%	(savings – basic rate)	904.80
34,500			
1,476	× 40%	(savings – higher rate)	590.40
35,976			
Income tax liability			7,390.40

(W2) Employment income

	£
Salary	37,900
Car benefit	5,700
	43,600
Less: Pension contributions (6% × £37,900)	(2,274)
Employment income	41,326

Test your understanding 5

Briony

Income tax computation – 2018/19

	Total £	Non-savings £	Dividends £
Employment income	39,295	39,295	
Trading income	15,415	15,415	
Property income	6,500	6,500	
Dividends	6,710		6,710
Net income	67,920	61,210	6,710
Less: PA	(11,850)	(11,850)	
Taxable income	56,070	49,360	6,710

Income tax

£			£
34,500	× 20%	(non-savings – basic rate)	6,900.00
14,860	× 40%	(non-savings – higher rate)	5,944.00
49,360			
2,000	× 0%	(dividend allowance)	0.00
4,710	× 32.5%	(dividends – higher rate)	1,530.75
56,070			

		£
Income tax liability		14,374.75
Less: Tax deducted at source		
PAYE		(6,700.00)
Income tax payable		7,674.75

Test your understanding 6

Sally

The correct answer is £7,546.00.

Income tax computation – 2018/19

	£
Net income	47,965
Less: PA	(11,850)
Taxable income	36,115

Income tax

	£
34,500 × 20% (non-savings – basic rate)	6,900.00
1,615 × 40% (non-savings – higher rate)	646.00
Income tax liability	7,546.00

Note: The question asks for the income tax liability not the income tax payable so there is no need to deduct the PAYE.

Test your understanding 7

Jon

Income tax computation – 2018/19

	Total	Non-savings	Savings	Dividends
	£	£	£	£
Employment income – Salary	43,180	43,180		
NS&I Savings Certificates	Exempt			
Gambling winnings	Exempt			
Building society interest	900		900	
Dividends	3,100			3,100
Net income	47,180	43,180	900	3,100
Less: PA	(11,850)	(11,850)		
Taxable income	35,330	31,330	900	3,100

Income tax

£			
31,330	× 20%	(non-savings – basic rate)	6,266.00
500	× 0%	(savings allowance)	0.00
400	× 20%	(savings – basic rate)	80.00
2,000	× 0%	(dividend allowance)	0.00
270	× 7.5%	(dividend – basic rate)	20.25
34,500			
830	× 32.5%	(dividend – basic rate)	269.75
35,330			

Income tax liability		6,636.00
Less: Tax deducted at source PAYE		(5,650.00)
Income tax payable		986.00

Note: the savings allowance is £500 because Jon is a higher rate taxpayer.

Test your understanding 8

Marcel

Income tax computation – 2018/19

	Total	Non-savings	Savings	Dividends
	£	£	£	£
Pension income	16,980	16,980		
Interest on NS&I Certificates	Exempt			
Government stocks	9,410		9,410	
Bank interest	2,480		2,480	
Dividends	6,200			6,200
Net income	35,070	16,980	11,890	6,200
Less: PA	(11,850)	(11,850)		
Taxable income	23,220	5,130	11,890	6,200

Income tax

£		£
5,130	× 20% (non-savings – basic rate)	1,026.00
1,000	× 0% (savings allowance)	0.00
10,890	× 20% (savings – basic rate)	2,178.00
2,000	× 0% (dividend allowance)	0.00
4,200	× 7.5% (dividends – basic rate)	315.00
23,220		

Income tax liability	3,519.00
Less: Tax deducted at source PAYE	(1,280.00)
Income tax payable	2,239.00

Note: the savings allowance is £1,000 because Marcel is a basic rate taxpayer.

Test your understanding 9

Mr Black

Income tax computation – 2018/19

	Total £	Non-savings £	Savings £	Dividends £
Employment income	47,150	47,150		
Bank interest	728		728	
Dividends	330			330
Net income	48,208	47,150	728	330
Less: PA	(11,850)	(11,850)		
Taxable income	36,358	35,300	728	330

Income tax

£				£
34,500	× 20%	(non-savings – basic rate)		6,900.00
800	× 40%	(non-savings – higher rate)		320.00
35,300				
500	× 0%	(savings allowance)		0.00
228	× 40%	(savings – higher rate)		91.20
330	× 0%	(dividend allowance)		0.00
36,358				

	£
Income tax liability	7,311.20
Less: Tax deducted at source PAYE	(6,420.00)
Income tax payable	891.20

Note: the savings allowance is £500 because Mr Black is a higher rate taxpayer.

Test your understanding 10

1   **True**

2   **False** – The first £1,000 of savings income is only taxed at 0% if the person is a basic rate taxpayer.

3   **False** – where PAYE has resulted in an overpayment of tax, the taxpayer will receive a repayment.

4   **False**

 Test your understanding 11

Louis

Income tax computation – 2018/19

	Total	Non-savings	Savings	Dividends
	£	£	£	£
Employment income	146,400	146,400		
Bank interest	7,000		7,000	
Dividends	8,400			8,400
Net income	161,800	146,400	7,000	8,400
Less: PA (restricted)	(0)	(0)	(0)	(0)
Taxable income	161,800	146,400	7,000	8,400

Income tax

£			£
34,500	× 20%	(non-savings – basic rate)	6,900.00
111,900	× 40%	(non-savings – higher rate)	44,760.00
———			
146,400			
3,600	× 40%	(savings – higher rate)	1,440.00
———			
150,000			
3,400	× 45%	(savings – additional rate)	1,530.00
2,000	× 0%	(dividend allowance)	0.00
6,400	× 38.1%	(dividends – additional rate)	2,438.40
———			
161,800			———
———			

Income tax liability		57,068.40
Less: Tax deducted at source		
PAYE		(44,250.00)
		———
Income tax payable		12,818.40
		———

Note: there is no savings allowance because Louis is an additional rate taxpayer.

Pension payments and gift aid

Introduction

Tax relief is available in respect of these two types of payment. This chapter considers the amount of tax relief available and how it is given.

ASSESSMENT CRITERIA	CONTENTS
Apply occupational pension schemes (3.2)	1 Pension contributions
	2 Donations to charity
Apply private pension schemes (3.2)	3 Pension payments, gift aid and personal allowances
Apply charitable donations (3.2)	

1 Pension contributions

1.1 Tax efficiency

A tax efficient way of providing for retirement is to make contributions into a registered pension scheme.

It is tax efficient for the following reasons:

- The individual gets tax relief in respect of the contributions made.

- The employer gets tax relief in respect of any contributions made, but without there being a taxable benefit for the employee.

- The income and chargeable gains generated by the funds in a pension scheme are exempt from income tax and capital gains tax.

- Part of the pension may be taken as a **tax-free** lump sum.

Registered pension schemes are available to all individuals.

Certain employed persons have a choice of provision so the full details are included in this section for all individuals.

1.2 Options available to employees

An OPS is an option only if the employer has a scheme available.

An OPS is also known as a company pension scheme. Such schemes were considered briefly in Chapter 3.

A PPS is an option for an employee who:

- has no OPS available from his employer, or

- chooses the PPS in preference to his employer's OPS, or

- also contributes to an OPS.

1.3 Options available to other individuals

Other individuals may save through a PPS.

1.4 Tax relief for pension contributions

All registered pension schemes are governed by the same rules, regardless of whether they are occupational or personal pensions.

An individual may make a pension contribution of any amount into a registered pension scheme or may make contributions into a number of different schemes. Tax relief will however only be available for a maximum annual amount.

The maximum total annual contribution into **all** pension schemes that an individual can obtain tax relief for is the higher of:

- £3,600, and

- 100% of the individual's relevant earnings, chargeable to income tax in the tax year.

Relevant earnings include trading profits, employment income, but not investment income (although profits from furnished holiday lettings are specifically included in the definition of relevant earnings).

Note that an individual with no relevant earnings can still obtain tax relief on contributions of up to £3,600.

 Example

Rob has employment income of £2,500 and interest income of £10,000 (gross) in 2018/19.

What is the maximum pension contribution that Rob can get tax relief for in 2018/19?

Solution

The maximum pension contribution that Rob can get tax relief for in 2018/19 is £3,600 – being the higher of:

	£
– £3,600 and	3,600
– 100% of relevant earnings	
= employment income	2,500

1.5   Method of giving tax relief for pension contributions

The **amount of tax relief** that is given for pension contributions is the same whether the contributions are to a personal pension scheme or an occupational pension scheme.

However, the **method by which the tax relief is given** is different for the two types of scheme.

1.6   Tax relief for contributions to personal pension schemes

Personal pension contributions are paid net of basic rate tax (20%).

Higher rate and additional rate income tax relief is achieved by extending the basic rate and higher rate bands by the gross amount of the pension contribution.

For example, if an individual pays a premium of £8,000 (net) – equivalent to a gross premium of £10,000 (£8,000 × 100/80) – his basic rate threshold is extended to £44,500 (£34,500 + £10,000).

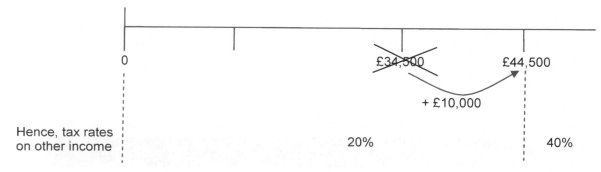

The limit at which he starts paying tax at the additional rates is also extended. The new limit is £160,000 (£150,000 + £10,000).

:Ö: **Example**

Pauline's income for 2018/19 is as follows:

	£
Salary	39,000
Benefits	4,440
Bank interest received	8,000

She made a personal pension contribution of £3,200 (net) in 2018/19.

Calculate Pauline's income tax liability for 2018/19.

Solution

	Total £	Non-savings £	Savings £
Employment income (£39,000 + £4,440)	43,440	43,440	
Bank interest	8,000		8,000
Net income	51,440	43,440	8,000
Less: PA	(11,850)	(11,850)	
Taxable income	39,590	31,590	8,000

Income tax

£			£
31,590	× 20%	(non-savings – basic rate)	6,318.00
500	× 0%	(savings allowance)	0.00
6,410	× 20%	(savings – basic rate)	1,282.00
38,500	(W)		
1,090	× 40%	(savings – higher rate)	436.00
39,590			
Income tax liability			8,036.00

Working:

	£
Basic rate band	34,500
Add: Personal pension contribution (£3,200 × 100/80)	
(maximum contribution = 100% × £43,440)	4,000
Extended basic rate band	38,500

1.7 Method of giving tax relief for occupational pension scheme contributions

The pension contribution paid is deducted from employment income in the year of payment.

Tax relief is obtained through the PAYE system, at all rates of tax, and no further tax adjustment is required in the income tax computation other than showing the deduction against employment income (i.e. it is an allowable expense).

Example

David received an annual salary of £43,300 and interest income of £12,000 in 2018/19.

Each year David pays 3% of his salary and his employer pays a further 5% into his employer's registered occupational pension scheme.

Explain how David will obtain tax relief for his pension contributions and calculate his income tax liability for 2018/19.

Solution

- David will pay a pension contribution of £1,299 (£43,300 × 3%) in 2018/19 on which he will obtain full tax relief, as it is less than the maximum available for tax relief of £43,300 (100% of earned income).

- David will obtain tax relief, at basic and higher rates, for the contribution through the PAYE system.

  His employer will deduct the pension contribution from David's taxable pay, in order to calculate the PAYE due.

David

Income tax computation – 2018/19

	Total	Non-savings	Savings
	£	£	£
Employment income	43,300		
Less: Pension contributions (3%)	(1,299)		
	42,001	42,001	
Interest income	12,000		12,000
Net income	54,001	42,001	12,000
Less: PA	(11,850)	(11,850)	
Taxable income	42,151	30,151	12,000

Income tax

£			£
30,151	× 20%	(non-savings – basic rate)	6,030.20
500	× 0%	(savings allowance)	0.00
3849	× 20%	(savings – basic rate)	769.80
34,500			
7,651	× 40%	(savings – higher rate)	3,060.40
42,151			
Income tax liability			9,860.40

The pension contributions made by David's employer are an exempt benefit.

📝 Test your understanding 1

Gabrielle has a salary of £50,000 per year. She pays 6% of her salary into her employer's pension scheme.

What is Gabrielle's income tax liability for 2018/19?

1.8   Annual allowance

Contributions into a registered pension scheme can be made by the scheme member or any other party (e.g. employer).

If the total contributions paid into the pension scheme exceed the annual allowance then the individual member is charged income tax on the excess.

The annual allowance is not within the scope of the assessment criteria.

1.9 Lifetime allowance

There is no restriction on the *total* contributions that an individual may make into a registered pension scheme. There is only a limit upon the annual contributions in respect of which *tax relief will* be available.

As funds in a registered pension scheme grow tax free there is also a limit, the 'lifetime allowance', which determines the maximum amount that an individual can accumulate in a pension scheme tax free.

The lifetime allowance is considered when a member becomes entitled to take benefits out of the scheme (e.g. when he becomes entitled to take a pension).

The lifetime allowance is not within the scope of the assessment criteria.

2   Donations to charity

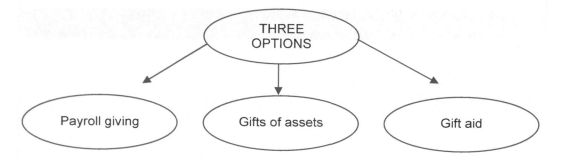

2.1 Options available to individuals

Payroll giving – an individual can have an amount deducted from salary/wages at each pay day.

This is treated as an allowable expense when calculating employment income (see Chapter 3).

Gifts of assets – an individual can make gifts of certain assets (mainly quoted shares and land and buildings).

The value of the asset gifted is deducted as a relief from total income (see Chapter 7).

Gift aid – an individual can make regular payments or one-off payments of cash directly to charity (see 2.2 below).

2.2 Gift aid

If an individual declares a charitable payment of cash to be under 'gift aid', the amount of the donation is treated as paid net of basic rate tax which is then recoverable by the charity:

	£
Donation actually paid, say	80
Basic rate tax (20/80)	20
Gross value of gift to charity	100
Charity claims direct from HMRC	20

If the individual is a basic rate taxpayer there is no effect on his personal taxation.

If the individual is a higher or additional rate taxpayer he will benefit from higher or additional rate relief by extending his basic rate band and higher rate band by the gross amount of the gift aid payment.

In the above example, the taxpayer would not be subject to the higher rates (40% or 32.5%) until his taxable income exceeded £34,600 (£34,500 + £100 gross gift aid).

This is the same as the mechanism that gives tax relief for personal pension payments.

Taxpayers can elect to treat a gift aid donation as if it were paid in the previous tax year.

Example

John earns £70,000 p.a. and pays a total of £4,800 to a number of charities in 2018/19 under the gift aid scheme.

Calculate his income tax liability for 2018/19.

Solution

	£
Net income	70,000
Less: PA	(11,850)
Taxable income	58,150

Basic rate band: £34,500 + (£4,800 × 100/80) = £40,500

	£	
Income tax:	40,500 × 20%	8,100.00
	17,650 × 40%	7,060.00
	———	
	58,150	
	———	
Income tax liability		15,160.00
		———

 Test your understanding 2

Imogen

Imogen has given you the following details relating to her tax affairs for 2018/19.

	£
Salary and benefits (PAYE = £59,180)	166,040
Bank interest received	3,100
Payroll giving	2,500
Personal pension payment	6,320

Imogen is not entitled to a personal allowance (see section 3 below).

Required:

Calculate Imogen's income tax payable or repayable for 2018/19.

Approach to a question

Step 1: Consider how to treat the gift to charity

- Payroll giving deduction against employment income; or

- Relief against total income for gifts of certain assets; or

- Gift aid: extend basic rate and higher rate tax bands.

Step 2: Consider how to treat the pension payment:

- Allowable expense against employment income (OPS); or

- Extend basic rate and higher rate tax bands (PPS).

Step 3: Now continue with the income tax computation.

3 Pension payments, gift aid and personal allowances

We saw in Chapter 7 that the personal allowance is reduced where a person's income exceeds £100,000.

When calculating this restriction, the figure of net income should be reduced by the grossed up amount of any gift aid payment or personal pension contributions.

Example

Rodney's only source of income is an annual salary of £115,000.

He makes personal pension contributions of £7,200 each year.

What is his personal allowance for 2018/19?

Solution

Net income for calculating the personal allowance restriction

	£
Salary	115,000
Less: Gross pension contributions (£7,200 × 100/80)	(9,000)
Adjusted net income	106,000

Personal allowance

Standard personal allowance	11,850
Less: 50% × (£106,000 − £100,000)	(3,000)
Reduced personal allowance	8,850

Test your understanding 3

Kurt receives a salary of £106,000 per year and pays £1,600 a year to Oxfam under gift aid.

What is Kurt's personal allowance for 2018/19?

4 Test your understanding

 Test your understanding 4

Mr Mars

Mr Mars has been self-employed for many years. His taxable trade profits in 2018/19 were £47,715.

He has the following investment income for 2018/19.

	£
Building society interest	600
Bank interest	1,750

Mr Mars paid a personal pension contribution of £2,800 on 13 December 2018.

Required:

Calculate Mr Mars' income tax liability for 2018/19.

 Test your understanding 5

Proctor

The following information is relevant to Proctor's taxation position for the year ended 5 April 2019.

(1)   His salary as managing director of Peter Proctor (Engineers) Limited was £40,975 and his Form P11D showed his taxable benefits totalled £1,800. The company does not have an occupational pension scheme.

(2)   During the year, Proctor paid £3,200 (net) and Peter Proctor (Engineers) Limited paid £10,000 into Proctor's personal pension scheme.

(3)   Other income:

(i)	Building society interest	£3,440
(ii)	Rental income	£6,010

Required:

Calculate Proctor's income tax liability for 2018/19.

Test your understanding 6

Ming Lee

Ming Lee is employed as a management consultant. For 2018/19 her taxable employment income is £37,600. Tax deducted under PAYE was £5,900.

Her only other income in 2018/19 is £7,875 of dividend income.

She has decided to start making pension contributions.

Required:

(a)   Calculate the maximum amount of tax deductible contributions that Ming could have made into a personal pension scheme for 2018/19 and the amount she would pay into the pension scheme in order to contribute the maximum.

(b)   Calculate Ming's income tax payable/repayable for 2018/19 assuming she had contributed the maximum amount to her personal pension.

 Test your understanding 7

Marjorie

Marjorie is employed at an annual salary of £17,000. PAYE of £1,350 was deducted in 2018/19. She was provided with a Peugeot car which gave rise to a taxable benefit of £2,330.

Other relevant information is as follows:

(1)   Marjorie has an account with the Halifax Building Society and £250 interest was credited on 31 January 2019.

(2)   Marjorie received dividends in 2018/19 of £1,500.

(3)   Marjorie paid contributions of £78 per month into her employer's occupational pension scheme throughout 2018/19.

Required:

Calculate Marjorie's tax payable for 2018/19.

Test your understanding 8

Peter

Peter is employed as a sales director by Neat Limited. He earned a salary of £157,350 in the year to 5 April 2019.

He makes personal pension contributions of £22,000 (net) each year. He also makes charitable payments under the gift aid scheme totalling £15,400.

He receives bank and building society interest of £2,500.

Required:

Calculate Peter's income tax liability for 2018/19.

 Test your understanding 9

Mark the following statements as true or false.

		True	False
1	Jessica has a salary of £50,000 and pays £4,000 to her employer's occupational pension scheme. Her basic rate band will be extended by £5,000.		
2	Making a gift aid payment never affects the tax liability of a taxpayer whose taxable income falls under the basic rate threshold.		
3	Employer contributions to a personal pension scheme are paid net of 20% tax.		
4	Payroll giving is paid gross and is an allowable employment income expense.		

5 Summary

- Pension contributions are a tax efficient way of providing for retirement.

- There are two types of pension scheme

Occupational Pension Schemes	Personal Pension Schemes
Tax relief given at source through the PAYE system	Paid net of basic rate tax Gross up by 100/80 Extend the tax rate bands to obtain higher rate tax relief

- There are three tax efficient ways of giving to charity:

  - Payroll giving

  - Gift of assets

  - Gift aid.

  You must be able to deal with all of these.

- If a taxpayer with net income of £100,000 or more makes a gift aid payment or personal pension payment, the gross amount of the payment is deducted from their net income for the purposes of calculating their personal allowance.

Test your understanding answers

Test your understanding 1

The correct answer is £8,000.

	£
Salary	50,000
Less: Pension contribution (£50,000 × 6%)	(3,000)
	47,000
Less: Personal allowance	(11,850)
Taxable income	35,150

Income tax

£	
34,500 × 20%	6,900.00
650 × 40%	260.00
35,150	
Income tax liability	7,160.00

Test your understanding 2

Imogen

Income tax computation – 2018/19

	Total £	Non-savings £	Savings £
Salary and benefits	166,040		
Less: Payroll giving	(2,500)		
	163,540	163,540	
Bank interest	3,100		3,100
Net income	166,640	163,540	3,100
Less: PA (restricted)	(0)	(0)	(0)
Taxable income	166,640	163,540	3,100

Income tax

£			£
42,400	× 20% (W)	(non-savings – basic rate)	8,480.00
115,500	× 40%	(non-savings – higher rate)	46,200.00
157,900	(W)		
5,640	× 45%	(non-savings – additional rate)	2,538.00
163,540			
3,100	× 45%	(savings – additional rate)	1,395.00
166,640			

Income tax liability	58,613.00
Less: Tax deducted at source	
PAYE	(59,180.00)
Income tax repayable	(567.00)

Working: Extended tax bands

Extend tax bands by £7,900 (£6,320 × $^{100}/_{80}$):

– Basic rate band £42,400 (£34,500 + £7,900)

– Higher rate band £157,900 (£150,000 + £7,900)

Note: Imogen is not entitled to a savings allowance as she is an additional rate taxpayer.

Test your understanding 3

The correct answer is £9,850.

Net income for calculating the personal allowance restriction

	£
Salary	106,000
Less: Gross gift aid (£1,600 × 100/80)	(2,000)
Adjusted net income	104,000

Personal allowance

Standard allowance	11,850
Less: 50% × (£104,000 – £100,000)	(2,000)
Reduced personal allowance	9,850

Test your understanding 4

Mr Mars

Income tax computation – 2018/19

	Total	Non-savings	Savings
	£	£	£
Trading income	47,715	47,715	
Building society interest	600		600
Bank interest	1,750		1,750
Net income	50,065	47,715	2,350
Less: PA	(11,850)	(11,850)	
Taxable income	38,215	35,865	2,350

Income tax £
35,865	× 20%	(non-savings – basic rate)	7,173.00
500	× 0%	(savings allowance)	0.00
1,635	× 20%	(savings – basic rate)	327.00
___			
38,000			
215	× 40%	(savings – higher rate)	86.00
___			
38,215			
___			

Income tax liability 7,586.00

Notes: Basic rate band is extended by £3,500 (£2,800 × 100/80) from £34,500 to £38,000.

Mr Mars is entitled to a savings allowance of £500 as he is a higher rate taxpayer.

Test your understanding 5

Proctor

Income tax computation – 2018/19

	Total	Non-savings	Savings
	£	£	£
Employment income (£40,975 + £1,800)	42,775	42,775	
Building society interest	3,440		3,440
Property income	6,010	6,010	
Net income	52,225	48,785	3,440
Less: PA	(11,850)	(11,850)	
Taxable income	40,375	36,935	3,440

Income tax

£				£
36,935	× 20%	(non-savings – basic rate)		7,387.00
500	× 0%	(savings allowance)		0.00
1,065	× 20%	(savings – basic rate)		213.00
___				
38,500				
1,875	× 40%	(savings – higher rate)		750.00
___				
40,375				
___				

Income tax liability   8,350.00
                                                                            _____

Notes: The full personal pension premium is allowable as it is less than the maximum amount allowed of £42,775 (100% of earned income).

The basic rate band is therefore extended by £4,000 (£3,200 × 100/80) to £38,500 (£34,500 + £4,000).

Proctor is entitled to a savings allowance of £500 as he is a higher rate taxpayer.

The contributions by Proctor's employer are an exempt benefit.

Test your understanding 6

Ming Lee

(a) Maximum pension contribution

The maximum personal pension contribution that Ming will obtain tax relief for is £37,600 being the higher of £3,600 and 100% of her earnings (£37,600).

Ming would pay the contribution net of basic rate tax:

i.e. (£37,600 × 80%) = £30,080.

(b) Income tax computation – 2018/19

	Total	Non-savings	Dividends
	£	£	£
Employment income	37,600	37,600	
Dividend income	7,875		7,875
Net income	45,475	37,600	7,875
Less: PA	(11,850)	(11,850)	
Taxable income	33,625	25,750	7,875

Income tax

£			£
25,750	× 20%	(non-savings – basic rate)	5,150.00
2,000	× 0%	(dividend allowance)	0.00
5,875	× 7.5%	(dividends – basic rate)	440.62
33,625			

Income tax liability	5,590.62
Less: Tax deducted at source	
PAYE	(5,900.00)
Income tax repayable	(309.38)

Notes: The basic rate band is extended by £37,600 to £72,100 (£34,500 + £37,600).

Test your understanding 7

Marjorie

Income tax computation – 2018/19

	Total	Non-savings	Savings	Dividends
	£	£	£	£
Employment income (£17,000 + £2,330)	19,330			
Less: Pension contributions (£78 × 12)	(936)			
	18,394	18,394		
Building society interest	250		250	
Dividends	1,500			1,500
Net income	20,144	18,394	250	1,500
Less: PA	(11,850)	(11,850)		
Taxable income	8,294	6,544	250	1,500

Income tax

£				£
6,544	× 20%	(non-savings – basic rate)		1,308.80
250	× 0%	(savings allowance)		0.00
1,500	× 0%	(dividend allowance)		0.00
8,294				

	£
Income tax liability	1,308.80
Less: Tax deducted at source PAYE	(1,350.00)
Income tax repayable	(41.20)

Note: Contributions into an occupational pension scheme are an allowable expense against employment income.

KAPLAN PUBLISHING

Test your understanding 8

Peter

Income tax computation – 2018/19

	Total	Non-savings	Savings
	£	£	£
Employment income	157,350	157,350	
Interest	2,500		2,500
Net income	159,850	157,350	2,500
Less: PA (W)	(5,300)	(5,300)	
Taxable income	154,550	152,050	2,500

Income tax

£				£
81,250	× 20%	(non-savings – basic rate)		16,250.00
70,800	× 40%	(non-savings – higher rate)		28,320.00
152,050				
500	× 0%	(savings allowance)		0.00
2,000	× 40%	(savings – higher rate)		800.00
154,550				

Income tax liability	45,370.00

Notes: The basic rate band is extended by £46,750 ((£22,000 + £15,400) × 100/80) to £81,250 (£34,500 + £46,750).

The higher rate band will also be extended by £46,750. This extends the band to £196,750 (£150,000 + £46,750).

The savings income nil rate band is £500 because Peter is a higher rate taxpayer.

Working: Personal allowance

The personal allowance is restricted because adjusted net income exceeds £100,000. The adjusted net income is calculated as follows:

	£
Net income	159,850
Less: Pension contributions (£22,000 × 100/80)	(27,500)
Gift aid (£15,400 × 100/80)	(19,250)
Adjusted net income	113,100
Less: Limit	(100,000)
Excess	13,100

The personal allowance is £5,300 (£11,850 − (£13,100 × 50%)).

Test your understanding 9

1   **False** – Payment to her employer's occupational pension scheme will be deducted from her salary. Her basic rate band is unaffected.

2   **True**

3   **False** – They are paid gross. Employee's contributions are paid net of 20% tax.

4   **True**

National insurance contributions

9

Introduction

Class 1 national insurance contributions (NICs) are paid by employers and employees in respect of the earnings (excluding benefits) of the employees.

Class 1A NICs are paid by employers in respect of benefits provided to employees.

NICs are likely to be tested in every assessment.

ASSESSMENT CRITERIA
Identify taxpayers who need to pay NICs (3.4)
Calculate NICs payable by employees (3.4)
Calculate NICs payable by employers (3.4)

CONTENTS
1 NICs payable in respect of employees
2 Earnings for class 1 NIC purposes
3 Calculating class 1 contributions
4 Class 1A contributions

1 NICs payable in respect of employees

1.1 Classes of NICs payable in respect of employees

The following national insurance contributions (NICs) are payable in respect of employees:

- Class 1 employee contributions (also known as primary)
- Class 1 employer's contributions (also known as secondary)
- Class 1A contributions.

1.2 Class 1 employee contributions

Class 1 employee contributions are a percentage based contribution levied on the 'gross earnings' of the employee.

Class 1 employee contributions are due in respect of employees:

- aged 16 or over until
- attaining state pension age.

The employer is responsible for:

- calculating the amount of class 1 employee NICs due and deducting them from the employee's wages and
- paying them to HMRC on behalf of the employees.

Note that class 1 employee contributions:

- are not an allowable deduction for the purposes of calculating the individual employee's personal income tax liability
- do not represent a cost to the business of the employer, as they are ultimately paid by the employee. Therefore, they are not a deductible expense when calculating the employer's tax adjusted trading profits.

1.3 Class 1 employer's contributions

Class 1 employer's contributions are a percentage based contribution levied on the 'gross earnings' of the employee.

Class 1 employer's contributions are paid by employers in respect of employees:

- aged 16 or over
- until the employee ceases employment.

There is no upper age limit for employer contributions; the employer is liable in full even where the employee's age exceeds state pension age.

Employer's contributions are an additional cost of employment and are a deductible expense when calculating the employer's taxable profit.

1.4 Class 1A contributions

Class 1A contributions are also paid by employers.

They are paid in respect of the taxable benefits provided to employees.

The contributions are calculated as:

- 13.8% on the value of the taxable benefits.

Class 1A contributions are an additional cost of employment and are a deductible expense when calculating the employer's tax adjusted trading profits.

2 Earnings for class 1 NIC purposes

2.1 The definition of earnings

'Earnings' consist of:

- any remuneration derived from the employment

- which is paid in cash or assets which are readily convertible into cash.

The calculation of class 1 NICs is based on **gross earnings** with **no allowable deductions** (i.e. earnings before deductions that are allowable for income tax purposes, such as employee occupational pension scheme contributions and subscriptions to professional bodies).

2.2 Amounts included in gross earnings

The following are **included** in gross earnings

- wages, salary, overtime pay, commission or bonus

- sick pay, including statutory sick pay

- tips and gratuities paid or allocated by the employer

- reimbursement of the cost of travel between home and work

- mileage allowances in excess of 45p per mile (45p limit applies even if mileage exceeds 10,000 per year)

- vouchers (exchangeable for cash or non-cash items, such as goods).

2.3 Amounts not included in gross earnings

The following are **not included** in gross earnings

- benefits (other than those listed above)

- tips directly received from customers

- business expenses paid for or reimbursed by the employer, including reasonable travel and subsistence expenses.

Note that dividends are not subject to NICs, even if they are drawn by a director/shareholder in place of a monthly salary.

 Example

Janet and John are employed by Garden Gnomes Ltd and both pay into the company's occupational pension scheme. Their remuneration for the tax year 2018/19 is as follows:

	Janet £	John £
Salary	30,000	55,000
Bonus	Nil	4,000
Car benefit	Nil	3,950
Employer's pension contribution	2,300	4,575
Employee's pension contribution	1,650	3,800

Calculate Janet and John's gross earnings for class 1 NIC purposes.

Solution

	Janet £	John £
Salary	30,000	55,000
Bonus	Nil	4,000
Gross earnings	30,000	59,000

Notes: The employer's pension contributions are excluded as they are an exempt benefit.

The employee's pension contributions are ignored as these are not deductible in calculating earnings for NIC purposes.

The car benefit is excluded as it is a non-cash benefit which will be assessed to class 1A NICs, not class 1.

3 Calculating class 1 contributions

3.1 Calculating class 1 employee contributions

Employee contributions are normally calculated by reference to an employee's earnings period:

- if paid weekly, the contributions are calculated on a weekly basis

- if paid monthly, the contributions are calculated on a monthly basis.

In the assessment, the class 1 NIC thresholds are provided on an annual basis and calculations can be performed on an annual basis if annual salary figures are provided. See below for details regarding how to deal with monthly or weekly figures.

The employee contributions payable are calculated as:

- 12% on gross earnings between £8,424 and £46,350

- 2% on gross earnings in excess of £46,350.

The class 1 employee rates and thresholds are available for you to refer to in the assessment.

3.2 Calculating class 1 employer's contributions

Employer's contributions are calculated as:

- 13.8% on all gross earnings above £8,424 per annum.

Note that there is:

- no upper earnings limit

- no change in the rate of NICs payable for employer contributions.

There are different rules for employees aged under 21 and for apprentices aged under 25. Class 1 employer's NICs are not payable on earnings below the upper threshold of £46,350.

Example

Millie is employed by Blue Forge Ltd and is paid an annual salary of £45,000. Millie is also provided with the following taxable benefits:

	£
Company car	5,000
Vouchers for the local gym	2,000

Calculate Millie's and Blue Forge Ltd's class 1 NIC liability due for the tax year 2018/19.

Solution

Class 1 NICs are due on annual earnings of £47,000 (salary £45,000 and vouchers £2,000). The company car is a non-cash benefit and is therefore not subject to class 1 NICs.

Millie's class 1 NICs	£
(£46,350 – £8,424) × 12%	4,551.12
(£47,000 – £46,350) × 2%	13.00
	4,564.12

Blue Forge Ltd's class 1 NICs	
(£47,000 – £8,424) × 13.8%	5,323.49

 Test your understanding 1

Alex

Alex is paid £9,950 per year and Betty is paid £48,440 per year.

Required:

Calculate the employee's and the employer's class 1 NIC liability for the tax year 2018/19.

3.3 Earnings periods

Class 1 is normally calculated on either a weekly or monthly basis, according to how frequently the employee is paid. This is known as the earnings period.

- Calculations should be done on a weekly or monthly basis, as appropriate, in the assessment, unless the earnings period is not given. If no earnings period is given, calculations can be done on an annual basis.

- For weekly or monthly calculations the annual thresholds given in the rates and allowances table should be divided by 52 (weekly) or 12 (monthly).

 Example

June is paid a wage of £250 a week. She was also paid a bonus of £10,000 in the last week of March 2019.

Calculate the total amount of NICs payable by June for the tax year 2018/19.

Solution

June will pay NICs on earnings of £250 a week for 51 weeks and earnings of £10,250 for the week in which the bonus was paid.

The lower and upper weekly thresholds for class 1 employee NICs are:

£8,424 ÷ 52 = £162

£46,350 ÷ 52 = £891

			£
(£250 – £162)	× 12% ×	51 weeks	538.56
(£891 – £162)	× 12% ×	1 week	87.48
(£10,250 – £891)	× 2% ×	1 week	187.18
			813.22

Therefore in the week in which her bonus is paid, £9,359 (£10,250 – £891) is charged at the rate of 2% as it exceeds the upper threshold for the week of payment.

Notes: This question only asked for the NICs payable by June and therefore it was not necessary to calculate the class 1 employer's NICs, which are payable by her employer. Be careful to only answer the question asked.

As this example shows, an employee may pay less national insurance by being paid a low weekly wage and a large bonus.

3.4 NIC employment allowance

Each employer is able to claim up to £3,000 relief per year from their total class 1 employer's NIC payments for the business. The allowance is the same for each employer, regardless of the number of employees.

This allowance cannot be used against any other classes of NICs (e.g. Class 1A).

The figure of £3,000 is available for you to refer to in the assessment.

 Test your understanding 2

Clare

Clare employs two full time assistants at a salary of £15,000 p.a. each. This salary is paid monthly, and in December 2018 she also paid each assistant a bonus of £5,000.

Required:

Calculate the total NICs that Clare must pay to HMRC for the tax year 2018/19 in respect of her employees.

3.5 Company directors

Special rules apply to company directors to prevent the avoidance of NICs by paying low weekly or monthly salaries, and then taking a large bonus in a single week or month.

Therefore, when an employee is a company director, his class 1 NICs are calculated as if he had an annual earnings period, regardless of how he is paid (e.g. monthly, weekly) or how long he has been employed as a director during the tax year.

4 Class 1A contributions

4.1 Class 1A contributions

Class 1A contributions are paid by employers in respect of the taxable benefits provided to employees.

No class 1A contributions are payable in respect of:

- exempt benefits (i.e. those benefits which are exempt from income tax
- benefits already treated as earnings and assessed to class 1 NICs, such as remuneration received in the form of non-cash vouchers.

The contributions are calculated as:

- 13.8% on the value of the taxable benefits.

Class 1A contributions are an additional cost of employment and are a deductible expense when calculating the employer's tax adjusted trading profits.

> ### Example
>
> Simon is employed by Dutton Ltd at an annual salary of £52,000.
>
> He was provided with the following benefits in the tax year 2018/19:
>
> | | £ |
> |---|---|
> | Company motor car | 3,900 |
> | Private fuel | 5,772 |
> | Subsidised meals in the company canteen | 360 |
>
> Calculate the employee's and the employer's class 1 and class 1A NIC liabilities due for the tax year 2018/19 in respect of Simon.
>
> Ignore the employment allowance.
>
> **Solution**
>
> **Class 1 NICs**
>
> | | £ |
> |---|---|
> | Employee's class 1 NICs | |
> | (£46,350 − £8,424) × 12% | 4,551.12 |
> | (£52,000 − £46,350) × 2% | 113.00 |
> | | ———— |
> | | 4,664.12 |
> | | ———— |

Employer's class 1 NICs	
(£52,000 – £8,424) × 13.8%	6,013.49

Class 1A NICs

Simon's taxable benefits for class 1A purposes are as follows:

	£
Company motor car	3,900
Private fuel	5,772
Taxable benefits for class 1A	9,672
Employer's class 1A NICs (£9,672 × 13.8%)	1,334.74

Notes: The subsidised canteen is an exempt benefit and is therefore not subject to class 1A NICs.

The employment allowance is deducted from the employer's total class 1 employer's NICs, not from the liability relating to one individual.

 Test your understanding 3

Sally

Sally is paid £25,000 per year and had taxable benefits for the tax year 2018/19 of:

	£
Company motor car	5,250
Private fuel provided by company	4,200
Beneficial loan	2,600
Vouchers to be used at the local department store	250

The company also provided Sally with a mobile phone, which cost £135.

Contributions into her personal pension scheme were as follows:

Employer's contribution	£2,540
Employee's contribution	£1,380

Required:

Calculate the employee's and the employer's class 1 and class 1A NIC liabilities for the tax year 2018/19 in respect of Sally.

Ignore the employment allowance.

---

5 Test your understanding

Test your understanding 4

Keith

Keith is an employee of K Ltd. Keith receives cash earnings of £31,400 and a car benefit valued at £5,800 in the tax year 2018/19.

Required:

How much class 1 (employee) national insurance contributions (NIC) does Keith suffer in respect of the tax year 2018/19?

Test your understanding 5

Mr Khan

Mr Khan is employed and received the following from his employer for the tax year 2018/19.

	£
Salary	35,000
Employer pension contributions	3,250
A company car – assessable benefit	3,570

In addition, Mr Khan incurred business travel expenses of £400.

Required:

What are Mr Khan's earnings for the purpose of calculating his class 1 national insurance contributions?

Test your understanding 6

Daniel

Daniel is employed by A Ltd and earns a salary of £50,000 per year. In addition, Daniel receives taxable non-cash benefits of £3,000 every year.

Ignore the employment allowance.

Required:

What are A Ltd's class 1 employer's national insurance contributions for the tax year 2018/19?

6 Summary

The main issues to beware of in relation to NICs are:

- Class 1 NICs are paid by employers and employees in respect of earnings (excluding benefits).

- The meaning of earnings for these purposes.

- How to calculate class 1 NICs.

- Class 1A NICs are paid by employers in respect of benefits provided to employees.

Test your understanding answers

Test your understanding 1

Alex

	£
Employee's class 1 NICs (£9,950 – £8,424) × 12%	183.12
Employer's class 1 NICs (£9,950 – £8,424) × 13.8%	210.59

Betty

Employee's class 1 NICs

	£
(£46,350 – £8,424) × 12% (maximum)	4,551.12
(£48,440 – £46,350) × 2%	41.80
	4,592.92

Employer's class 1 NICs

	£
(£48,440 – £8,424) × 13.8%	5,522.21

Test your understanding 2

Clare

Employee contributions

Class 1 employee contributions are levied on the assistants. However, it is Clare's responsibility to deduct the NICs from the assistants' salaries and pay them to HMRC along with the class 1 employer's contributions.

The contributions will be based on her assistants' salaries of £15,000 and bonus of £5,000.

In 11 months the assistants receive £1,250 (£15,000 ÷ 12), and in December they receive £6,250 (£1,250 + £5,000).

The lower and upper monthly thresholds for class 1 employee NICs are:

£8,424 ÷ 12   = £702

£46,350 ÷ 12   = £3,862

Employee class 1 NICs (each)	£
(£1,250 − £702) = £548 × 12% × 11 months	723.36
(£3,862 − £702) = £3,160 × 12% × 1 month	379.20
(£6,250 − £3,862) = £2,388 × 2% × 1 month	47.76
	1,150.32

Employer's contributions

Class 1 employer's contributions are payable as Clare is an employer.

The monthly employer's threshold is £702 (£8,424 ÷ 12).

Employer's class 1 NICs (each)	£
(£1,250 − £702) = £548 × 13.8% × 11 months	831.86
(£6,250 − £702) = £5,548 × 13.8% × 1 months	765.62
	1,597.48

Total NICs payable to HMRC in 2018/19:

	£
Class 1 employee NICs (£1,150.32 × 2)	2,300.64
Class 1 employer's NICs (£1,597.48 × 2)	3,194.96
Annual employment allowance	
(against class 1 employer's NICs only)	(3,000.00)
	2,495.60

Test your understanding 3

Sally

Class 1 NICs

	£
Salary	25,000
Vouchers	250
Cash earnings for class 1 NICs	25,250
Employee's class 1 NICs (£25,250 − £8,424) × 12%	2,019.12
Employer's class 1 NICs (£25,250 − £8,424) × 13.8%	2,321.99

Notes: The provision of one mobile phone per employee, and employer pension contributions, are excluded as they are exempt benefits.

The employee pension contributions are not allowable deductions in calculating earnings for NIC purposes.

The car, fuel and beneficial loan benefits are excluded as they are non-cash benefits which are assessed to class 1A NICs, not class 1.

Class 1A NICs

	£
Company motor car	5,250
Private fuel provided by company	4,200
Beneficial loan	2,600
Taxable benefits for class 1A	12,050
Employer's class 1A NICs (£12,050 × 13.8%)	1,662.90

Note: The employment allowance is deducted from the employer's total class 1 employer's NICs, not from the liability relating to one individual.

Test your understanding 4

Keith

The correct answer is £2,757.12

Class 1 employee contributions: (£31,400 – £8,424) × 12% = £2,757.12

Benefits are not liable to class 1 contributions. They are liable to class 1A which is payable by the employer.

 Test your understanding 5

Mr Khan

The correct answer is £35,000.

Class 1 employee contributions are not payable on either exempt benefits (the employer pension contributions) or taxable benefits, (i.e. the company car).

No deduction is made for allowable expenses in arriving at the earnings figure.

 Test your understanding 6

Daniel

The correct answer is £5,737.49.

Class 1 employer's national insurance contributions (NIC) are calculated on cash earnings only, but not benefits. The first £8,424 is exempt and the remainder is charged at 13.8%.

The NIC is therefore: (£50,000 – £8,424) × 13.8%   £5,737.49
                                                                                    ―――――

Introduction to capital gains tax

Introduction

In the assessment there will be a number of tasks covering various aspects of capital gains tax (CGT).

This chapter determines when we need to perform a CGT computation and how to calculate the CGT payable.

The following chapters will describe how to calculate chargeable gains.

ASSESSMENT CRITERIA	CONTENTS
Chargeable and exempt assets (4.1)	1 Capital gains tax computation
Chargeable and exempt persons (4.1)	2 Chargeable disposal
Apply current exemptions (4.4)	3 Chargeable person
Treat capital losses (4.4)	4 Chargeable asset
Apply rates of capital gains tax (4.4)	5 Calculating CGT
Identify the date on which capital gains tax is due (4.4)	

1 Capital gains tax computation

1.1 The three essential elements

A capital gains tax (CGT) computation is only required if there is a:

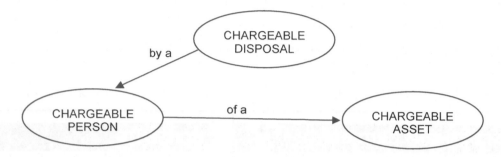

2 Chargeable disposal

2.1 Disposals

A chargeable disposal includes:

- a sale of an asset (whole or part of an asset)
- a gift of an asset
- an exchange of an asset
- the loss or destruction of an asset.

Where a gift is made the sale proceeds are deemed to be the asset's market value.

Where an asset is lost or destroyed the sale proceeds are likely to be nil or the insurance proceeds.

2.2 Exempt disposals

The following occasions are exempt disposals and so no CGT computation is required:

- disposals on the death of a taxpayer
- gifts of assets to charities.

3 Chargeable person

3.1 Chargeable person

A chargeable person is:

- an individual, or

- a company (only dealt with in Business Tax).

Individuals who are UK resident in the tax year in which the disposal takes place are subject to capital gains tax on their worldwide gains.

Non-UK residents only pay UK CGT on residential property situated in the UK. Therefore if a non-UK resident has no UK residential property they will have no UK CGT liability.

In the assessment you should assume that all individuals are UK resident in questions requiring the calculation of tax, unless you are told otherwise.

3.2 Exempt persons

Charities do not pay capital gains tax on their disposals.

4 Chargeable asset

4.1 Exempt assets

All assets are chargeable unless they are in the list of exempt assets.

The main types of exempt asset are listed below.

Those most likely to be in an assessment are marked *.

(a) *Principal private residences (see Chapter 11).

(b) Gilts (e.g. treasury stock or government stock) and qualifying corporate bonds (i.e. loan notes, also known as debentures).

(c) *Wasting chattels – a wasting asset is one with an expected life of not more than 50 years, a chattel is tangible moveable property (e.g. a racehorse) (see Chapter 11). All animals in the assessment are wasting chattels.

(d) *Other chattels sold at a gain where the cost and consideration is ≤ £6,000 or less (see Chapter 11), (e.g. an antique table costing £4,000 sold for £4,500).

(e) *Private motor cars, including vintage and veteran cars.

(f)   NS&I Savings Certificates, Premium Bonds and SAYE certificates.

(g)   Shares held in an ISA (individual savings account).

(h)   Cash, legal tender in the UK.

(i)   Foreign currency bank accounts.

(j)   Medals awarded for valour, unless acquired by purchase.

(k)   Betting and lottery winnings.

(l)   Compensation or damages for any wrong or injury suffered by an individual in his person or in his profession or vocation.

Test your understanding 1

Which of the following disposals requires a CGT computation?

Select yes or no for each disposal.

1	Sale of a greyhound	Yes/No
2	Gift of shares in a limited company	Yes/No
3	Gift of a Picasso painting in a will	Yes/No
4	Sale of a vintage motor car for a substantial profit	Yes/No
5	Gift of a computer to a local charity	Yes/No
6	Sale of a holiday home in Cornwall	Yes/No

---

5   Calculating CGT

5.1   Introduction

Capital gains tax (like income tax) is calculated for the tax year.

For each individual we must undertake the following steps.

Step 1 (Chapters 11 and 12)

Calculate the gains or losses on disposals of individual assets for 2018/19 (i.e. disposals between 6 April 2018 and 5 April 2019).

For example, if four chargeable assets are disposed of, four calculations of gains or losses must be made.

Step 2

Bring together all gains and losses of the tax year and deduct the annual exempt amount to determine the taxable gains.

Step 3

Calculate the capital gains tax payable.

5.2 The annual exempt amount

An individual has an annual exempt amount which is applied to net chargeable gains after deduction of capital losses.

The annual exempt amount for 2018/19 is £11,700. This figure is available for you to refer to in the assessment.

The annual exempt amount can only be relieved against chargeable gains of the current tax year. Any unused amount cannot be offset against taxable income or carried forward or back.

5.3 Calculation of taxable gains

The pro forma shows how chargeable gains and capital losses are brought together to calculate taxable gains.

The calculation of individual gains and losses is covered in the next chapter.

	£
Chargeable gains for the year	X
Less: Current year capital losses	(X)
	―――
Net chargeable gains for the year	X
Less: Capital losses brought forward	(X)
	―――
Net chargeable gains	X
Less: Annual exempt amount	(11,700)
	―――
Taxable gains	X
	―――

The treatment of capital losses is explained in detail below.

Test your understanding 2

Manuel made chargeable gains and allowable losses for 2018/19:

Gain of £60,000

Gain of £12,000

Capital loss of £4,000

Required:

Calculate Manuel's taxable gains for 2018/19.

5.4 Treatment of capital losses

There is a difference in the treatment of current year capital losses and brought forward capital losses.

Current year capital losses are automatically deducted from the chargeable gains of the year. Where this results in net capital losses for the year, they will be carried forward for relief in the future.

Capital losses brought forward are automatically deducted from the net chargeable gains for the year.

However, the maximum amount of brought forward losses that will be deducted is restricted to the amount required to reduce the net chargeable gains for the year to the level of the annual exempt amount.

Accordingly, brought forward losses are not used to the extent that this would lead to wastage of the annual exempt amount.

Finally, a capital loss arising on a disposal to a connected person (Chapter 11) can only be used against a gain on a disposal to that same connected person.

 Example

Mica has the following chargeable gains and losses for the two years ended 5 April 2019.

	2017/18	2018/19
	£	£
Gains	12,500	13,900
Losses	(14,000)	(2,000)

What gains (if any) are taxable after considering all reliefs and exemptions?

Solution

	2017/18 £	2018/19 £
Current gains	12,500	13,900
Current losses	(12,500)	(2,000)
		11,900
Brought forward losses*		(200)
Net chargeable gains	Nil	11,700
Annual exempt amount	Wasted	(11,700)
Taxable gains		Nil
Loss carried forward		
(£14,000 – £12,500)	1,500	
(£1,500 – £200)		1,300

*Utilised to reduce gains to annual exempt amount.

Test your understanding 3

Gabi has the following chargeable gains and losses for the two years ended 5 April 2019.

	2017/18 £	2018/19 £
Gains	15,000	16,400
Losses	(17,000)	(4,000)

1   What are the losses carried forward (if any) at the end of 2017/18?

2   What are the losses carried forward (if any) at the end of 2018/19?

5.5 Calculation of CGT payable

Taxable gains are treated as an additional amount of income in order to determine the rates of CGT. However, the gains must not be included in the income tax computation.

Where the taxable gains fall within any remaining basic rate band they are taxed at 10%.

The balance of the taxable gains is taxed at 20%.

These rates are available for you to refer to in the assessment.

 Example

In 2018/19 Basil has taxable gains of £14,600 in respect of quoted shares. His taxable income for the year, after deducting the personal allowance, is £32,500.

Calculate Basil's capital gains tax liability for 2018/19.

Solution

	£
£2,000 (£34,500 – £32,500) × 10%	200.00
£12,600 (£14,600 – £2,000) × 20%	2,520.00
Capital gains tax liability	2,720.00

Note that 'taxable gains' are the gains after the deduction of the annual exempt amount.

5.6 Payment of CGT

- CGT is payable by 31 January following the end of the tax year (31 January 2020 for 2018/19).

6 Test your understanding

 Test your understanding 4

Which of the following transactions carried out by an individual may give rise to a chargeable gain? Select yes or no for each disposal.

1	Sale of shares	Yes/No
2	Sale of a motor car	Yes/No
3	Gift of a holiday home	Yes/No
4	Sale of an antique ring (which cost £4,000) for £5,000	Yes/No
5	Gift of an antique chair (which cost £4,000) when it was valued at £15,000	Yes/No

 Test your understanding 5

Read the following statements and state whether they are true or false.

1 Capital losses are deducted before the annual exempt amount.

2 Excess capital losses can be offset against taxable income.

3 Any available capital losses must always be relieved in full.

4 Capital gains are taxed at 40% for higher rate taxpayers.

Test your understanding 6

1 Mary made a capital loss of £4,000 in 2017/18. In 2018/19 she made a chargeable gain of £12,600 and a capital loss of £3,000.

How much capital loss is carried forward at the end of 2018/19?

2 What would your answer be if Mary had only made the chargeable gain of £12,600 in 2018/19 and not the capital loss?

Test your understanding 7

Carl sold three paintings in 2018/19 and made two chargeable gains of £9,900 and £11,400 and a capital loss of £2,400. Carl has capital losses brought forward as at 6 April 2018 of £3,400.

Required:

What are Carl's taxable gains for 2018/19?

 Test your understanding 8

Misha has sold two paintings in 2018/19 and made two chargeable gains of £16,900 and £12,100. Her taxable income for the year, after deducting the personal allowance, is £26,175.

Required:

What is Misha's capital gains tax liability for 2018/19?

7 Summary

7.1 Essential elements

There are three essential elements for CGT to apply:

- chargeable disposal, by a
- chargeable person, of a
- chargeable asset.

7.2 Order of calculation

To calculate CGT for the tax year:

Step 1 Calculate individual gains and losses.

Step 2 Calculate taxable gains by deducting losses (as appropriate) and the annual exempt amount.

Step 3 Calculate the CGT payable.

Test your understanding answers

Test your understanding 1

1 **No** A greyhound is a wasting chattel (tangible moveable property with a life of < 50 years) and is therefore exempt.

2 **Yes** Gifts are still chargeable disposals and shares are a chargeable asset.

3 **No** Disposals on death are not chargeable disposals.

4 **No** Cars are exempt assets regardless of whether they are sold for a profit or a loss.

5 **No** Gifts to charity are not chargeable disposals.

6 **Yes** PPR relief only applies to an individual's main home, therefore the sale of a holiday home is not exempt (see Chapter 11).

Test your understanding 2

The correct answer is £56,300.

Explanation

Taxable gains are defined as net chargeable gains after the deduction of the annual exempt amount, as follows:

	£
Total chargeable gains (£60,000 + £12,000)	72,000
Less: Capital loss	(4,000)
Net chargeable gains	68,000
Less: Annual exempt amount	(11,700)
Taxable gain	56,300

Test your understanding 3

1   The correct answer is £2,000.

2   The correct answer is £1,300.

Explanation

	2017/18 £	2018/19 £
Current gains	15,000	16,400
Current losses	(15,000)	(4,000)
		12,400
Brought forward losses*		(700)
	Nil	11,700
Annual exempt amount	Wasted	(11,700)
		Nil
Loss carried forward		
(£17,000 – £15,000)	2,000	
(£2,000 – £700)		1,300

*Utilised to reduce gains to annual exempt amount.

Test your understanding 4

1   **Yes**   Shares are a chargeable asset.

2   **No**   Motor cars are exempt assets.

3   **Yes**   A gift is a chargeable disposal and principal private residence relief only applies to an individual's main home, therefore the gift of a holiday home is not exempt.

4   **No**   Chattels sold at a gain where the cost and consideration is £6,000 or less are exempt assets.

5   **Yes**   A gift is a chargeable disposal. The antique chair is treated as having been sold for its market value of £15,000.

Test your understanding 5

1   **True**

2   **False** – Capital losses can only be set against gains.

3   **False** – Current year losses must be relieved in full but brought
    forward losses are only utilised to the extent that they reduce net
    gains to the level of the annual exempt amount.

4   **False** – Gains are taxed at 20% for higher rate taxpayers.

 Test your understanding 6

Mary

1   The correct answer is £4,000.

2   The correct answer is £3,100.

Explanation

1   Net chargeable gains for 2018/19 are £9,600 (£12,600 – £3,000).
    As this is less than the annual exempt amount, the loss brought
    forward of £4,000 is carried forward to 2019/20.

2   If Mary had only made the chargeable gain of £12,600 in 2018/19,
    losses brought forward of £900 would have been offset to reduce
    the gain to the level of the annual exempt amount. The balance of
    the capital losses of £3,100 (£4,000 – £900) would have been
    carried forward.

Test your understanding 7

Carl

The correct answer is £3,800.

	£
Chargeable gains for the year (£9,900 + £11,400)	21,300
Less: Current year capital losses	(2,400)
Net chargeable gains for the year	18,900
Less: Capital losses brought forward	(3,400)
Net chargeable gains	15,500
Less: Annual exempt amount	(11,700)
Taxable gains	3,800

Test your understanding 8

Misha

The correct answer is £2,627.50.

	£
Chargeable gains (£16,900 + £12,100)	29,000
Less: Annual exempt amount	(11,700)
Taxable gains	17,300
£8,325 (£34,500 − £26,175) × 10%	832.50
£8,975 (£17,300 − £8,325) × 20%	1,795.00
Capital gains tax liability	2,627.50

Calculation of individual gains and losses

Introduction

It is likely that one of the CGT tasks will require a calculation of gains on assets other than shares.

This chapter looks at the standard calculations, followed by some special rules. At least one of the special rules is likely to be included in the assessment.

ASSESSMENT CRITERIA	CONTENTS
Connected persons (4.1)	1 Pro forma calculation of gains and losses
Calculate chargeable gains and allowable losses on normal capital disposals (4.2)	2 Special rules
Apply part disposals rules (4.2)	3 Principal private residence exemption
Apply chattels and wasting chattel rules (4.2)	
Determine principal private residence relief (4.2)	

1 Pro forma calculation of gains and losses

1.1 Pro forma

The following pro forma is used to calculate a chargeable gain:

	Notes	£
Gross sale proceeds	(a)	X
Less: Selling costs	(b)	(X)
Net sale proceeds		NSP
Less: Allowable cost	(c)	(X)
Chargeable gain	(d)	X

1.2 Notes to the pro forma

(a) Sale proceeds are usually obvious. However, where a transaction is not at arm's length (e.g. a gift) then the market value of the asset is used.

(b) Selling costs incurred on the disposal of an asset are an allowable deduction. Examples of such costs include valuation fees, advertising costs, legal fees, auctioneer's fees.

(c) The allowable cost of an asset is its purchase price plus any incidental purchase costs (for example legal fees) together with any capital expenditure subsequently incurred, known as enhancement expenditure, that increases the value of the asset.

If the asset was received as a gift then its cost = market value at the date of the gift.

If the asset was inherited on someone's death then the cost = probate value (market value at the date of the death, which is used for inheritance tax purposes).

(d) The gain after deducting the costs above is known as a chargeable gain.

Test your understanding 1

Paul

On 23 April 2018, Paul sold a property that was not his main residence for £145,000. He had purchased the property on 3 June 2010 for £108,000. The seller incurred fees in June 2010 of £2,000.

Required:

What is the chargeable gain arising on this disposal?

2 Special rules

2.1 Situations when special rules apply

Special rules apply in the following situations.

- Part disposals (2.2 below).

- Chattels (2.3 below).

- Connected persons (2.4 below).

- Transfers between spouses and civil partners (2.5 below).

- Assets lost, destroyed or damaged (2.6 below).

2.2 Part disposals

When there is a disposal, it is necessary to match costs with proceeds in order to calculate the gain.

When **part of an asset is disposed of** we need some method of deciding how much of the initial purchase cost relates to the part just disposed of, so that we can calculate a gain.

Example

Graham disposes of part of a field which cost £6,000 as a whole.
He sold one corner of the field for £8,000 incurring £200 legal costs.
We need to calculate the gain.

```
                              ┌──────────────┐
                              │  Proceeds    │
                              │  £8,000      │
        Cost of entire field  │              │
               £6,000         └──────────────┘
```

We know the sale proceeds but not the cost of the part sold.

To calculate the gain it is necessary to **apportion part of the overall cost to the part disposed of**.

This could be done in a number of ways, e.g. based on the area of the land sold.

However, in order to make the calculation standard for all types of disposal, the following proportion of the cost is used for tax purposes:

$$\frac{A}{A+B}$$

where   A = the value of the part sold (if a sale then use sale proceeds **before** deducting selling expenses)

B = the value of the unsold remainder

Solution

Thus, if the remainder of the land was worth £15,000 then the chargeable gain would be calculated as follows:

	£
Proceeds	8,000
Less: Selling expenses	(200)
	———
Net sale proceeds	7,800
Less: Cost (£6,000) × $\dfrac{£8,000}{£8,000 + £15,000}$	(2,087)
	———
Chargeable gain	5,713
	———

2.3   Chattels

Chattels are tangible, moveable property; for example a picture or a table.

A building is not a chattel as it is not moveable. Similarly, shares are not chattels – a share certificate may be tangible and moveable but the asset of value is the underlying rights conferred by the certificate.

Wasting chattels (expected life not exceeding 50 years) are exempt.

Machinery is always treated as wasting. However, it will only be a wasting chattel if it is moveable.

All animals which appear in the assessment are regarded as wasting chattels.

Non-wasting chattels (expected life of more than 50 years) are likely to be items such as antiques, works of art, jewellery, etc.

The treatment of non-wasting chattels is based on the £6,000 rules.

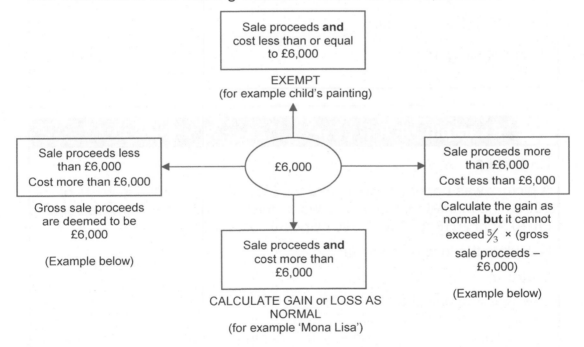

Example

Chattels 1

Marjory bought two antique tables in March 1994 for £1,000 each. She sold them both in June 2018 for £6,400 and £13,600 respectively.

Calculate the chargeable gains on the disposals.

Solution

	Table A £	Table B £
Proceeds	6,400	13,600
Less: Cost	(1,000)	(1,000)
Chargeable gain	5,400	12,600

The gains calculated above cannot exceed:

5/3 × (£6,400 – £6,000)	667	
5/3 × (£13,600 – £6,000)		12,667
Chargeable gain	667	12,600

 Example

Chattels 2

A picture was bought in April 1992 for £10,000 plus purchase costs of £500. The market for the artist's work slumped and the picture was sold on 10 April 2018 for £500, less disposal costs of £50.

Calculate the loss on disposal.

Solution

The loss is as follows:

	£
Gross sale proceeds (£500 but deemed to be £6,000)	6,000
Less: Selling costs	(50)
Net proceeds	5,950
Less: Cost (including acquisition expenses)	(10,500)
Allowable loss	(4,550)

Notice that it is the gross sale proceeds **before** deducting selling costs that are deemed to be £6,000.

Test your understanding 2

Mr Windsor

Mr Windsor has made the following disposals in 2018/19.

(1) A painting was sold in July 2018 for £6,600. He originally bought it in February 2000 for £3,500.

(2) A house which he bought in April 1993 for £5,000 (an investment property) was sold in September 2018 for £75,000. In June 1998 an extension costing £10,000 was built.

(3) He sold a car for £20,000 in June 2018 that had originally cost him £43,000 in June 2009.

(4) He bought a plot of land for £8,000 in August 2002. He sold part of the land for £20,000 in January 2019. At that time the remaining land was worth £60,000.

Required:

Calculate his total chargeable gains.

2.4 Connected persons

Where a disposal is between connected persons:

(i) sale proceeds are deemed to be market value (any actual sale proceeds are ignored), and

(ii) if a loss arises on a disposal to a connected person it can only be offset against a gain made on a disposal to the **same** connected person.

Connected persons are mainly relatives and their spouses/civil partners or relatives of your spouse/civil partner.

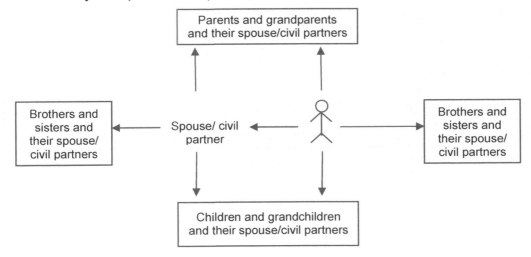

An individual is also connected with a company he controls and a partner is connected with his other business partners as well as their business partner's spouse/civil partner and relatives.

2.5 Transfers between spouses and civil partners

Whilst spouses are clearly connected persons, the tax treatment of assets disposed of by one to the other is different.

On disposals between spouses, sales proceeds are deemed to be equal to the seller's cost such that no gain or loss arises.

This figure is also used for the purchaser's cost when calculating a gain on a future sale by the purchaser.

This treatment also applies to disposals between civil partners.

🔆 Example

David purchased some jewellery in August 2008 for £50,000. In June 2017 he gave the jewellery to his wife Victoria when it was worth £200,000. Victoria sold the jewellery in May 2018 for £220,000.

Calculate Victoria's chargeable gain.

Solution

Disposal by David

	£
Deemed proceeds (equal to cost)	50,000
Less: Cost	(50,000)
	———
No gain or loss arises	Nil
	———

Sale by Victoria

	£
Proceeds	220,000
Less: Deemed cost	(50,000)
	———
Chargeable gain	170,000
	———

Test your understanding 3

For each statement below, tick the appropriate treatment.

		Actual proceeds used	Market value used	No gain or loss basis
1	Jamie gives an asset to his sister in law			
2	Husband sells an asset to his wife at market value			
3	Eloise sells an asset on EBay for £8,000 when the market value is £12,000			

2.6 Assets lost, destroyed or damaged

A capital transaction usually has two parties, a buyer and a seller.

However, when an asset is damaged, destroyed or lost and the asset's owner receives compensation (either from the perpetrator or an insurance company) the position is different. The owner has received a capital sum without disposing of the asset and the payer has received nothing in return.

Consequently, a special set of rules is required.

The rules vary according to whether:

- the asset has been completely lost/destroyed or merely damaged

- the owner has replaced or restored the asset.

2.6.1 Assets lost or destroyed

There is a deemed disposal for capital gains tax purposes as follows:

(a) **No insurance proceeds**

Compute a capital loss using the normal CGT computation:

- Disposal proceeds will be £Nil.

- Deduction of the allowable expenditure will create a loss.

(b) **Insurance proceeds received – no replacement of asset**

Chargeable gain/loss is computed using the normal CGT computation pro forma.

(c) **Insurance proceeds received – asset replaced within 12 months**

The taxpayer can claim that no gain or loss will arise on the destruction/loss of the asset (as for transfers between spouses).

If the insurance proceeds are greater than the original cost of the asset, the excess is deducted from the replacement asset's allowable cost.

2.6.2 Asset damaged

(a) **No compensation**

There are no implications for capital gains tax purposes unless compensation (i.e. insurance proceeds or damages) is received.

(b) **Compensation received – no restoration of asset**

Where an asset is damaged and compensation is received there is a part disposal for capital gains tax purposes (as in section 2.2 above).

The allowable cost is calculated using the normal part disposal formula:

$$\text{Cost} \times A/A + B$$

Where   A = Compensation received

            B = Market value of the remainder at the time of the part disposal (i.e. value in its damaged condition).

(c) **Compensation received – used to restore asset**

If the compensation is used to fully restore the damaged asset the taxpayer may claim to deduct the compensation from the cost of the asset rather than be treated as having made a part disposal.

3   Principal private residence exemption

3.1   General exemption

Other than business reliefs (which we do not need to consider for the Personal Tax paper) the main CGT relief available to individuals is the *principal private residence* (PPR) exemption.

If the owner occupies his PPR throughout his period of ownership, the gain is exempt.

If there have been periods where the owner has not lived in the property, part of the gain may be taxable.

An individual who lives in more than one residence may elect for one of them to be treated as his main residence. This election must be made to HM Revenue and Customs within two years of commencing to live in the second residence.

3.2 Principal private residence relief

Where there has been a period of absence, the procedure is as follows.

(a) Calculate the gain on the sale of the house.

(b) Compute the total period of ownership in months.

(c) Calculate periods of occupation in months.

(d) PPR exemption = $\frac{(c)}{(b)} \times (a)$ The PPR exemption must be given before deducting capital losses.

Example

Jim bought a house on 1 January 2001. Initially the house remained empty. He started to live in the house on 1 October 2008, and lived in it until he sold it on 30 September 2018.

The gain on disposal before deduction of principal private residence relief was £167,500.

Calculate the chargeable gain after principal private residence relief.

Solution

Step 1: Calculate the gain before relief.

Given = £167,500.

Step 2: Identify the total period of ownership and the period the house was occupied (lived in by Jim).

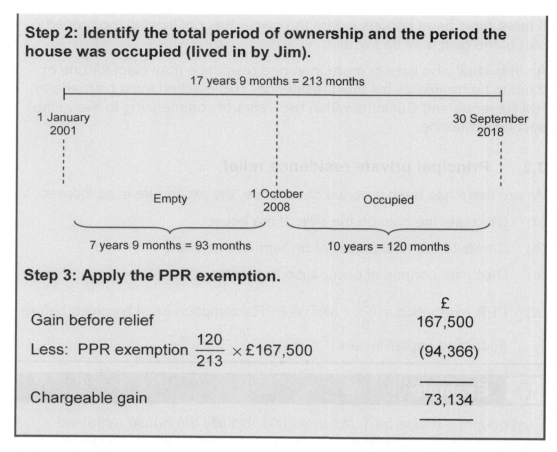

17 years 9 months = 213 months

1 January 2001

30 September 2018

Empty

1 October 2008

Occupied

7 years 9 months = 93 months

10 years = 120 months

Step 3: Apply the PPR exemption.

	£
Gain before relief	167,500
Less: PPR exemption $\frac{120}{213} \times £167,500$	(94,366)
Chargeable gain	73,134

3.3 Periods of deemed occupation

Exemption is also available for the following periods of 'deemed occupation'.

(a) The last 18 months of ownership.

(b) Up to three years of absence for any reason.

(c) Any period spent working abroad.

(d) Up to four years of absence while working elsewhere in the UK.

To be allowed, the absences in (b), (c) and (d) above must be preceded and followed by a period of actual occupation. No such condition applies to absence under (a) above.

Even for (c) and (d) the condition of actual occupation after a period of absence is relaxed where an employer requires the owner to work elsewhere immediately, thus making it impossible to resume occupation.

Example

Arthur bought a house on 1 January 2000 and sold it on 30 September 2018 making a gain before deduction of reliefs of £275,000.

During this time:

1 January 2000	– 31 December 2001	Lived in house
1 January 2002	– 30 June 2008	Employed overseas
1 July 2008	– 31 December 2012	Travelled the world
1 January 2013	– 30 September 2018	Lived in house

Solution

Step 1: Calculate the gain before relief.

Given = £275,000

Step 2: Identify:

- period of ownership

- periods of actual occupation

- periods of deemed occupation (remember preceded and followed by actual occupation).

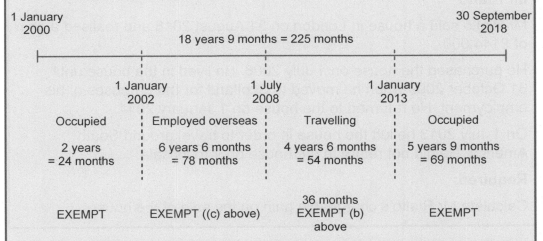

The periods of occupation before and after deemed occupation do **not** need to be **immediately** before and after (for example the employment overseas ended on 30 June 2008 and is followed by actual occupation which did not start until 1 January 2013).

Step 3: Apply PPR exemption.

		£
Gain before relief		275,000
PPR exemption		
	Months	
Occupied	24	
Employed overseas	78	
Any reason	36	
Occupied	69	
	207 out of 225	

$$\frac{207}{225} \times £275,000 \qquad\qquad (253,000)$$

Chargeable gain	22,000

 Test your understanding 4

Mr Rialto

Mr Rialto sold a house in London on 31 August 2018 and realised a gain of £144,000.

He purchased the house on 1 July 2006. He lived in the house until 31 October 2009 when he moved to Scotland for the purposes of his employment. He returned to the house on 1 January 2011.

On 1 July 2013 he left the house in order to travel around South America. He did not return to the house prior to its sale.

Required:

Calculate Mr Rialto's chargeable gain on the sale of the house.

4 Test your understanding

Test your understanding 5

Alfie bought a chargeable asset in August 2015 for £120,000. He spent £25,000 on improving the asset in February 2017. He sold the asset for £170,000 in February 2019.

The gain on this asset is:

Test your understanding 6

Lisa bought a chargeable asset in November 2007 for £32,500, selling it in October 2018 for £56,250. She paid auctioneers commission of 2% when she bought the asset and 6% when she sold the asset.

The gain on this asset is:

Test your understanding 7

Read the following statements and state whether they are true or false.

1   Brian sold a quarter of a plot of land. A quarter of the original cost should be deducted when calculating the chargeable gain.

2   Advertising costs are not an allowable deduction as they are revenue expenses.

3   Market value should be substituted for disposal proceeds when an asset is gifted to someone other than the spouse.

4   If Sally bought a picture for £8,000 and sold it for £3,000 her allowable loss will be £2,000.

Test your understanding 8

Match the following statements to the correct asset details. All of the assets are chattels and none have a life of less than 50 years.

Match the statements below with the assets disposed of.

Asset	Sale proceeds	Cost	Statement
1	£8,000	£4,000	
2	£14,000	£20,000	
3	£16,000	£7,000	
4	£4,000	£9,000	
5	£3,000	£2,000	

Statements:

Exempt asset

Calculate gain as normal

Calculate loss as normal

Sale proceeds to be £6,000

Gain restricted to 5/3 rule

 Test your understanding 9

Whahid bought 20 acres of land on 3 May 2006 for £28,000. On 12 December 2018 he sold 10 acres for £45,000. The market value of the remaining land at that time was £15,000.

What is the chargeable gain arising on the disposal of the land in December 2018?

Test your understanding 10

Lionel disposes of a house which he had owned for 20 years making a gain of £200,000.

What would be the chargeable gain assuming:

1   he had always lived in the house

2   he had never lived in the house

3   he had lived in the house for three years, moved away for eight years whilst he was working elsewhere in the UK, and then lived in it for the final nine years of ownership?

 Test your understanding 11

Mitch bought a house on 1 July 2008 for £100,000.

He lived in the house until 30 June 2014 when he decided to travel the world. The house remained empty until he sold it on 30 September 2018 for £170,000. The house was Mitch's only property.

Which periods are treated as occupied and which are not?

Occupation	Non-occupation

5 Summary

In this chapter we have considered the pro forma calculation of the chargeable gain for an individual asset.

	£
Sale proceeds	X
Less: Allowable cost	(X)
Chargeable gain	X

In addition, special rules apply in certain situations.

For part disposals, the cost must be apportioned on the basis of the formula: A/(A + B).

For disposals of chattels, the rules depend on whether the asset is wasting and whether the cost or proceeds are less than £6,000.

For connected persons, market value must be used for disposal proceeds and there are restrictions on the loss relief available.

If a taxpayer has only one house at any one time and occupies it throughout, the gain is fully exempt. Certain periods of non-occupation are deemed to be occupation.

Test your understanding answers

Test your understanding 1

Paul

The correct answer is £37,000.

	£
Sales proceeds	145,000
Less: Allowable cost	(108,000)
Chargeable gain	37,000

Note: The fees of £2,000 in June 2010 were incurred by the seller, not Paul; therefore they are not an allowable deduction.

The **chargeable** gain is **before** deducting the annual exempt amount.

Test your understanding 2

Mr Windsor

	£	£
(1) Painting (non-wasting chattel)		
Sales proceeds	6,600	
Less:Allowable cost	(3,500)	
	3,100	
Chargeable gain cannot exceed:		
$\frac{5}{3}$ × (sale proceeds – £6,000)		
= $\frac{5}{3}$ × (£6,600 – £6,000)		1,000
Total gains c/f		1,000

		£	£
	Total gains b/f		1,000
(2)	**House**		
	Sale proceeds	75,000	
	Less: Allowable cost		
	Original	(5,000)	
	Enhancement	(10,000)	
	Chargeable gain		60,000
(3)	**Car – exempt asset**		Nil
(4)	**Plot of land (part disposal)**		
	Sale proceeds	20,000	
	Less: Allowable cost		

$$\frac{A}{A+B} \times £8,000$$

$$\frac{20,000}{20,000+60,000} \times £8,000 \qquad (2,000)$$

Chargeable gain		18,000
Total chargeable gains		79,000

📝 Test your understanding 3

1 Market value used as the disposal is between connected persons.

2 No gain or loss basis as a transfer between spouses. Actual proceeds are irrelevant.

3 Actual proceeds used as the sale is not between connected persons and not a deliberate sale at undervalue.

Test your understanding 4

Mr Rialto

		£
Gain before relief		144,000
PPR exemption		

		Months
1 July 2006 – 31 October 2009	Occupied	40
1 November 2009 – 31 December 2010	Employed in UK	14
1 January 2011 – 30 June 2013	Occupied	30
1 July 2013 – 31 August 2018	Absent (Note 1)	18
		____
		102
		____

102/146 (Note 2) × £144,000	(100,603)
	_____
Chargeable gain	43,397
	_____

Notes:

1   The last 18 months of ownership are always treated as a period of occupation. Accordingly, the period of absence from 1 March 2017 to 31 August 2018 is deemed occupation.

   None of the beginning of the period of absence, from 1 July 2013 to 28 February 2017, can be treated as a period of occupation as Mr Rialto did not live in the property both before and after the period of absence.

2   Mr Rialto owned the property for a period of 146 months from 1 July 2006 to 31 August 2018.

Test your understanding 5

Alfie

The correct answer is £25,000.

	£
Disposal proceeds	170,000
Less: Cost	(120,000)
Enhancement cost	(25,000)
	_____
Chargeable gain	25,000
	_____

Test your understanding 6

Lisa

The correct answer is £19,725.

	£
Disposal proceeds	56,250
Less: Selling costs (£56,250 × 6%)	(3,375)
	52,875
Less: Cost	(32,500)
Incidental purchase costs (£32,500 × 2%)	(650)
Chargeable gain	19,725

Test your understanding 7

1   **False** – The A/(A + B) formula should be used to calculate the allowable cost.

2   **False** – Advertising costs are an allowable selling cost.

3   **True**

4   **True** – Proceeds will be deemed to be £6,000 as a picture is a chattel and it has been sold for less than £6,000 but bought for more. The loss will therefore be (£6,000 – £8,000) = £2,000.

Test your understanding 8

Asset	Sale proceeds	Cost	Statement
1	£8,000	£4,000	Gain restricted to 5/3 rule
2	£14,000	£20,000	Calculate loss as normal
3	£16,000	£7,000	Calculate gain as normal
4	£4,000	£9,000	Sale proceeds to be £6,000
5	£3,000	£2,000	Exempt asset

Test your understanding 9

Whahid

The correct answer is £24,000.

Explanation

	£
Proceeds	45,000
Less: Cost	
£28,000 × £45,000/(£45,000 + £15,000)	(21,000)
Chargeable gain	24,000

 Test your understanding 10

1   £Nil – PPR exemption applies throughout.

2   £200,000, the house was never used as his PPR.

3   £10,000 (£200,000 × 1/20):

First 3 years – exempt – actual occupation

Next 4 years – exempt – working elsewhere in the UK

Next 3 years – exempt – absent for any reason

Next 1 year – chargeable under PPR rules

Next 9 years – exempt – actual occupation

 Test your understanding 11

Mitch

Occupation	Non-occupation
1 Jul 2008 – 30 Jun 2014	1 Jul 2014 – 31 Mar 2017
1 Apr 2017 – 30 Sep 2018 (last 18 months)	

Shares and securities

12

Introduction

As part of the assessment you may be required to calculate a gain on the disposal of some shares.

There are special rules applying to share disposals as it is necessary to determine which particular shares have been sold.

ASSESSMENT CRITERIA	CONTENTS
Apply matching rules for individuals (4.3)	1 The matching rules
	2 Same day and next 30 days
Account for bonus issues (4.3)	3 Share pool
Account for rights issues (4.3)	4 Bonus issues and rights issues
	5 Approach to assessment questions

1 The matching rules

What distinguishes a share disposal from other asset disposals is the need for matching rules.

The main reason why matching rules are needed is because the same type of shares in a company may be bought at different times and at different prices.

Hence, if only some of the shares are sold we need to know which they are in order to identify their cost.

The matching rules for companies making disposals are different to those for individuals and are covered in Business Tax.

In relation to individuals, we match shares disposed of in the following order:

- first, with shares acquired on the same day as the disposal

- second, with shares acquired within the following 30 days (using the earliest acquisition first, i.e. on a FIFO basis)

- third, with the share pool (all the shares bought by the individual before the date of disposal).

Example

Frederic had the following transactions in the shares of DEF plc, a quoted company.

1 June 1996	Bought	4,000 shares for	£8,000
30 July 2003	Bought	1,800 shares for	£9,750
20 May 2011	Bought	1,000 shares for	£8,500
15 March 2019	Sold	3,500 shares for	£36,000
20 March 2019	Bought	400 shares for	£3,900

You are required to match the shares sold with the relevant acquisitions.

Solution

		Number	Number
Shares sold			3,500
(1)	Shares acquired same day		Nil
(2)	Shares acquired following 30 days (20 March 2019)		(400)
			3,100
(3)	Share pool		
	1 June 1996	4,000	
	30 July 2003	1,800	
	20 May 2011	1,000	
		6,800	
	The disposal from the pool is therefore 3,100 out of 6,800		(3,100)
			Nil

Test your understanding 1

Petra sold 200 shares in Red plc on 13 December 2018. She had acquired her shares in the company as follows:

	Number of shares
1 January 2009	650
14 February 2010	250
5 January 2019	50

In accordance with the share matching/identification rules the 200 shares sold by Petra are correctly identified as follows.

A   The 50 shares acquired on 5 January 2019 and then 150 of the remaining 900 shares in the pool.

B   The 50 shares acquired on 5 January 2019 and then 150 of the shares acquired on 14 February 2010.

C   200 of the shares acquired on 1 January 2009.

D   200 shares in the share pool which includes all 950 shares acquired.

Once the correct acquisition is identified, then the computation of the gains can be carried out. This is looked at in detail over the next few sections.

2 Same day and next 30 days

2.1 Calculation of the gain

The calculation of the gain on disposal is straightforward.

	£
Sale proceeds or market value	X
Less: Allowable cost	(X)
Chargeable gain	X

Example

Using the example details above (Frederic) calculate the gain on the sale of the shares acquired in the 30 days following the sale.

Solution

This consists of the sale of 400 shares.

Sale proceeds of £36,000 relates to 3,500 shares so must be apportioned.

The proceeds relating to 400 shares will be:

$$\frac{400}{3,500} \times £36,000 = £4,114$$

	£
Sale proceeds	4,114
Less: Cost	(3,900)
Chargeable gain	214

The balance of the proceeds (£36,000 − £4,114 = £31,886) will be applied to shares sold from the share pool.

3 Share pool

3.1 Calculation of the pooled cost

The share pool consists of all shares in a particular company purchased before the date of disposal. It is used to calculate the cost of shares sold by reference to the average cost of all shares purchased.

The pool is set up with two columns; number (of shares) and cost. Shares purchased are added to the pool and shares sold are deducted.

- For a purchase, add the number of shares acquired to the number column and the cost to the cost column.

- For a sale, deduct the number of shares sold from the number column and an appropriate proportion of the cost from the cost column.

Example

Using the example details above (Frederic), calculate the cost to be eliminated from the pool.

Solution

Share pool

		Number	Cost £
June 1996	purchase	4,000	8,000
July 2003	purchase	1,800	9,750
20 May 2011	purchase	1,000	8,500
		6,800	26,250
March 2019	disposal		
3,100 out of 6,800 (Note 1)		(3,100)	(11,967)
Pool balance carried forward		3,700	14,283

Note:

(1) To calculate the amount to eliminate on disposal, multiply the total cost by $\dfrac{\text{Number of shares sold}}{\text{Total shares in pool}}$

3.2 Calculation of the gain on the share pool

The gain is calculated as proceeds less cost in the normal way:

	£
Sale proceeds	X
Less: Allowable cost	(X)
Chargeable gain	X

 Example

Using the details from the example Frederic, what is the gain on the share pool disposals?

Solution

Sale proceeds are £31,886 (£36,000 × 3,100/3,500).

	£
Sale proceeds	31,886
Less: Allowable cost (above)	(11,967)
Chargeable gain on share pool shares	19,919

Hence, the total chargeable gain on disposal of the 3,500 shares = (£214 + £19,919) = £20,133.

Test your understanding 2

Ken has carried out the following transactions in shares in CYZ plc.

	Number	Cost
		£
Purchase (8 February 2002)	1,800	3,100
Purchase (12 September 2011)	1,200	4,400
Purchase (10 October 2018)	400	6,000
	Number	**Proceeds**
Sale (10 October 2018)	2,000	33,000

Required:

What is the chargeable gain on the sale of shares?

4 Bonus issues and rights issues

A bonus issue is the distribution of free shares to existing shareholders based on existing shareholdings.

The number of shares acquired is added to the number column in the share pool but there is no cost to add to the cost column.

A rights issue involves shareholders acquiring new shares in proportion to their existing shareholdings. The shares are not free but are usually priced at a rate below the market price.

The number of shares acquired is added to the number column in the share pool and the cost to the cost column. Accordingly, a rights issue is treated the same as any other purchase of shares in the share pool.

 Example

Alma acquired shares in S plc, a quoted company, as follows.

2,000 shares acquired in June 1997 for £11,500.

In October 2007 there was a 1 for 2 bonus issue.

In December 2009 there was a 1 for 4 rights issue at £3 per share.

Alma sold 1,350 shares in November 2018 for £30,000.

What is the chargeable gain?

Solution

	£
Sale proceeds	30,000
Less: Cost (W)	(4,950)
	———
Chargeable gain	25,050
	———

Working: Share pool

	Number	Cost £
June 1997 purchase	2,000	11,500
October 2007 bonus issue (1 for 2)		
No cost so simply add in new shares	1,000	–
	3,000	11,500
December 2009 rights issue		
(1 for 4) (£3 × 750)	750	2,250
	3,750	13,750
November 2018 disposal		
$\frac{1,350}{3,750}$ × £13,750	(1,350)	(4,950)
Pool carried forward	2,400	8,800

 Test your understanding 3

Mr Jones

In October 2018 Mr Jones sold 3,000 shares in Smith plc for £36,000. He had purchased 4,200 shares in June 1995 for £11,600. In August 2009 there was a 1 for 3 rights issue at £5.60 per share.

Required:

Calculate the chargeable gain on disposal.

5 Approach to assessment questions

In the assessment you are likely to be asked to calculate a gain on shares. If so, this question will be manually marked. Hence it is important that you enter your answer correctly into the table supplied and show your workings.

In the sample assessment a four column table is supplied. The first column is for description and narrative whilst the three other columns are for numerical entry.

This should allow you to enter your answer in the same layout as used throughout this chapter although with a little less detail. You will not be able to type in lines to indicate totals and subtotals.

 Example

Jason bought 1,000 shares in VZ plc for £4.20 each in December 2008.

In July 2017 he received a 1 for 5 rights issue at £6.52 each.

In May 2018 he sold 400 shares for £45,000.

What is the chargeable gain? Your answer should clearly show the balance of shares carried forward. Show all workings.

Solution

		£	
Proceeds		45,000	
Less cost (pool)		(1,835)	
Gain		43,165	
Pool		Number	Cost (£)
Dec 2008 Purchase		1,000	4,200
Jul 2017 Rights issue	1,000/5 × £6.52	200	1,304
		1,200	5,504
May 2018 Sale	400/1,200 × £5,504	(400)	(1,835)
Balance c/f		800	3,669

6 Test your understanding

Test your understanding 4

Ben bought 1,000 shares in XYZ plc on 1 May 2009 and a further 500 shares on 5 September 2018. He sold 750 shares on 25 August 2018.

Which shares are the shares sold identified with?

A   750 of the shares acquired on 1 May 2009

B   500 of the shares acquired on 1 May 2009 and 250 of the shares acquired on 5 September 2018

C   The 500 shares acquired on 5 September 2018 and then 250 of the remaining 1,000 shares in the pool

D   750 shares in the share pool which includes 1,500 shares acquired

Test your understanding 5

Tony bought 15,000 shares in Last Chance Ltd for £6 per share in August 2007. He received a bonus issue of 1 for 15 shares in January 2010.

In November 2018 Tony sold 9,000 shares for £14 per share.

Required:

Calculate the gain made on the sale of the shares and show the balance of shares and their cost to carry forward.

All workings must be shown in your calculations.

Test your understanding 6

Conrad sold all of his 2,145 ordinary shares in Turnip plc on 19 November 2018 for net sale proceeds of £8,580.

His previous dealings in these shares were as follows:

July 2014	purchased 1,750 shares for £2,625
May 2015	purchased 200 shares for £640
June 2016	took up 1 for 10 rights issue at £3.40 per share

What is the amount of the chargeable gain/allowable loss arising on the disposal?

 Test your understanding 7

David bought 2,000 shares in PQR plc for £4,000 on 6 October 2005 and a further 1,000 shares for £3,000 in March 2011.

PQR plc made a rights issue of 1 new share for every 5 held at £4 per share in February 2013. David sold 400 shares in September 2018 for £7,000.

What is the cost of the shares sold?

7 Summary

Share disposals require special matching rules.

Shares sold are matched with:

*   purchases on the same day
*   purchases within the following 30 days
*   share pool.

Bonus issues increase the number of shares held in the pool.

Rights issues affect both the number of shares held in the pool and the pool cost.

Test your understanding answers

 Test your understanding 1

Petra

The correct answer is **A**.

Explanation

A is the correct answer because the share identification rules match shares in the following priority.

1   Shares acquired on the same day as the disposal – not applicable here.

2   Shares acquired in the following 30 days – 50 shares acquired on 5 January 2019.

3   Shares in the share pool (all acquisitions prior to date of disposal).

Test your understanding 2

Ken

October 2018 disposal of 2,000 shares identified with:

		£
(a)	Shares acquired on the same day	400
(b)	Shares from share pool	1,600
		─────
		2,000
		─────

Sale proceeds are £33,000 for 2,000 shares

(a)   10 October 2018 acquisition

	£
Sale proceeds ($\frac{400}{2,000} \times £33,000$)	6,600
Less: Cost	(6,000)
	─────
Chargeable gain	600

(b)   Share pool

	£
Sale proceeds ($\frac{1,600}{2,000} \times £33,000$)	26,400
Less: Cost (W)	(4,000)
	──────
Chargeable gain	22,400
Total chargeable gains	23,000
	──────

Working: Share pool		**Number**	**Cost**
			£
February 2002	purchase	1,800	3,100
September 2011	purchase	1,200	4,400
		─────	─────
		3,000	7,500
October 2018	disposal	(1,600)	(4,000)
		─────	─────
Pool balance c/f		1,400	3,500
		─────	─────

Test your understanding 3

Mr Jones

	£
Sale proceeds	36,000
Less: Cost (W)	(10,414)
Chargeable gain	25,586

Workings: Share pool	Number	Cost £
June 1995 purchase	4,200	11,600
August 2009 rights issue ($\frac{1}{3}$ × 4,200) = 1,400 × £5.60	1,400	7,840
	5,600	19,440
October 2018 disposal $\frac{3,000}{5,600}$ × £19,440	(3,000)	(10,414)
Pool balance c/f	2,600	9,026

Test your understanding 4

Ben

The correct answer is **C**.

Explanation

The share identification rules match shares in the following priority.

1   Shares acquired on the same day as the disposal – not applicable here.

2   Shares acquired in the following 30 days – 500 shares acquired on 5 September 2018.

3   Shares in the share pool.

Test your understanding 5

Tony

	£
Sale proceeds (9,000 × £14)	126,000
Less: Cost (W)	(50,625)
Chargeable gain	75,375

Workings: Share pool	**Number**	**Cost**
		£
August 2007 purchase (15,000 × £6)	15,000	90,000
January 2010 bonus issue	1,000	
	16,000	90,000
November 2018 disposal $\frac{9,000}{16,000}$ × £90,000	(9,000)	(50,625)
Pool balance c/f	7,000	39,375

Test your understanding 6

Conrad

The correct answer is £4,652.

Explanation

	£
Proceeds	8,580
Less: Cost (W)	(3,928)
Chargeable gain	4,652

Working: Share pool	Shares number	Cost £
July 2014 purchase	1,750	2,625
May 2015 purchase	200	640
	1,950	3,265
June 2016 rights issue (1 for 10) @ £3.40	195	663
	2,145	3,928
November 2018 sale	(2,145)	(3,928)
	Nil	Nil

Test your understanding 7

David

The correct answer is £1,044.

Explanation

Working: Share pool	Shares number	Cost £
October 2005 purchase	2,000	4,000
March 2011 purchase	1,000	3,000
	3,000	7,000
February 2013 rights issue (1 for 5) @ £4.00	600	2,400
	3,600	9,400
September 2018 sale	(400)	(1,044)
	3,200	8,356

Inheritance tax

Introduction

Most inheritance tax (IHT) is collected on the death of an individual based on the value of their death estate. Some lifetime gifts may also result in an IHT liability.

This chapter covers the principles that underpin IHT, the ways in which an individual is liable to IHT and considers the IHT payable on lifetime gifts. Finally, it covers the IHT payable on the death estate.

IHT will always be tested in the assessment.

ASSESSMENT CRITERIA
Chargeable lifetime transfers (5.1)
Exempt transfers (5.1)
Potential exempt transfers (5.1)
Calculate tax payable on death (5.2)
Calculate tax payable on lifetime transfers (5.2)
Identify who is responsible for payment of inheritance tax (5.2)

CONTENTS

1   The charge to IHT
2   Lifetime gifts
3   Exemptions
4   IHT payable during an individual's lifetime on CLTs
5   IHT payable on lifetime gifts as a result of death
6   IHT payable on the death estate

1 The charge to IHT

1.1 Introduction

IHT is charged on:

- a **transfer of value**
- of **chargeable property**
- by a **chargeable person**.

A charge to IHT may arise:

- on the death of an individual
- on lifetime gifts where the donor dies within seven years of the date of a gift
- on certain lifetime gifts which are taxed at the date of the gift.

The donor is the person who makes the transfer of the asset.

The donee is the person who receives the asset.

1.2 Transfer of value

A transfer of value is a **gift of any asset** which results in a reduction in the value of the donor's estate.

To be treated as a transfer of value the transfer must be a 'gratuitous disposition'. This basically means a gift.

A bad business deal will therefore not be liable to IHT, even though there is a fall in value of the estate, as it was not the donor's intention to give anything away.

To calculate the transfer of value for IHT purposes, the **loss to donor** principle is used (also referred to as the **diminution in value** concept).

The loss to the donor, is the difference between the value of the donor's estate before and after the gift, and is the starting point for IHT calculations:

	£
Value of estate before gift	X
Less: Value of estate after gift	(X)
Diminution in value or transfer of value	X

The loss to the donor is usually the **open market value** of the asset gifted.

However, in some circumstances, the transfer of value from the donor's point of view is not necessarily the same as the value of the asset received from the donee's point of view.

This is most common with unquoted shares, where a controlling shareholding has a higher value per share than a minority shareholding.

 Example

Linda owns 6,000 shares which represents a 60% holding in Loot Ltd. On 31 December 2018 she gave a 20% holding in the company to her friend, Bob.

The values of shareholdings in Loot Ltd on 31 December 2018 have been agreed for IHT purposes as follows:

Holding	Value per share
Up to 25%	£9
26% to 50%	£15
51% to 74%	£26
75% or more	£45

Calculate the transfer of value relating to the gift of unquoted shares for IHT purposes.

Solution

	£
Value of estate before transfer (6,000 × £26)	156,000
Less: Value of estate after transfer (4,000 × £15)	(60,000)
	————
Transfer of value	96,000
	————

Note that a lifetime gift will have both IHT and CGT consequences.

The diminution in value concept is very important but unique to IHT.

The value of the asset gifted; a 20% interest in these shares (i.e. 2,000 × £9 = £18,000):

- is not relevant for IHT purposes; it is the diminution in the value of the estate from the donor's point of view which is important, but

- is important for CGT purposes; the market value of the asset gifted is always the consideration used as the starting point of the chargeable gain computation.

1.3 Chargeable property

All property to which a person is beneficially entitled is deemed to form part of their estate. Therefore, a gift of **any asset** is a transfer of value.

1.4 Chargeable persons

A chargeable person is an individual. All individuals are potentially liable to IHT. Companies and partnerships are not subject to IHT.

An individual who is domiciled in the UK (see Chapter 1) is liable to IHT in respect of their worldwide assets.

If not UK domiciled, they are liable in respect of UK assets only.

Note that spouses and partners in a registered civil partnership are chargeable to IHT separately.

2 Lifetime gifts

2.1 Types of lifetime gifts

There are three categories of lifetime gifts that can be made by an individual. The three categories, and their IHT implications are:

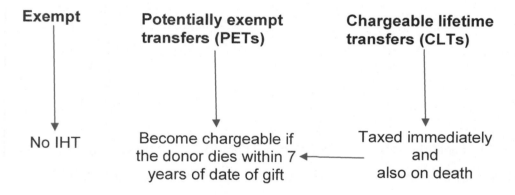

The definition of each type of gift and an overview of the way in which they are taxed is summarised in the following table.

Exempt transfers	Potentially exempt transfers (PETs)	Chargeable lifetime transfers (CLTs)
Definition		
A gift that is specifically deemed to be exempt from IHT (see below)	A gift by an individual to another individual	No definition = residual category (i.e. a gift which is not exempt nor a PET) Therefore a CLT will be a gift into most types of trust such as a discretionary trust
During lifetime		
No IHT payable	No IHT payable	IHT to pay calculated using the lifetime rates of tax
If donor lives seven years		
No IHT payable	No IHT payable Gift becomes exempt	No further IHT payable
If donor dies within seven years		
No IHT payable	The PET becomes chargeable on death for the first time	Possibly extra IHT, calculated using the death rates of tax

It is important to note that in practice, the majority of lifetime transfers made by individuals are either:

- exempt transfers, or

- transfers from one individual to another (i.e. a PET).

Individuals should ensure that they keep a record of the lifetime gifts they have made so that IHT can be calculated at death if necessary.

2.2 Chargeable lifetime transfers (CLTs)

A CLT is a gift which is not exempt and not a PET. They are not common in practice, but appear in assessments because they are chargeable to IHT at the time of the gift, i.e. while the donor is still alive.

In the assessment a lifetime transfer by an individual into a trust should be treated as a CLT.

A trust is an arrangement where property is transferred by a person (known as the settlor) to the trustees, to be held for the benefit of one or more specified persons (known as the beneficiaries) on specified terms.

The most common example of a trust is where parents wish to give assets to their children, but not until they are adults. They therefore put the assets into a trust with the children as beneficiaries, and the assets are controlled by the trustees until the children reach a specified age.

It is not necessary to understand the workings of trusts for the assessment, only to learn that gifts into trusts are CLTs.

2.3 Potentially exempt transfers (PETs)

PETs derive their name from the fact that if the donor lives for seven years after making the gift, then the transfer is exempt (i.e. free from IHT). Therefore, at the time of such transfer, it has the potential to be exempt.

However, if the donor dies within seven years of making the gift, then IHT may become chargeable on these gifts.

Note that transfers on death can never be PETs.

Test your understanding 1

Mark the following statements as true or false.

		True	False
1	A potentially exempt transfer is chargeable to IHT unless the donor dies within seven years of the gift.		
2	IHT may be charged on both potentially exempt transfers and chargeable lifetime transfers at the time of a person's death.		
3	IHT is only ever payable when a person dies.		
4	An IHT liability may arise in respect of a gift made more than seven years prior to death.		

---

3 Exemptions

3.1 Overview

There is no IHT payable where a gift is covered by an exemption.

The following table summarises the exemptions available for IHT that may feature in the assessment.

Exemptions available against:	
Lifetime gifts only	**Lifetime gifts and death estate**
• Small gifts exemption • Marriage exemption • Normal expenditure out of income • Annual exemption	• Inter spouse exemption • UK charities exemption • Political parties exemption • Museums and art galleries exemption

3.2 Exemptions available for lifetime gifts only

The following exemptions are available to reduce lifetime transfers only. They do not apply to the death estate.

The limits for these exemptions are included in the tax rates and allowances provided for you to refer to you in the assessment.

Small gifts exemption

Lifetime gifts are exempt if they are:

- an outright gift to an individual of no more than £250

- per recipient

- per tax year.

The small gift exemption does not apply to a gift or gifts to an individual of more than £250.

Therefore, a gift of £300 will not qualify. Similarly, if an individual makes a gift of £240 to a person followed by another gift of £100 to the same person in the same tax year, neither gift will be exempt.

However, the donor can make gifts of up to £250 to any number of different recipients and they will all be exempt.

Marriage exemption

A lifetime transfer made 'in consideration of a marriage' (or registration of a civil partnership) is exempt up to the following maximum limits:

- £5,000 by a parent

- £2,500 by a grandparent or remoter ancestor

- £2,500 by a party to the marriage or civil partnership (e.g. from the groom to the bride)

- £1,000 by anyone else.

The exemption is conditional on the marriage taking place.

Normal expenditure out of income

IHT is levied on transfers of capital wealth.

Therefore, a lifetime transfer will be exempt if it can be shown that the gift:

- is made as part of a person's normal expenditure out of income, and

- does not affect the donor's standard of living.

To be treated as 'normal', gifts must be habitual (i.e. there is a regular pattern of giving). For example, payment of school fees for a grandchild or annual payments into a life insurance policy for the benefit of a child are usually exempted under this rule.

The annual exemption

The annual exemption (AE) is an exemption available against lifetime transfers and operates as follows:

- The AE:

    - exempts the **first £3,000** of lifetime transfers in any one tax year

    - is applied chronologically to the first gift in the tax year, then (if there is any left) the second gift and so on

    - must be applied to the first gift each year, even if the first gift is a PET and never becomes chargeable.

- Any unused AE:

    - may be carried forward to the next year

    - however, it can be carried forward for one year only, and

    - can only be used after the current year's AE.

- The maximum AE in any one year is therefore £6,000 (£3,000 × 2).

- If other exemptions are available they are given before the AE.

Example

Julie made the following lifetime gifts:

(a) 31 August 2016, £600, to her son

(b) 31 October 2016, £800, to a trust

(c) 31 May 2017, £2,100, to a trust

(d) 30 November 2017, £1,100, to a trust

(e) 30 April 2018, £5,000, to her daughter.

Calculate the transfer of value after AEs for each of the gifts.

Solution

	PET 31.8.16	CLT 31.10.16	CLT 31.5.17	CLT 30.11.17	PET 30.4.18
Tax year of gift	2016/17	2016/17	2017/18	2017/18	2018/19
	£	£	£	£	£
Transfer of value	600	800	2,100	1,100	5,000
Less: AE					
2016/17	(600)	(800)			
2015/16 b/f	(–)	(–)			
2017/18			(2,100)	(900)	
2016/17 b/f				(200)	
2018/19					(3,000)
2017/18 b/f					(Nil)
Transfer of value	Nil	Nil	Nil	Nil	2,000

The 2015/16 AE brought forward is available in full (£3,000) however in can only be carried forward for one year and is not utilised in 2016/17, therefore it is lost.

The 2016/17 AE carried forward is £1,600 (£3,000 – £600 – £800). £200 of that is utilised in 2017/18, and the remaining £1,400 is lost.

The 2017/18 AE is utilised in full in 2017/18 therefore there is no brought forward AE available in 2018/19 to offset against the gift in that year.

Test your understanding 2

Calculate the chargeable amount (i.e. after the deduction of all available exemptions) in respect of each of the following cash gifts which were made on 1 June 2018.

		Gift £
1	Lance Lance's gift was to his brother. Lance had not made any gifts prior to 1 June 2018.	7,400
2	Carrie Carrie's gift was to her daughter at the time of her wedding. Carrie's only previous gift was £2,300 to her son on 1 October 2017.	12,200
3	Pinto Pinto's gift was to a friend. On 1 May 2018 Pinto gave £14,000 to his brother.	£170

3.3 Exemptions available for lifetime transfers and the death estate

Inter spouse exemption

Transfers between spouses or between partners in a registered civil partnership are exempt:

- regardless of the value of the transfer, and
- whether they are made during the individual's lifetime or on death.

Other exemptions

All gifts to the following, regardless of their value, are exempt from IHT.

- UK charities
- Qualifying political parties
- Museums and art galleries.

This means that where an individual leaves a gift to one or more of these organisations in their will, the amount of the gift(s) must be deducted from the value of the assets in the death estate.

Test your understanding 3

In the situations set out below it should be assumed that no annual exemptions are available to the donor.

Tick the appropriate column for each of the gifts

	Gift	Not exempt	Partly exempt	Fully exempt
1	£520 from Tim to his friend Martha.			
2	£218,000 from Serena to her husband.			
3	£1,600 from Marie to her friend Eric on his wedding day.			
4	A painting worth £1,700,000 from Brenda to The National Gallery.			

4 IHT payable during an individual's lifetime on CLTs

4.1 The procedure to calculate the lifetime IHT on a CLT

Lifetime IHT may be payable when an individual makes a gift into a trust.

The lifetime tax should be calculated on each gift separately, in chronological order, as follows:

(1) Calculate the chargeable amount of the gift:

	£
Value of estate before gift	X
Less: Value of estate after gift	(X)
Transfer of value	X
Less: Specific exemptions (e.g. spouse/charity)	(X)
Marriage exemption	(X)
Annual exemptions	(X)
Chargeable amount	X

The transfer of value in the above calculation will often be simply the value of the gift.

(2)   Calculate the amount of nil rate band available after deducting gross chargeable transfers in the previous seven years (see below).

(3)   Calculate the excess of the chargeable amount over the available nil rate band.

(4)   Calculate tax on this excess at either 20% or 25% depending on whether the donor or the donee will pay the tax (see below).

(5)   Calculate the gross amount of the gift to carry forward for future computations.

4.2   The nil rate band (NRB)

All individuals are entitled to a NRB and are taxed on the value of gifts in excess of the NRB at different rates depending on who has agreed to pay the lifetime tax.

The NRB is the maximum value of lifetime and death gifts, which can be gifted without incurring any IHT liability.

For lifetime calculations, the NRB applicable at the time of the gift should be used.

The current NRB of £325,000 is included in the tax rates and allowances provided to you in the assessment.

4.3   The appropriate rate of tax

The appropriate rate of tax to apply to lifetime gifts depends on who has agreed to pay the tax due.

Donee pays the tax

If the trustees of the trust (i.e. the donee) agree to pay the tax:

- the gift is referred to as a **gross gift**, and

- the appropriate rate of tax is 20%.

Donor pays the tax

If the donor agrees to pay the tax:

- The gift is referred to as a **net gift**.

- As a result of the gift, the estate of the donee is being reduced by:

    - the value of the gift, and

    - the associated tax payable on the gift.

- Accordingly the amount of the gift needs to be 'grossed up' to include the tax that the donor has to pay.

- The appropriate rate of tax is therefore 25% (i.e. 20/80ths of the net gift).

- The gross transfer to carry forward is the net chargeable amount plus any IHT paid by the donor.

In summary, the rate of tax on the value of CLTs in excess of the NRB is:

Payer		Appropriate rate
Trustees of the trust	Gross gift	20%
Donor	Net gift	25% (or 20/80)

Note that the tax due on a CLT is primarily the responsibility of the donor.

☀ Example

Charlotte made a gift into a trust on 13 June 2018 of £366,000.

She has made no previous gifts.

Calculate the amount of lifetime IHT due on the gift, assuming:

(a) the trustees of the trust have agreed to pay the tax.

(b) Charlotte has agreed to pay the tax.

Solution

(a) Trustees have agreed to pay the tax

	£
Gift	366,000
Annual exemption 2018/19	(3,000)
Annual exemption 2017/18 brought forward	(3,000)
	———
Chargeable amount	360,000
NRB	(325,000)
	———
Excess of chargeable amount over NRB	35,000
	———
IHT (£35,000 × 20%)	7,000
	———

(b) Charlotte has agreed to pay the tax

	£
Excess of chargeable amount over NRB as in (a)	35,000
	———
IHT (£35,000 × 25%)	8,750
	———

Note: Gross amount to carry forward for future computations (£360,000 + £8,750)   368,750

4.4 The seven year accumulation period

The NRB is available for a 'seven year accumulation period'.

In order to calculate the IHT liability in respect of a CLT it is necessary to look back seven years and calculate how much NRB is available to set against that particular gift.

For lifetime calculations, to calculate the NRB available at any point in time, it is necessary to deduct the total of the gross amounts of all other CLTs made within the previous seven years from the NRB.

However, you will only be tested on basic calculations in the assessment.

 Test your understanding 4

Dana made a gift into a trust on 1 September 2018 of £380,000. This was Dana's only gift in 2018/19.

She has made gross chargeable transfers of £86,000 in the seven years prior to 2018/19 including gifts of more than £3,000 in 2017/18.

Calculate the amount of lifetime IHT due on the gift, assuming:

(a)   the trustees of the trust have agreed to pay the tax.

(b)   Dana has agreed to pay the tax.

4.5 Summary of lifetime calculations

Remember, whilst the donor is alive:

• only calculate IHT on CLTs

• tax is due at 20% if the trustees pay, and 25% if the donor pays

• PETs are not chargeable at this stage, but they do use the annual exemptions.

---

5 IHT payable on lifetime gifts as a result of death

5.1 IHT on gifts within seven years of death

On the death of an individual, an IHT charge may arise in relation to lifetime gifts made **within seven years of death** as follows:

• PETs become chargeable for the first time.

• Additional tax may be due on CLTs.

The IHT payable on lifetime gifts as a result of death is always paid by the recipient of the gift:

Type of gift:	Paid by:
CLT	Trustees of the trust
PET	Donee

5.2 The available NRB

The NRB available on the death of an individual is:

- the NRB for the tax year of death (rather than the tax year of the gift)

- plus any unused proportion of the NRB of their spouse or civil partner who has already died

- less any gross chargeable transfers in the previous seven years (you will not be required to calculate this figure).

Note that the unused proportion of a spouse's NRB can only be utilised when calculating tax at death, **not** during the donor's lifetime.

Example

Erica was widowed on the death of her husband Arnie on 21 June 2008.

35% of Arnie's NRB was used when calculating the IHT due at the time of his death.

Erica died on 23 May 2018.

Erica had made gross chargeable transfers of £40,000 in the seven years prior to her death.

Calculate Erica's available NRB at the time of her death.

Solution

	£
NRB at the date of death	325,000
NRB transferred from Arnie (£325,000 × 65%)	211,250
Erica's gross chargeable transfers in the seven years prior to death	(40,000)
NRB available to Erica	496,250

5.3 Calculating the death IHT on lifetime gifts

The death tax should be calculated on a gift within seven years of death as follows:

(1) Calculate the **gross chargeable amount** of the gift.

(2) Calculate the **available NRB** (as set out above).

(3) Deduct the available NRB from the gross chargeable amount of the gift.

(4) Calculate the **death tax** on the excess at 40%.

(5) Calculate and deduct any **taper relief** available (see below).

(6) For CLTs, deduct any **lifetime IHT paid**.

(7) If required by the question, state who will pay the tax (see below).

5.4 Taper relief

Note that taper relief applies to both CLTs and PETs.

Where IHT is chargeable on any lifetime transfer due to death, the amount of IHT payable on death will be reduced by taper relief:

- where more than three years have elapsed since the date of the gift

- by a percentage reduction according to the length of time between

  – the date of the gift, and

  – the date of the donor's death.

The rates of taper relief are provided in the rates and allowances available to you in the assessment and are as follows:

	% reduction
3 years or less	0
Over 3 years but less than 4 years	20
Over 4 years but less than 5 years	40
Over 5 years but less than 6 years	60
Over 6 years but less than 7 years	80

For gifts made seven or more years before death there is no IHT payable on death, so taper relief is not relevant.

5.5 Deduction of lifetime IHT paid

For CLTs, any lifetime IHT already paid can be deducted from the liability calculated on death.

However, no refund is made if the tax already paid is higher than the amount now due on death.

At best, the deduction of lifetime tax paid will bring the liability on death down to £Nil.

Example

On 15 July 2011 Paula made a transfer of £365,000 into a trust. Paula agreed to pay the IHT due in respect of this gift. She has made no other lifetime transfers.

Paula died on 30 May 2018.

Solution

Lifetime IHT payable

	£
Transfer of value	365,000
Less:	
AE – 2011/12	(3,000)
AE – 2010/11	(3,000)
	———
Net chargeable amount	359,000
NRB at date of gift (no gifts in the previous seven years)	(325,000)
	———
Taxable amount	34,000
	———
Lifetime IHT due (£34,000 × 25%)	8,500
	———
Gross amount to carry forward for future computations (£359,000 + £8,500)	367,500
	———

IHT payable on death

	£
Gross chargeable amount (above)	367,500
NRB at death (no gifts in the previous seven years)	(325,000)
Taxable amount	42,500
IHT due on death (£42,500 × 40%)	17,000
Less: Taper relief (£17,000 × 80%)	(13,600)
(15 July 2011 to 30 May 2018 is 6 – 7 years)	
	3,400
Less: IHT paid in lifetime on CLT – restricted	(3,400)
IHT payable on death	Nil

Note: Deducting lifetime IHT cannot result in a repayment, and so the deduction is restricted to the amount required to reduce the liability to nil.

6 IHT payable on the death estate

6.1 The death estate computation

On the death of an individual, an IHT charge arises on the value of their estate at the date of death.

The death estate includes all assets held at the date of death.

The value of assets brought into an individual's estate computation is normally the open market value (OMV) of the asset at the date of death (known as the probate value).

The gross chargeable value of an individual's estate is calculated using the following pro forma:

Pro forma death estate computation	£	£
Freehold property		X
Less: Mortgage		(X)
		——
		X
Business owned by sole trader/partnership		X
Stocks and shares (including ISAs)		X
Government securities		X
Insurance policy proceeds		X
Leasehold property		X
Motor cars		X
Personal chattels		X
Debts due to the deceased		X
Cash at bank and on deposit (including ISAs)		X
		——
		X
Less: Debts due by the deceased	X	
Outstanding taxes (e.g. IT, CGT due)	X	
Funeral expenses	X	
	——	
		(X)
Less: Exempt legacies		(X)
Gross chargeable estate		X

Exempt legacies

The only exempt legacies are to:

- spouse or civil partner
- UK charities
- qualifying political parties
- museums and art galleries.

6.2 The procedure to calculate the IHT on the death estate

The procedure to calculate the IHT on the death estate is as follows.

(1) Deal with the IHT on lifetime gifts within seven years of the date of death first before looking at the estate computation.

(2) Calculate the gross chargeable estate value.

(3) Calculate the amount of the residence nil rate band (RNRB) available.

(4) Calculate the amount of NRB available after deducting the figure for GCTs in the previous seven years (you will not be required to calculate this figure).

(5) Calculate the tax on the excess at 40%.

(6) If required by the question, state who will pay the tax.

6.3 Further points regarding IHT payable on the death estate

The RNRB

The RNRB is available if the deceased leaves a home in their death estate that they have lived in at some point to a direct descendant, e.g. son or granddaughter. It applies from 6 April 2017 and is deducted in the death estate computation before applying the NRB.

The RNRB is not available against lifetime gifts and is restricted to the lower of:

- £125,000

- the value of the property (net of any repayment mortgage).

The RNRB is provided in your tax tables.

The NRB

The NRB available to an individual on death of £325,000 is first used to calculate the death tax on lifetime gifts, and then any remainder is set against the death estate.

The seven year accumulation period

The seven year accumulation period applies in a similar way to the death calculations on lifetime gifts. The NRB must be reduced by the total of the gross amounts of all chargeable gifts made within the previous seven years. In the assessment you will not be required to calculate this figure.

The death rate of tax

The death rate of IHT is 40%. This is charged on the excess of the estate over the NRB available.

💡 Example

Sara died on 15 June 2018 leaving a gross chargeable estate valued at £427,000 which was bequeathed to her brother.

(a) Calculate the IHT liability arising on Sara's estate assuming she made no lifetime transfers.

(b) What if Sara had gross chargeable transfers of £147,000 in the seven years prior to her death?

(c) How would your answer to part b have changed if Sara had bequeathed a property of £100,000 included in the estate above and left everything to her daughter?

Solution

(a) No lifetime transfers

	£	£
Gross chargeable estate value		427,000
NRB at death:	325,000	
Less: GCTs in 7 years pre-death	(Nil)	
	———	
NRB available		(325,000)
		———
Taxable amount		102,000
		———
IHT due on death (£102,000 × 40%)		40,800
		———

(b) Lifetime transfers = £147,000

	£	£
Gross chargeable estate value		427,000
NRB at death:	325,000	
Less: GCTs in 7 years pre-death	(147,000)	
	———	
NRB available		(178,000)
		———
Taxable amount		249,000
		———
IHT due on death (£249,000 × 40%)		99,600
		———

(c)   Lifetime transfers = £147,000 plus availability of the RNRB

	£	£
Gross chargeable estate value		427,000
RNRB lower of £125,000 and £100,000		(100,000)
NRB at death:	325,000	
Less: GCTs in 7 years pre-death	(147,000)	
	————	
NRB available		(178,000)
		————
Taxable amount		149,000
		————
IHT due on death (£149,000 × 40%)		59,600
		————

 Test your understanding 5

Timothy died on 23 April 2018 leaving a gross chargeable estate valued at £627,560 which included a home valued at £150,000, which he bequeathed to his girlfriend.

Timothy had made gross chargeable transfers of £222,000 in the seven years prior to his death.

Calculate the IHT liability arising on Timothy's estate.

6.4   Transfer of NRB and RNRB

Any unused NRB and/or RNRB can be transferred to the surviving spouse/civil partner on the death of the first spouse/civil partner.

It is always an unused percentage that is transferred and you will be told what proportion of the RNRB was utilised on the first spouse's death in the assessment.

Where the spouse/civil partner died before 6 April 2017 100% of the RNRB will be available to transfer to the second spouse, since the RNRB was not yet available on the first spouse's death.

The second spouse therefore has a maximum RNRB of £250,000 and a maximum NRB of £650,000 to set against their death estate.

Test your understanding 6

David died on 1 July 2018 and left an estate of £900,000, including a home valued at £300,000 to his son. David's civil partner James had passed away in 2013 and 58% of his NRB was used when calculating the IHT at the time of his death.

David had made gross chargeable transfers of £92,000 in the seven years prior to his death.

Calculate the IHT liability arising on David's estate.

6.5 Payment of IHT on the death estate

IHT on the death estate is initially paid by the executors.

The tax is paid from the estate, and so it is effectively borne by the person who inherits the residue of the assets (known as the residual legatee) after the specific legacies have been paid.

A summary of the payment of tax is shown below:

Recipient/asset	Paid by	Suffered by
Spouse	N/A – exempt	N/A – exempt
Specific UK assets	Executors	Residual legatee
Residue of estate	Executors	Residual legatee

7 Summary

IHT may be charged on:

- chargeable lifetime transfers whilst the donor is alive
- all gifts within seven years of death
- the death estate.

The taxable amount is:

- the transfer of value
- less exemptions
- less the available NRB.

It is important to learn:

- the meaning of chargeable lifetime transfer and potentially exempt transfer
- when the exemptions are available
- the calculation of the available NRB
- the rate at which IHT is paid in the different situations.

You should then practise calculating:

- lifetime IHT due in respect of a chargeable lifetime transfer
- IHT due on death in respect of a lifetime gift
- IHT due in respect of the death estate.

Test your understanding answers

Test your understanding 1

1   **False** – A potentially exempt transfer is chargeable to IHT unless the donor **survives the gift by at least seven years**.

2   **True** – All gifts within the seven years prior to death may give rise to an IHT charge.

3   **False** – IHT may be payable whilst a person is alive in respect of a chargeable lifetime transfer.

4   **True** – A chargeable lifetime transfer may result in an IHT liability at any time in a person's life and not just in the seven years prior to death.

Test your understanding 2

Chargeable amounts

		£
1	**Lance**	
	Gift	7,400
	Annual exemption 2018/19	(3,000)
	Annual exemption 2017/18 b/f	(3,000)
	Chargeable amount	1,400
2	**Carrie**	
	Gift	12,200
	Marriage exemption	(5,000)
	Annual exemption 2018/19	(3,000)
	Annual exemption 2017/18 b/f (£3,000 – £2,300)	(700)
	Chargeable amount	3,500
3	**Pinto**	
	Gift	170
	Small gifts exemption	(170)
	Chargeable amount	Nil

Test your understanding 3

	Gift	Not exempt	Partly exempt	Fully exempt
1	£520 from Tim to his friend Martha.	✓		
2	£218,000 from Serena to her husband.			✓
3	£1,600 from Marie to Eric on his wedding day.		✓	
4	A painting worth £1,700,000 from Brenda to The National Gallery.			✓

1 This gift exceeds £250, such that the small gifts exemption is not available.

2 The whole of this gift is covered by the spouse exemption.

3 A marriage exemption of £1,000 is available in respect of this gift.

4 The whole of this gift is covered by the exemption available in respect of gifts to museums and art galleries.

Test your understanding 4

Dana

(a) **Trustees have agreed to pay the tax**

	£
Gift	380,000
Annual exemption 2018/19	(3,000)
Chargeable amount	377,000
NRB (£325,000 – £86,000)	(239,000)
Excess of chargeable amount over NRB	138,000
IHT (£138,000 × 20%)	27,600

The annual exemption for 2017/18 will have been used against the gifts in 2017/18.

(b) **Dana has agreed to pay the tax**

	£
Excess of chargeable amount over NRB as in (a)	138,000
IHT (£138,000 × 25%)	34,500

Note: Gross amount to carry forward for future computations (£377,000 + £34,500) — 411,500

Test your understanding 5

Timothy – IHT on death estate

	£
Gross chargeable estate	627,560
NRB (£325,000 – £222,000)	(103,000)
Taxable amount	524,560
IHT due on death (£524,560 × 40%)	209,824

Note: The RNRB did not apply as although Tim left a home in his death estate he did not leave it to a direct descendent.

 Test your understanding 6

David – IHT on death estate

	£
Gross chargeable estate	900,000
RNRB (£125,000 × 2)	(250,000)
NRB ((£325,000 × 1.42) – £92,000)	(369,500)
Taxable amount	280,500
IHT due on death (£280,500 × 40%)	112,200

Note: David was able to make use of James' RNRB and the unused 42% of James' NRB to reduce his death estate.

He could make full use of the total RNRB of £250,000 as the home he bequeathed was worth more than £250,000 and was left to his son.

MOCK ASSESSMENT
AQ2016

1 Mock Assessment Questions

This assessment contains 13 tasks and you should attempt to complete every task.

Each task is independent. You will not need to refer to your answers in previous tasks.

Read every task carefully to make sure you understand what is required.

Where the date is relevant, it is given in the task data.

You may use minus signs or brackets to indicate negative numbers UNLESS task instructions say otherwise.

You must use a full stop to indicate a decimal point.
For example, write 100.57 NOT 100,57 or 100 57

You may use a comma to indicate a number in the thousands, but you don't have to.

For example, 10000 and 10,000 are both acceptable.

If rounding is required, normal mathematical rounding rules should be applied UNLESS task instructions say otherwise.

Task 1 (10 marks)

You work for a firm of accountants. You have become aware that one of your clients, Alexander, purchased a second home recently and that, occasionally, he may be renting out the property.

Using the AAT guidelines 'Professional conduct in relation to taxation', explain your responsibilities in relation to this matter.

(10 marks)

Task 2 (8 marks)

(a) **What percentage would be used to calculate the benefit for the following diesel cars (none of which meet the RDE2 standards) provided to employees for a mixture of business and private use during 2018/19?**   **(4 marks)**

    (i)   112 g/km

    (ii)   179 g/km

    (iii) 82 g/km

    (iv) 35 g/km

(b)   Jake is provided with the use of a Toyota car on 6 November 2018 by his employer. The list price of the car is £16,000 and Jake made a capital contribution of £1,800 towards the cost of the car. The CO_2 emissions are 114 g/km and it has a petrol engine. The company pays for all the running costs of the car including private fuel.

Complete the following sentences regarding Jake's taxable benefits for the car for 2018/19. Show your answers in whole pounds only.   **(4 marks)**

The benefit for 2018/19 for the use of the car is £

The fuel benefit for 2018/19 is £

Task 3   (8 marks)

(a)   On 6 June 2018, Sue was provided with a flat to live in, purchased by her employer in 2017 for £126,000. The flat had an annual value of £2,500 and is not job related accommodation. It has furniture supplied by her employer and valued at £15,000 when Sue moved in. Her employer also paid her gas bill of £125.

Complete the following sentences regarding Sue's taxable benefits for the accommodation for 2018/19. Show your answers in whole pounds only.   **(4 marks)**

The accommodation benefit (only) for 2018/19 is £

The total ancillary benefits for 2018/19 are £

(b)   On 10 December 2016, Rona was provided with a loan of £18,000 from her employer. The interest rate charged is 0.9%. Rona repaid £1,500 of the loan during 2018/19.

Using the average method, how much is the taxable benefit for the loan for 2018/19? Show your answer in whole pounds only.
                              (1 mark)

£

(c) Engelbert is loaned the use of a television by his employer. The television cost £650 when first provided on 1 May 2018. Engelbert does not have any business use of the television but he does pay £5 per month to his employer for the use of the television from 1 May 2018.

What is Engelbert's taxable benefit for the use of the television during 2018/19? Show your answer in whole pounds only.

(1 mark)

£

(d) **Mark the following benefits as taxable or exempt.** **(2 marks)**

	Taxable	Exempt
Childcare vouchers provided to an employee of £45 per week. The employee, who is a basic rate taxpayer, spent the vouchers with an approved child minder.		
A second mobile phone provided to an employee.		
A car parking space in a multi-storey car park near the place of work.		
An employer contribution to an employee's pension scheme.		

Task 4 (6 marks)

(a) **Mark the following statements as true or false.** **(3 marks)**

	True	False
Income tax is always charged at 0% on the first £5,000 of a taxpayer's dividend income.		
There is no upper limit on the amount of tax-free dividend income which can be received by a taxpayer in a tax year in respect of shares held in an ISA.		
An additional rate taxpayer is entitled to a savings allowance of £500.		

(b) **Calculate the total tax payable by the following individuals in respect of their investment income in 2018/19. Show your answer in whole pounds only.** **(3 mark)**

	Total tax payable on investment income £
Maisie earned an annual salary of £140,000 and received dividend income of £1,700.	
Nathan received interest income of £4,000. He also received an annual salary, after deduction of the personal allowance of £41,000.	

Task 5 (6 marks)

Joan Miller has two properties that she rents out monthly, payment is in arrears:

(1) Two bedroom unfurnished flat. This was occupied throughout 2018/19. The monthly rent, was £620 until 31 December 2018 and then it increased to £680. The tenant was late in paying the rent for March 2019 and did not pay it until 10 April 2019.

Joan paid an agents fee of 5% of the total rental income, gardening fees of £200 for 2018/19 and had a new en-suite bathroom installed at a cost of £5,000.

(2) Three bedroom furnished house. This was occupied until 5 November 2018 at a monthly rent of £750 and was not re-occupied for the rest of 2018/19.

During 2018/19, Joan sold the lounge furniture in this property for £240. She could have purchased replacement furniture of a similar standard for £900, but instead she chose to purchase higher quality furniture costing £1,300.

Joan has a property loss brought forward of £1,500 from 2018/19.

Calculate the property income to be entered into the income tax computation for 2018/19 for both properties under the cash basis using the following table. Show your answers in whole pounds only. (Ignore the property allowance)   (6 marks)

	Flat £	House £
Income		
Expenses		

Task 6 (12 marks)

During 2018/19 Lauren had a gross salary of 101,600 from which £30,600 of PAYE had been deducted. She also received dividends of £7,100. Lauren pays £1,640 to Oxfam each year through the gift aid scheme.

Calculate her total income tax payable or repayable for 2018/19 using the table set out below. **(12 marks)**

Task 7 (4 marks)

Mark the following statements as true or false.   (4 marks)

	True	False
No class 1 national insurance contributions are payable in respect of a person who has attained state pension age.		
Class 1A national insurance contributions are payable by employees in respect of the benefits they receive.		
The employment allowance can only be deducted from the employer's class 1 national insurance contributions, not the employee's class 1 contributions.		
Earnings for the purposes of calculating class 1 national insurance contributions are before the deduction of pension contributions.		

Task 8 (7 marks)

(a) Statham is a basic rate taxpayer.

He pays £3,000 per year to be a member of a health club and £2,800 per year to park near his place of work.

His employer has offered to either pay for the membership of the health club or provide Statham with a free parking space near his place of work.

Mark the benefit which is worth the most to Statham.   (2 marks)

Membership of the health club	
Free parking space	

(b) Nadia is a higher rate taxpayer. She is provided with a company car, which has a scale charge percentage of 23%.

Nadia is also provided with free petrol for both business and private use. The cost of the petrol used by Nadia for private purposes is £1,800 per year.

How much better off would Nadia be each year if she stopped receiving private petrol from her employer? **(3 marks)**

£

(c) **Mark the following statements as true or false.** **(2 marks)**

	True	False
Portia earns an annual salary of £80,000. In 2018/19 she received bank interest of £520. She will not have to pay any income tax in respect of this interest income.		
Rowan has had to move house following the relocation of his job. His removal expenses of £9,700 have been paid by his employer. Rowan will pay income tax on the whole of the £9,700 because it exceeds £8,000.		

Task 9 (12 marks)

(a) Romana sold a painting for £11,500 in October 2018. She had originally purchased the painting in August 2004 for £4,800. She had the painting professionally cleaned at a cost of £150 in August 2018 to prepare it for sale.

What is the gain or loss on the sale of this asset? **(4 marks)**

£

(b) Stefan sold a necklace for £2,800 in September 2018, which had originally been purchased for £1,900 in June 1998.

What is the gain or loss on the sale of this asset? **(1 mark)**

£

(c) Paula sold a painting to her brother for £15,000. The painting cost Paula £11,520 in June 2010. The market value of the painting at the date of the sale was £17,200.

What is the gain or loss on the sale of this asset? **(1 mark)**

£ [_____]

(d) Alex attends a party with the following people.

His girlfriend, his brother, his sister and her husband, his cousin and finally Alex's grandfather also attends.

How many of these people are connected with Alex for capital gains purposes? **(2 marks)**

A   6

B   5

C   4

D   3

(e) Sally sold a diamond ring for £5,200 in August 2018. She had purchased the ring for £7,150 in November 2017.

Which of the following applies to calculating the gain/loss on disposal? **(1 mark)**

A   The loss is calculated as normal

B   The sales proceeds are deemed to be £6,000

C   There is a restriction on the gain of:
5/3 × (gross sales proceeds − £6,000)

D   The gain is calculated as normal

E   Rings are exempt from tax

(f) Sheena sold 3 acres of land for £28,000. She bought 10 acres in July 1997 for £32,000. The value of the remaining 7 acres at the date of sale was £90,000.

What is the gain/loss on this disposal? **(3 marks)**

£ [_____]

Task 10 (8 marks)

Mai sold 4,200 shares in Toby Ltd for £8.50 per share in May 2018. She purchased 3,500 shares in Toby Ltd for £16,800 in April 2014, she purchased a rights issue of 1 for 4 at £3.60 per share in November 2016 and she received a bonus issue of 1 for 3 in January 2018.

Clearly showing the balance of shares and their value to carry forward, calculate the gain made on the sale in May 2018.

All workings must be shown in your calculations. (8 marks)

Task 11 (7 marks)

(a) John bought a house for £52,000 on 1 February 2003. He lived in the house until 31 March 2004 when he went travelling. He returned to the house on 1 June 2012 and lived in it until 30 November 2017 when he moved into his girlfriend's flat. The house was sold for £180,000 on 1 June 2018.

Complete the following sentences. **(3 marks)**

The total period of ownership is [   ] months

The total period of actual and deemed residence is [   ] months

The chargeable gain on sale is [£   ]

(b) **Mark the following statements as true or false.** **(2 marks)**

	True	False
Capital losses can be offset against taxable income if the taxpayer has no capital gains in the year.		
Current year capital losses must be deducted from current year capital gains even where the gains are less than the annual exempt amount.		

(c) Jenna had gains of £36,000 for 2018/19 in respect of quoted shares sold on the stock market. She also had capital losses brought forward of £4,000 from 2017/18 which arose when she sold a painting to her brother. She has taxable income, after deduction of the personal allowance, of £49,500 in 2018/19.

What is Jenna's capital gains tax liability for 2018/19? **(2 marks)**

[£   ]

Task 12 (6 marks)

(a) **Mark the following statements as true or false** (3 marks)

	True	False
No IHT liability can arise in respect of a gift made more than seven years prior to death.		
In 2018/19 Ryan made a single gift to Danielle of £420. The small gifts exemption will not be available in respect of this gift.		
A chattel with a value of no more than £6,000 is exempt from IHT.		

(b) Ellie died on 15 October 2018. She was not domiciled in the UK. At the time of her death, Ellie owned UK assets with a value of £840,000 and overseas assets with a value of £310,000. She left the whole of her estate to her son.

What is the value of Ellie's gross chargeable estate for the purposes of IHT? (1 mark)

£

(c) On 1 May 2018 Guiseppe gave his niece £8,000 on her wedding day. Guiseppe's only previous gift was £7,000 to his grandson on 1 November 2017.

What is the chargeable amount (after the deduction of all available exemptions) of the gift made on 1 May 2018?

(2 marks)

£

Task 13 (7 marks)

(a) On 1 August 2018, Vladimir made a gift of £482,000 to a trust. This was the first gift made by Vladimir. He agreed to pay any IHT due in respect of this gift.

Calculate the IHT payable by Vladimir in respect of the gift on 1 August 2018.

All workings must be shown in your calculations. (3 marks)

(b) Petra died on 1 December 2018. Her estate was valued at £1,700,000. In her will Petra left £1,200,000 to her husband, £35,000 to a UK charity, and the residue of her estate to her son.

Petra did not make any lifetime transfers.

Calculate the IHT payable in respect of Petra's estate.

All workings must be shown in your calculations. (3 marks)

2 Mock Assessment Answers

Task 1

Alexander – Professional conduct in relation to taxation

It is first necessary to establish the facts. We need to know if Alexander really does own a property and, if so, if he has been renting it out.

If there is an irregularity here in the form of undeclared income, and it cannot be regarded as trivial, we must advise Alexander to disclose this income to HM Revenue and Customs. We should advise him of any interest or penalties which may be imposed and the implications for him of not disclosing this information.

If Alexander refuses to disclose this information, we must cease to act for him. We should inform HM Revenue and Customs that we no longer act for him but we should not provide them with any reasons for our actions.

Finally, we should consider our obligations under the anti-money laundering legislation and the necessity to make a suspicious activity report.

Task 2

(a) Appropriate percentage – Diesel car

  (i) 27% (20% + 1/5 (110 – 95) + 4%)

  (ii) 37% (20% + 1/5 (175 – 95) + 4%) = 40% so restricted to 37%

  (iii) 23% (19% + 4%)

  (iv) 17% (13% + 4%)

(b) Jake

The benefit for 2018/19 for the use of the car is **£1,361**

(£16,000 – £1,800) = £14,200 × 23% (W) × 5/12

Working for % = 20% + 1/5(110 – 95) = 23%

The fuel benefit for 2018/19 is **£2,242**

(£23,400 × 23% × 5/12)

Task 3

(a) Sue

The answer is **£3,146**.

(£2,500 + 2.5% (£126,000 – £75,000)) × 10/12 = £3,146

The answer is **£2,625**.

(£15,000 × 20% × 10/12) + £125 = £2,625

(b) Rona

The answer is **£276**.

(£18,000 + £16,500)/2 × (2.5% – 0.9%) = £276

(c) Engelbert

The answer is **£64**.

(£650 × 20%) × 11/12 – (£5 × 11) = £64

(d) Taxable or exempt

	Taxable	Exempt
Childcare vouchers provided to an employee of £45 per week. The employee, who is a basic rate taxpayer, spent the vouchers with an approved child minder.		✓
A second mobile phone provided to an employee.	✓	
A car parking space in a multi-storey car park near the place of work.		✓
An employer contribution to an employee's pension scheme.		✓

Notes:

Childcare vouchers for use with an approved childcare provider are exempt up to £55 per week for a basic rate taxpayer.

The use of one mobile phone is an exempt benefit but the provision of any further mobile phones will give rise to a taxable benefit.

A car park space at or near the place of work is an exempt benefit.

Employer's pension contributions are an exempt benefit.

Task 4

(a) Investment income

	True	False
Income tax is always charged at 0% on the first £5,000 of a taxpayer's dividend income		✓
There is no upper limit on the amount of tax-free dividend income which can be received by a taxpayer in a tax year in respect of shares held in an ISA.	✓	
An additional rate taxpayer is entitled to a savings allowance of £500.		✓

Notes:

Income tax is only charged at 0% on the first £2,000 of a taxpayer's dividend income.

Additional rate taxpayers are not entitled to a savings allowance.

(b) Total tax payable in respect of investment income

Maisie

The answer is £nil.

The first £2,000 of a taxpayer's dividend income is taxed at 0%.

Nathan

The answer is £1,400.

Nathan is a higher rate taxpayer. The first £500 of his interest income is taxed at 0%. The remainder is taxed at 40%. The total tax payable is therefore £1,400 ((£4,000 – £500) × 40%).

Task 5

Joan Miller

	Flat £	House £
Income		
(£620 × 9) + (£680 × 2)	6,940	
(£750 × 7)		5,250
Expenses		
Agents fees (5% × £6,940)	(347)	
Gardening fees	(200)	
New bathroom is capital	Nil	
Lounge furniture (note)		(660)
Property income	6,393	4,590
Total property income		10,983
Less: Loss b/f		(1,500)
Taxable property income		9,483

Note: As the tenant didn't pay the March 2019 rent until 10 April 2019 this will be assessable in 2019/20 rather than 2018/19 as it was not received in the tax year.

The allowable deduction in respect of the replacement of the lounge furniture is restricted to £660 (£900 – £240), being the cost of furniture of a similar standard less the proceeds received in respect of the sale of the old furniture.

Task 6

Lauren – Income tax payable

	Total	Non-savings income	Dividends
	£	£	£
Salary	101,600	101,600	
Dividends	7,100		7,100
Net income	108,700		
Less: PA £11,850			
Less: ½ (£108,700 – £2,050 – £100,000)	(8,525)	(8,525)	
Taxable income	100,175	93,075	7,100
Basic rate band:			
(£34,500 + £2,050)			
Non-savings – basic rate	£36,550	× 20%	7,310.00
Non-savings – higher rate	£56,525	× 40%	22,610.00
Dividends – allowance	£2,000	× 0%	0.00
Dividends – higher rate	£5,100	× 32.5%	1,657.50
Income tax liability			31,577.50
PAYE			(30,600.00)
Income tax payable			977.50

The gift aid payment is grossed up to £2,050 (£1,640 × 100/80) and reduces the net income for the purpose of calculating the personal allowance and extends the basic rate band.

Task 7

National insurance contributions

	True	False
No class 1 national insurance contributions are payable in respect of a person who has attained state pension age.		✓
Class 1A national insurance contributions are payable by employees in respect of the benefits they receive.		✓
The employment allowance can only be deducted from the employer's class 1 national insurance contributions, not the employee's class 1 contributions.	✓	
Earnings for the purposes of calculating class 1 national insurance contributions are before the deduction of pension contributions.	✓	

Notes:

1   Class 1 employer's contributions are payable regardless of the age of the employee.

2   Class 1A contributions are paid by the employer and not by employees.

Task 8

(a) Statham

The correct answer is the free parking space.

Payment of the health club membership would result in an income tax liability of £600 (£3,000 × 20%). The net benefit to Statham of this payment would therefore be £2,400 (£3,000 – £600).

The provision of free parking is an exempt benefit. The benefit to Statham would therefore be £2,800.

(b) Nadia

The correct answer is £353.

Nadia's income tax liability in respect of the free petrol is:

£23,400 × 23% × 40% = £2,153.

If she stopped receiving the free petrol she would be £353 (£2,153 – £1,800) better off.

(c) True or false

	True	False
Portia earns an annual salary of £80,000. In 2018/19 she received bank interest of £520. She will not have to pay any income tax in respect of this interest income.		✓
Rowan has had to move house following the relocation of his job. His removal expenses of £9,700 have been paid by his employer. Rowan will pay income tax on the whole of the £9,700 because it exceeds £8,000.		✓

Notes:

1   Portia is a higher rate taxpayer and is therefore entitled to a savings income allowance of £500.

2   The exemption of £8,000 will be deducted from the amount paid by Rowan's employer.

Task 9

(a) Romana

	£
Proceeds	11,500
Less: Selling costs	(150)
Net sales proceeds	11,350
Less: Cost	(4,800)
Gain	6,550

5/3 (£11,500 – £6,000) = £9,167

	£
Chargeable gain	£6,550

(b) Stefan

This is an exempt disposal as the necklace is a non-wasting chattel bought and sold for less than £6,000.

(c) Paula

	£
Proceeds = Market value	17,200
Less: Cost	(11,520)
Chargeable gain	5,680

Market value has been used because Paula and her brother are connected persons.

(d) Alex

The answer is C.

Alex is connected with everyone except his girlfriend and his cousin.

(e) Sally

The answer is B.

When a chattel is sold for less than £6,000 but was purchased for more than £6,000, the gross proceeds of sale are deemed to be £6,000.

(f) Sheena

The answer is £20,407.

	£
Proceeds	28,000
Less: Cost £32,000 × (£28,000/(£28,000 + £90,000))	(7,593)
Chargeable gain	20,407

The cost of the land sold must be found using the A/A+B formula
A = £28,000 B = £90,000

Task 10

Shares

		£	
Sales proceeds	(£8.50 × 4,200)	35,700	
Less: Cost (pool)		(14,365)	
Chargeable gain		21,335	
Pool		Number	Cost (£)
Apr 2014 Purchase		3,500	16,800
Nov 2016 Rights	1 for 4 at £3.60	875	3,150
		4,375	19,950
Jan 2018 Bonus	1 for 3	1,458	Nil
		5,833	19,950
May 2018 Sale		(4,200)	(W)(14,365)
Balance c/f		1,633	5,585
Working	4,200/5,833		
	× £19,950	= £14,365	

Task 11

(a) John

The total period of ownership is **184** months

The total period of actual and deemed residence is **122** months

The chargeable gain on sale is **£43,130**

	£
Sales proceeds	180,000
Less: Cost	(52,000)
Gain before relief	128,000
Less: PPR exemption (W) (122/184 × £128,000)	(84,870)
Chargeable gain	43,130

Date	Total months	Exempt months	Comments
1 Feb 2003 – 31 Mar 2004	14	14	Occupation
1 Apr 2004 – 31 Mar 2007	36	36	3 years any reason
1 Apr 2007 – 31 May 2012	62		
1 Jun 2012 – 30 Nov 2017	66	66	Occupation
1 Dec 2017 – 31 May 2018	6	6	Last 18 months
Total	184	122	

(b) True or false

	True	False
Capital losses can be offset against taxable income if the taxpayer has no capital gains in the year.		✓
Current year capital losses must be deducted from current year capital gains even where the gains are less than the annual exempt amount.	✓	

(c) **Jenna**

The answer is £4,860

	£
Gains	36,000
Less: Annual exempt amount	(11,700)
Taxable gains	24,300
CGT at 20%	4,860

Jenna cannot use the loss in respect of the disposal to her brother against gains generally, but only against future gains on assets sold to her brother.

The rate of CGT is 20% because Jenna is a higher rate taxpayer.

Task 12

(a) **True or false**

	True	False
No IHT liability can arise in respect of a gift made more than seven years prior to death.		✓
In 2018/19 Ryan made a single gift to Danielle of £420. The small gifts exemption will not be available in respect of this gift.	✓	
A chattel with a value of no more than £6,000 is exempt from IHT.		✓

Notes:

1   An IHT liability can arise in respect of a chargeable lifetime transfer at any time in the donor's lifetime.

2   The small gifts exemption is only available in respect of gifts of no more than £250 per donee per tax year.

3   Such an asset would be exempt for the purposes of CGT but not for IHT.

(b) Ellie

The answer is £840,000.

Ellie will only be subject to IHT on her UK assets because she is not domiciled in the UK.

(c) Guiseppe

The answer is £4,000.

	£
Gift	8,000
Less: Marriage exemption	(1,000)
Annual exemption – 2018/19	(3,000)
Annual exemption – 2017/18 b/f	(Nil)
Chargeable amount	4,000

The annual exemption for 2017/18 will have been offset against the gift on 1 November 2017.

Task 13

(a) Vladimir

	£
Gift	482,000
Less: Annual exemption – 2018/19	(3,000)
Annual exemption – 2017/18	(3,000)
Chargeable amount	476,000
Nil rate band	(325,000)
Taxable amount	151,000
IHT (£151,000 × 25%)	37,750

The rate of IHT is 25% because the donor, Vladimir, is paying the tax.

(b) Petra

	£
Value of estate	1,700,000
Less: Exempt legacy to spouse	(1,200,000)
Exempt legacy to charity	(35,000)
Chargeable amount	465,000
Nil rate band	(325,000)
Taxable amount	140,000
IHT (£140,000 × 40%)	56,000

SAMPLE ASSESSMENT 1
AQ 2016

1 Sample Assessment 1 Questions

This assessment has been provided by AAT and has enhanced answers prepared by Kaplan Publishing.

You have 2 hours and 30 minutes to complete this practice assessment.

This assessment contains 13 TASKS and you should attempt to complete every task.

Each task is independent. You will not need to refer to your answers to previous tasks. Read every task carefully to make sure you understand what is required.

Task 1 requires extended writing as part of your response to the question. You should make sure you allow adequate time to complete this task.

Where the date is relevant, it is given in the task data.

You may use minus signs or brackets to indicate negative numbers unless task instructions say otherwise.

You must use a full stop to indicate a decimal point.

For example, write 100.57 NOT 100,57 or 100 57

You may use a comma to indicate a number in the thousands, but you don't have to.

For example, 10000 and 10,000 are both acceptable.

If your answer requires rounding, apply normal mathematical rounding rules unless the task instructions say otherwise. If your answer is a calculation of VAT and requires rounding, apply the relevant VAT rounding rules.

Task 1 (10 marks)

You work for a small firm of chartered accountants. You have received an email from a whistleblower stating that one of your clients owns a very busy carwash located in the car park of a restaurant. You have checked the client's file and the only business which is being declared to HMRC is a restaurant.

(a) Using the AAT guidelines 'Professional conduct in relation to taxation', explain what steps you should take regarding this possible irregularity. **(7 marks)**

Another one of your clients, Rupinder, is 25 years old. She was born in the UK but her domicile of origin was not in the UK. She lived abroad until she was two years old but she has resided in the UK since then.

(b) **Explain to Rupinder whether she will have deemed domicile status for the 2018/19 tax year based upon the information she has provided. Explain why you have made that decision.**

(3 marks)

(Total: 10 marks)

Task 2 (8 marks)

Sam had the use of two company cars during 2018/19 and his employer paid the running costs for each car, including all fuel. The table below details all of the necessary information in respect of each car.

Car	Number of months	List price £	Cost price £	Contribution to the cost made by Sam £	Scale charge %
Car 1	5	28,150	25,130	6,000	26
Car 2	7	18,920	17,100	1,500	16

(a) **Complete the following sentences to show Sam's taxable benefit in kind for the cars for 2018/19. Show your answers in whole pounds only.** **(6 marks)**

The benefit in kind for the use of Car 1 for 2018/19 is:

£ _____

The benefit in kind for the provision of fuel for Car 1 for 2018/19 is:

£ _____

The benefit in kind for the use of Car 2 for 2018/19 is:

£ _____

The benefit in kind for the provision of fuel for Car 2 for 2018/19 is:

£ _____

Cars 3 and 4 were both registered after 1 September 2017.

(b) **Complete the following table by inserting the scale charge for 2018/19 for each of the cars shown below.** **(2 marks)**

	Engine type	CO$_2$ emissions	Scale charge %
Car 3	Petrol	185	
Car 4	Diesel – certified to the Real Driving Emissions 2 (RDE2) standards.	132	

(Total: 8 marks)

Task 3 (8 marks)

Below is a list of benefits that Clartt Ltd provides to its employees.

Enter the amount that would be taxable for 2018/19 for each benefit in the box provided. If you answer is zero, enter '0'. Enter your answer in whole pounds only. **(8 marks)**

Details	Taxable benefit in kind £
Joe is a higher rate taxpayer and Clartt Ltd pays £40 per week (for 52 weeks) to a registered childminder for Joe's daughter. This arrangement commenced in November 2016.	
Jules moved into a house provided by Clartt Ltd on 1 August 2015 when its market value was £320,500. The house cost Clartt Ltd £236,000 in January 2010. The house has an annual value of £6,900 Jules pays Clartt Ltd £500 per month towards the use of the house.	
A television and cinema system costing Clartt Ltd £15,500 was bought for Ranjit's use on 1 September 2018.	
All employees had the use of a subsidised canteen. The cost to Clartt Ltd was £580 per employee.	
George moved 150 miles due to a promotion and received £9,500 to help with his removal expenses.	
On 1 July 2018, James was given a loan of £12,000 on which he paid 3.5% interest. He has not repaid any of this loan yet.	
Margaret received a watch as her 25 year long service award. This was Margaret's first long service award and the watch cost Clartt Ltd £1,450.	

(Total: 8 marks)

Task 4 (6 marks)

The information below relates to the investment income received during 2018/19 by three taxpayers.

Complete the following sentences for each taxpayer. If your answer is zero, enter '0'. Enter your answer in whole pounds only. (6 marks)

Doris received a dividend of £10,000. Her other taxable income, after personal allowances, totalled £21,500.

The tax payable by Doris on these dividends is:

£ [   ]

Honey received £2,500 in interest from her building society account and £310 in interest from her individual savings account. Her other taxable income, after personal allowances, totalled £45,800.

Honey's income from investments on which tax will be paid is:

£ [   ]

The total payable on this interest by Honey is:

£ [   ]

Ivanka receiving building society interest of £3,200. Her other taxable income, after personal allowances, totalled £125,900.

Ivanka's income from investments on which tax will be paid is:

£ [   ]

The total tax payable on this interest by Ivanka is:

£ [   ]

(Total: 6 marks)

Task 5 (6 marks)

Sam owns and rents out three properties in 2018/19.

Sam will make elections as appropriate to minimise his taxable income.

Information on the properties is shown in the table below.

Complete the table below to show taxable rent and allowable expenses for these properties in 2018/19. If your answer is zero, enter '0'. Enter your answers in whole pounds only.   **(6 marks)**

Property	Details	Taxable rent £	Allowable expenses £
Green Cottage	Green Cottage was let from 8 June 2018 for the remainder of the tax year for £830 per month. Rent was paid on the same date each month starting 8 June 2018. Sam paid 10% commission to a letting agent and paid £600 in advertising costs.		
Yellow Gardens	Yellow Gardens was let from 7 January 2019 for the remainder of the tax year at £550 per month. Rent was paid the same date each month starting 7 January 2019. Sam paid £2,850 in August 2018 to replace the single glazed windows with double glazed windows.		
Lime Lane	Lime Lane was let for the whole of 2018/19 at £770 per month. Sam paid for the building insurance on 1 January 2018, which cost him £1,200 for the year from 1 January 2018 and he paid £1,375 on 1 January 2019 for the year from 1 January 2019.		

(Total: 6 marks)

Task 6 (12 marks)

John has the following income for 2018/19:

	£
Income from employment	58,000
Profits from property	15,500
Building society interest received	1,200
Dividends received	3,000

John has losses from property brought forward of £9,250 from 2017/18.

During 2018/19, John paid £224 per month into a private pension scheme.

(a) Calculate John's total income tax liability for 2018/19, entering your answer and workings into the blank table below.

You have been given more space than you will need.   (9 marks)

Joy's only income during 2018/19 was her gross salary of £110,000. She is confused why her personal allowance is only £6,850 for 2018/19.

(b) **Clearly explain in the box below why the personal allowance for Joy of £6,850 for 2018/19 is correct.** **(3 marks)**

(Total: 12 marks)

Task 7 (4 marks)

During 2018/19, Jonny received a gross salary of £58,000 and total benefits in kind (none of which are convertible into cash) of £6,850. Jonny is 49 years of age and he is not an apprentice.

Complete the following sentences by typing your answer, in whole pounds, into the boxes provided. Ignore the employment allowance. If your answer is zero, enter '0'. **(4 marks)**

The total class 1 national insurance contributions payable by Jonny in 2018/19 are:

£

The total class 1 national insurance contributions payable by Jonny's employer in 2018/19 are:

£

The total class 1A national insurance contributions payable by Jonny's employer in 2018/19 are:

£

(Total: 4 marks)

Task 8 (7 marks)

(a)   Tick to show if the following statements are true or false.

(2 marks)

Statement	True	False
Henry has always wanted to invest in shares but he does not own any. He has just won £4,000 on the lottery, so he decides to invest this win in an ISA. Henry currently has no investments in ISA's. There will be no income tax implications on this investment.		
An employee is provided with his first £20,000 loan by his employer. For this loan to be tax free, the employer must charge interest above 0%.		

(b)   **Complete the following sentences. Enter your numerical answers in whole pounds only.**   **(5 marks)**

∇ Drop down list for task 1.8 (b)

move the investment into Julia's name only.
leave the investment in his name only.
move the investment into joint names.

Michael and Julia are married. For 2018/19, Michael has a total employment income of £87,000 and Julia has a total employment income of £8,000. During 2018/19 Michael received investment income of £2,000 from a building society account. To minimise their total tax liability, Michael should [∇]

Ruby has a total income of £105,000. She wants to pay into her private pension scheme so that she can protect her full personal allowances of £11,850. She therefore needs to pay at least

£ [   ] into her private pension scheme.

Chen is a basic rate taxpayer. He has a company car for the whole of 2018/19. The car has a scale charge percentage of 20% and an assessable benefit in kind of £3,200. He has been offered an alternative car which costs the same as the original, but with a scale charge percentage of 13%. If Chen chose the alternative car on 6 April 2018, this will save him £ [ ] in income tax for 2018/19.

(Total: 7 marks)

Task 9 (10 marks)

During 2018/19, Sue sold five assets to unconnected persons.

The proceeds and cost of each asset are shown in the table below.

(a) **Show whether the selling of each asset below will result in a taxable gain or an allowable loss, or be exempt from capital gains tax, and then indicate the amount of gain/loss in the final column. If you think the asset is exempt, enter a zero '0' in the final column. Do not leave any cells blank. Do not use brackets or minus signs.** **(5 marks)**

▽ Drop down list for task 1.9 (a)

Allowable loss
Exempt
Taxable gain

Asset	Proceeds £	Cost £	Taxable gain, allowable loss, or exempt?	Amount of gain/loss £
Desk	8,980	7,140	▽	
Chair	6,240	5,600	▽	
Mirror	5,140	6,330	▽	
Ring	3,810	4,600	▽	
Race horse	10,560	5,500	▽	

(b) **Complete the following sentences.** **(2 marks)**

▽ Drop down list for task 1.9 (b) – both sentences

Would
Would not

Roly and his brother-in-law [▽] be treated as connected persons.

A 70-year-old vintage car [▽] be treated as a chargeable asset.

Elizabeth bought a painting for £32,400 in June 2009 and was charged 10% commission by the auctioneer. She sold the painting in January 2019 for £58,500, spending £1,200 on advertising it for sale. Throughout the period of ownership, Elizabeth spent £2,200 on insuring the painting.

(c) **Complete the following table to show the gain made on the sale of the painting.**

Do not use brackets or minus signs. **(3 marks)**

	£
Proceeds	
Total cost	
Gain	

(Total: 10 marks)

Task 10 (10 marks)

Keith bought and sold numerous shares in Helle plc as follows:

Event date	Detail
1 January 2013	Keith purchased 800 shares at a cost of £6.10 per share.
1 July 2015	There was a 1 for 5 rights issue at a cost of £3.80 per share.
12 August 2015	Keith sold 400 shares for £8.00 per share.
25 March 2016	There was a 1 for 10 bonus issue when the shares had a market value of £6.90 each.
14 April 2016	Keith bought 500 shares at a cost of £8.20 per share.
19 October 2018	Keith sold 250 shares for £10.10 per share.

Clearly showing the balance of shares and their value to carry forward, calculate the gain Keith made on the sale of the shares for 2018/19.

All workings must be shown in your calculations.

You have been given more space that you will need. **(10 marks)**

(Total: 10 marks)

Task 11 (7 marks)

The following information is available about four taxpayers who sold capital assets during 2018/19. These are the only assets that they sold during 2018/19, none of which relate to residential property.

Taxpayer	Sold to	Proceeds £	Market value £	Cost £	Other taxable income £
Alex	Husband	28,750	42,600	12,000	47,500
Donna	Brother	19,000	23,000	7,500	32,000
Carl	Stranger	64,800	64,000	44,050	54,600
Bridget	Friend	26,000	28,000	9,500	18,430

Calculate the amount of capital gains tax payable for each taxpayer. Your answer must be in whole pounds only. If your answer is zero, enter '0'.   **(7 marks)**

Taxpayer	Amount of capital gains tax payable £
Alex	
Donna	
Carl	
Bridget	

(Total: 7 marks)

Task 12 (6 marks)

(a) **Complete the following sentences that relate to inheritance tax (IHT).**

If appropriate, enter your answer in whole pounds only. If your answer is zero, enter '0'. **(4 marks)**

∇ Drop down list for task 1.12 (a) – box 1 & 2

would
would not

∇ Drop down list for task 1.12 (a) – box 3

carried back to be used in the previous tax year only
carried forward to be used in the next tax year only
carried forward indefinitely

Richard transferred the ownership of a boat into his wife's name in May 2015. In December 2018, Richard died. The transfer of the boat [∇] be exempt from IHT on Richard's death.

Samantha received £10,000 from her grandfather on the occasion of her marriage on 22 March 2019. The maximum value of the transfer that may be liable to IHT when her grandfather dies is £ [ ]

Hugo transferred a valuable painting to a charity in April 2015. In January 2019, Hugo died. The painting [∇] be exempt from IHT on Hugo's death.

Where a person does not use all of their annual exempt amount in a tax year, the unused excess can be [∇]

(b) **Tick to show if the following statements are true or false.(2 marks)**

Statement	True	False
Partnerships are treated as chargeable persons for IHT purposes.		
The £250 small gift exemption is per transferee per tax year.		

(Total: 6 marks)

Task 13 (6 marks)

Ian died on 12 January 2019 leaving an estate valued in total at £1,550,000. This included his home which was valued at £420,000.

His will shows that the entire estate is to be left to his grandchildren and he made no gifts during his lifetime.

Ian's wife died on 22 September 2012. Her estate on death used 30% of the nil rate tax band.

Calculate the inheritance tax payable on Ian's estate, entering your answer and workings into the blank table below. You have been given more space than you will need. (6 marks)

(Total: 6 marks)

1 Sample Assessment 1 Answers

Task 1 (10 marks)

(a) Using the AAT guidelines 'Professional conduct in relation to taxation', explain what steps you should take regarding this possible irregularity. (7 marks)

Firstly, it needs to be established that he is the owner. If not then no further action needs to be taken. If there does appear to be an irregularity, is the amount involved trivial (unlikely as it is said to be "busy")? It would suggest not, in which case the client needs to be approached to find out the facts.

If indeed the client has monetary gains from the carwash, then they must be advised that it needs to be disclosed to HMRC. If the client agrees to disclose to HMRC this business, then the client needs to be advised on the potential for penalties, interest, surcharges and other consequences. If the client does not agree to disclose, then the client needs to be advised, in writing, of the consequences of failure to disclose.

If the client still does not agree to disclose to HMRC, then you must cease to act for the client and inform HMRC of the withdrawal. However, because of the need to maintain client confidentiality, HMRC should not be provided with an explanation of the reasons why you have ceased to act. This may also be money laundering and the Money Laundering Officer duly advised.

(b) **Explain to Rupinder whether she will have deemed domicile status for the 2018/19 tax year based upon the information she has provided. Explain why you have made that decision.**

(3 marks)

For deemed domicile status Rupinder must satisfy all of Condition A or Condition B

Rupinder does not satisfy Condition A. She satisfies two of the three necessary conditions for A i.e. was born in the UK and has lived in the UK for 2017 to 2018 or later years

Rupinder does satisfy Condition B because in the 20 years immediately prior to the tax year 2018/19 Rupinder has been UK resident

Rupinder would have deemed domicile status

(Total: 10 marks)

Task 2 (8 marks)

These model answers show both rounded up and rounded down options. Both options are equally valid for the purposes of this assessment.

(a) **Complete the following sentences to show Sam's taxable benefit in kind for the cars for 2018/19. Show your answers in whole pounds only.** **(6 marks)**

The benefit in kind for the use of Car 1 for 2018/19 is:

£	2507 or 2508

The benefit in kind for the provision of fuel for Car 1 for 2018/19 is:

£	2535

The benefit in kind for the use of Car 2 for 2018/19 is:

£	1626 or 1625

The benefit in kind for the provision of fuel for Car 2 for 2018/19 is:

£	2184

Workings

(i) The annual benefit is £6,019 ((£28,150 – 5,000) × 26%). The annual benefit is then multiplied by 5/12 to reflect five months of usage in 2018/19. (£6,019 × 5/12) = £2,508.

(ii) The fuel benefit of £2,535 is worked out using the base charge of £23,400. Again this has to be adjusted to reflect five months of usage. (£23,400 × 26%) × (5/12) = £2,535

(iii) The annual benefit is £2,787.20 ((£18,920 – 1,500) × 16%). The annual benefit is then multiplied by 7/12 to reflect seven months of usage in 2018/19. (£2,787.20 × 7/12) = £1,626.

(iv) The fuel benefit of £2,184 is worked out using the base charge of £23,400. Again this has to be adjusted to reflect seven months of usage. (£23,400 × 16%) × (7/12) = £2,184.

Notes

Car benefits are calculated as follows:

- Appropriate percentage × List price × n/12

- Where n = number of months the car is available in the tax year.

The scale percentage is found from the following calculation:

- 20% + (CO_2 emissions – 95) × 1/5

- CO_2 emissions are rounded down to the next number ending in 0 or 5

- Diesel cars attract an extra 4%

- Maximum scale percentage is 37%.

Fuel benefit is calculated as follows:

- Appropriate percentage × £23,400 × n/12

- Where n = number of months the benefit is available in the tax year.

If an employee contributes towards the running costs of the car this is an allowable deduction, but partial contributions towards the cost of private fuel are NOT an allowable deduction.

If an employee contributes towards the capital cost of the car this is an allowable deduction from the list price up to a maximum of £5,000.

(b) **Complete the following table by inserting the scale charge for 2018/19 for each of the cars shown below.** **(2 marks)**

	Engine type	CO_2 emissions	Scale charge %
Car 3	Petrol	185	37
Car 4	Diesel – certified to the Real Driving Emissions 2 (RDE2) standards.	132	27

(Total: 8 marks)

Notes

The cars have CO_2 emissions in excess of 95 g/km.

The appropriate percentage is therefore calculated in the normal way (i.e. a percentage of 20% for petrol cars and 24% for diesel cars, plus 1% for each 5 complete emissions above 95 g/km up to a maximum percentage of 37%).

Diesel cars do not attract the 4% supplement if they meet RDE2 standards. So a base figure of 20% is used for the diesel car above.

Task 3 (8 marks)

Enter the amount that would be taxable for 2018/19 for each benefit in the box provided. If you answer is zero, enter '0'. Enter your answer in whole pounds only. (8 marks)

Details	Taxable benefit in kind £
Joe is a higher rate taxpayer and Clartt Ltd pays £40 per week (for 52 weeks) to a registered childminder for Joe's daughter. This arrangement commenced in November 2016.	624
Jules moved into a house provided by Clartt Ltd on 1 August 2015 when its market value was £320,500. The house cost Clartt Ltd £236,000 in January 2010. The house has an annual value of £6,900 Jules pays Clartt Ltd £500 per month towards the use of the house.	4,925
A television and cinema system costing Clartt Ltd £15,500 was bought for Ranjit's use on 1 September 2018.	1,808 or 1,809
All employees had the use of a subsidised canteen. The cost to Clartt Ltd was £580 per employee.	0
George moved 150 miles due to a promotion and received £9,500 to help with his removal expenses.	1,500
On 1 July 2018, James was given a loan of £12,000 on which he paid 3.5% interest. He has not repaid any of this loan yet.	0
Margaret received a watch as her 25 year long service award. This was Margaret's first long service award and the watch cost Clartt Ltd £1,450.	200

(Total: 8 marks)

Workings

(i) Childcare vouchers benefit = 52 × (40–28) = 624

(ii)

	£
Annual value	6,900
Additional charge for 'expensive' accommodation: (£236,000 – £75,000) × 2.5% (Note)	4,025
	10,925
Less: Rent paid by Jules (£500 × 12 months)	(6,000)
Taxable benefit – 2018/19	4,925

(iii) Use of asset benefit = (£15,500 × 20% × 7/12) = £1,808

(v) Relocation expenses are an exempt benefit up to £8,000. Thus the excess of £1,500 is taxable

(viii) Long service award benefit = 1,450 – (25 × 50) = 200

Notes

(i) Childcare vouchers up to £28 per week are tax free for higher rate taxpayers. It is presumed that Joe had been making use of childcare provision from his employer prior to 6 April 2017 and thus was still entitled to childcare support in the form of vouchers rather than via an account.

(ii) Where an employee is provided with living accommodation which the employer owns there will be an additional benefit if the property cost over £75,000. To calculate the benefit the excess of the cost is multiplied by the official rate of interest. The market value when moving in would only be used in place of cost if the employee moved in more than six years after the employer purchased the property.

(iv) Use of a subsidised canteen is an exempt benefit as long as some sort of provision is made available to all staff.

(v) The first £8,000 of removal expenses is exempt.

(vi)   James has a loan of £12,000 for part of 2018/19. This would normally lead to a taxable benefit, but as he pays interest above the official rate of interest of 2.5% there is no benefit on this occasion.

(vii) Long service awards are exempt up to £50 per year provided service is at least 20 years. The award must not be in cash and the recipient must not have had an award within the previous 10 years.

Task 4 (6 marks)

Complete the following sentences for each taxpayer. If your answer is zero, enter '0'. Enter your answer in whole pounds only. (6 marks)

Doris received a dividend of £10,000. Her other taxable income, after personal allowances, totalled £21,500.

The tax payable by Doris on these dividends is:

£	600

Honey received £2,500 in interest from her building society account and £310 in interest from her individual savings account. Her other taxable income, after personal allowances, totalled £45,800.

Honey's income from investments on which tax will be paid is:

£	2,000

The total payable on this interest by Honey is:

£	800

Ivanka receiving building society interest of £3,200. Her other taxable income, after personal allowances, totalled £125,900.

Ivanka's income from investments on which tax will be paid is:

£	2,700

The total tax payable on this interest by Ivanka is:

£	1,080

(Total: 6 marks)

Workings

(i)

	£
Taxable dividend income	10,000
£2,000 × 0%	0.00
£8,000 × 7.5%	600.00
Income tax liability	600.00

(iii)

	£
Taxable investment income	2,000
£500 × 0%	0.00
£2,000 × 40%	800.00
Income tax liability	800.00

(v)

	£
Taxable investment income	2,700
£500 × 0%	0.00
£2,700 × 40%	1,080.00
Income tax liability	1,080.00

Notes

(i)   All taxpayers are entitled to a dividend allowance of £2,000.

(ii)   Honey is a higher rate taxpayer and is entitled to a personal savings allowance of £500. As all her taxable savings income falls into the higher rate band it will all be taxed at 40%. The interest generated by an ISA is exempt from income tax.

(iv)   Ivanka is a higher rate taxpayer and is entitled to a personal savings allowance of £500. As all her taxable savings income falls into the higher rate band it will all be taxed at 40%.

Task 5 (6 marks)

Complete the table below to show taxable rent and allowable expenses for these properties in 2018/19. If your answer is zero, enter '0'. Enter your answers in whole pounds only. (6 marks)

Property	Details	Taxable rent £	Allowable expenses £
Green Cottage	Green Cottage was let from 8 June 2018 for the remainder of the tax year for £830 per month. Rent was paid the same date each month starting 8 June 2018. Sam paid 10% commission to a letting agent and paid £600 in advertising costs.	8,300	1,430
Yellow Gardens	Yellow Gardens was let from 7 January 2019 for the remainder of the tax year at £550 per month. Rent was paid the same date each month starting 7 January 2019. Sam paid £2,850 in August 2018 to replace the single glazed windows with double glazed windows.	1,650	2,850
Lime Lane	Lime Lane was let for the whole of 2018/19 at £770 per month. Sam paid for the building insurance on 1 January 2018, which cost him £1,200 for the year from 1 January 2018 and he paid £1,375 on 1 January 2019 for the year from 1 January 2019.	9,240	1,375

(Total: 6 marks)

Notes

As Sam's gross rents do not exceed £150,000 he will use the cash basis for preparing his property income. Therefore only rent received in the tax year is assessed and only allowable expenses paid in the tax year are deductible.

Task 6 (12 marks)

(a) Calculate John's total income tax liability for 2018/19, entering your answer and workings into the blank table below.

You have been given more space than you will need.   (9 marks)

		£
Employment income		58,000
Property income	(£15,500 – £9,250)	6,250
Building society interest		1,200
Dividends		3,000
		68,450
Personal allowance		11,850
		56,600
Basic rate:	£34,500 + (£224 × 12 × 100/80) = £37,860	
£37,860 × 20%		7,572
(£52,400 – £37,860) × 40%	(£58,000 + £6,250 – £11,850)	5,816
£500 × 0%		0
£700 × 40%		280
£2,000 × 0%		0
£1,000 × 32.5%		325
Total		13,993

Notes

The basic rate band is extended by the gross personal pension contribution.

As a higher rate taxpayer John is entitled to a savings allowance of £500.

All taxpayers are entitled to a dividend allowance of £2,000.

You may find it useful to do the computation on paper first before inputting on screen. This will be especially useful for this task as you are only given three columns to complete.

On paper you can analyse the taxable income into 'non-savings income', 'savings' and 'dividends' as different rates of tax apply to the different sources of income.

Joy's only income during 2018/19 was her gross salary of £110,000. She is confused why her personal allowance is only £6,850 for 2018/19.

(b)   Clearly explain in the box below why the personal allowance for Joy of £6,850 for 2018/19 is correct.   **(3 marks)**

> As Joy has total income over £100,000 her personal allowance will be reduced by £1 for every £2 over £100,000.
>
> Therefore, the computation for her personal allowance would be £11,850 − ((£110,000 − £100,000)/2) = £6,850.

(Total: 12 marks)

Task 7 (4 marks)

During 2018/19, Jonny received a gross salary of £58,000 and total benefits in kind (none of which are convertible into cash) of £6,850. Jonny is 49 years of age and he is not an apprentice.

Complete the following sentences by typing your answer, in whole pounds, into the boxes provided. Ignore the employment allowance. If your answer is zero, enter '0'.   **(4 marks)**

The total class 1 national insurance contributions payable by Jonny in 2018/19 are:

£	4784 or 4785

The total class 1 national insurance contributions payable by Jonny's employer in 2018/19 are:

£	6841 or 6842

The total class 1A national insurance contributions payable by Jonny's employer in 2018/19 are:

£	945 or 946

(Total: 4 marks)

(i)

	£
Working	
(£46,350 – £8,424) × 12%	4,551
(£58,000 – £46,350) × 2%	233
	—————
	4,784
	—————

(ii)

Working	
(£58,000 – £8,424) × 13.8%	£6,841
	—————

(iii)

Working	
£6,850 × 13.8%	£945
	—————

Task 8 (7 marks)

(a) **Tick to show if the following statements are true or false.(2 marks)**

Statement	True	False
Henry has always wanted to invest in shares but he does not own any. He has just won £4,000 on the lottery, so he decides to invest this win in an ISA. Henry currently has no investments in ISAs. There will be no income tax implications on this investment.	✓	
An employee is provided with his first £20,000 loan by his employer. For this loan to be tax free, the employer must charge interest above 0%.		✓

Notes

Lottery winnings and ISA income are exempt from income tax.

An employee can be provided with loans up to £10,000 without tax implications. If an employee is provided with one loan or a number of loans that add up to over £10,000 there is normally tax implications unless the rate of interest charged by the employer is greater than the official rate of interest – 2.5%.

(b) **Complete the following sentences. Enter your numerical answers in whole pounds only.** (5 marks)

∇ Drop down list for task 1.8 (b)

move the investment into Julia's name only.
leave the investment in his name only.
move the investment into joint names.

Michael and Julia are married. For 2018/19, Michael has a total employment income of £87,000 and Julia has a total employment income of £8,000. During 2018/18 Michael received investment income of £2,000 from a building society account. To minimise their total tax liability, Michael should

> Move the investment into Julia's name only∇

Ruby has a total income of £105,000. She wants to pay into her private pension scheme so that she can protect her full personal allowances of £11,850. She therefore needs to pay at least

£ | 4000   into her private pension scheme.

Chen is a basic rate taxpayer. He has a company car for the whole of 2018/19. The car has a scale charge percentage of 20% and an assessable benefit in kind of £3,200. He has been offered an alternative car which costs the same as the original, but with a scale charge percentage of 13%. If Chen chose the alternative car on 6 April 2018, this will save him £ 224 in income tax for 2018/19.

(Total: 7 marks)

Workings

(i)   To preserve her personal allowance in full Ruby will need to reduce her adjusted net income to £100,000.

	£	£
Personal allowance		11,850
Net income (= Total income)	105,000	
Less: Gross personal pension contribution		
(£4,000 × 100/80)	(5,000)	
Adjusted net income	100,000	
Less: Limit	(100,000)	
Excess	0 × 50%	(0)
Adjusted PA		11,850

(iii)   If Chen has a benefit in kind of £3,200 on the car then the list price must be £16,000 (£3,200/0.20). The alternative will therefore have a benefit in kind of £2,080 (£16,000 × 13%). This will lead to a tax saving of £224.00 ((£3,200 – £2,080) × 20%).

Notes

As Michael is a higher rate taxpayer he only has a personal savings allowance of £500. Julia is a basic rate taxpayer and has a personal savings allowance of £1,000. Therefore the investments should primarily be located with Julia to maximise the usage of the personal savings allowance.

Task 9 (10 marks)

During 2018/19, Sue sold five assets to unconnected persons.

The proceeds and cost of each asset are shown in the table below.

(a) **Show whether the selling of each asset below will result in a taxable gain or an allowable loss, or be exempt from capital gains tax, and then indicate the amount of gain/loss in the final column. If you think the asset is exempt, enter a zero '0' in the final column. Do not leave any cells blank. Do not use brackets or minus signs.** **(5 marks)**

∇ Drop down list for task 1.9 (a)

Allowable loss
Exempt
Taxable gain

Asset	Proceeds £	Cost £	Taxable gain, allowable loss, or exempt?	Amount of gain/loss £
Desk	8,980	7,140	Taxable gain ∇	1840
Chair	6,240	5,600	Taxable gain ∇	400
Mirror	5,140	6,330	Allowable loss∇	330
Ring	3,810	4,600	Exempt ∇	0
Race horse	10,560	5,500	Exempt ∇	0

Notes

Non wasting chattels with a cost and sale proceeds both exceeding £6,000 will have a normal gain calculated.

A non-wasting chattel with proceeds exceeding £6,000 but with a cost of no more than £6,000 will have a gain restricted to 5/3 × (Gross proceeds – £6,000).

Non wasting chattels with a cost of over £6,000 but proceeds of no more than £6,000 will have a restricted loss by using £6,000 as gross sale proceeds.

(b) Complete the following sentences. **(2 marks)**

∇ Drop down list for task 1.9 (b) – both sentences

Would
Would not

Roly and his brother-in-law | Would ∇ | be treated as connected persons.

A 70-year-old vintage car | Would not ∇ | be treated as a chargeable asset.

Elizabeth bought a painting for £32,400 in June 2009 and was charged 10% commission by the auctioneer. She sold the painting in January 2019 for £58,500, spending £1,200 on advertising it for sale. Throughout the period of ownership, Elizabeth spent £2,200 on insuring the painting.

(c) Complete the following table to show the gain made on the sale of the painting.

Do not use brackets or minus signs. **(3 marks)**

	£
Proceeds	58,500
Total cost (£32,400 + £3,240 + £1,200)	36,840
Gain	21,660

(Total: 10 marks)

Notes

Auction commission is an allowable acquisition cost and advertising costs are allowable as a selling expense (although it has been shown here as part of the total cost figure). Insurance costs are an example of revenue expenditure as they will not enhance the value of the asset. Therefore insurance is not an allowable expense.

Task 10 (10 marks)

Keith bought and sold numerous shares in Helle plc as follows:

Event date	Detail
1 January 2013	Keith purchased 800 shares at a cost of £6.10 per share.
1 July 2015	There was a 1 for 5 rights issue at a cost of £3.80 per share.
12 August 2015	Keith sold 400 shares for £8.00 per share.
25 March 2016	There was a 1 for 10 bonus issue when the shares had a market value of £6.90 each.
14 April 2016	Keith bought 500 shares at a cost of £8.20 per share.
19 October 2018	Keith sold 250 shares for £10.10 per share.

Clearly showing the balance of shares and their value to carry forward, calculate the gain Keith made on the sale of the shares for 2018/19.

All workings must be shown in your calculations.

You have been given more space that you will need.   (10 marks)

	Event	Shares	£
1 January 2013	Purchase	800	4,880
1 July 2015	Rights issue	160	608
		960	5,488
12 August 2015	Disposal	(400)	(2,287)
		560	3,201
25 March 2016	Bonus issue	56	0
		616	3,201
14 April 2016	Purchase	500	4,100
		1,116	7,301
19 October 2018	Disposal	(250)	(1,636)
Pool to carry forward		866	5,665
Proceeds		2,525	
Cost		(1,636)	
Gain		889	

(Total: 10 marks)

Task 11 (7 marks)

Calculate the amount of capital gains tax payable for each taxpayer. Your answer must be in whole pounds only. If your answer is zero, enter '0'.   (7 marks)

Taxpayer	Amount of capital gains tax payable £
Alex	0
Donna	510
Carl	1,810
Bridget	480

(Total: 7 marks)

Workings

(ii)

	£
Proceeds (Market value)	23,000
Cost	(7,500)
Gain	15,500
AEA	(11,700)
Taxable gain	3,800

(£34,500 - £32,000 = £2,500)	
£2,500 × 10%	250
£1,300 × 20%	260
Total capital gains tax liability	510

(iii)

	£
Proceeds	64,800
Cost	(44,050)
Gain	20,750
AEA	(11,700)
Taxable gain	9,050

£9,050 × 20%	1,810

(iv)

	£
Proceeds	26,000
Cost	(9,500)
Gain	16,500
AEA	(11,700)
Taxable gain	4,800

£4,800 × 10%	480

Notes

Where a capital transaction takes place between spouses/civil partners it is always a nil gain nil loss transaction.

If a chargeable disposal is made to a connected person then market value must be used as proceeds.

Connected people would not include friends or strangers, so actual proceeds must be used in these circumstances.

Where a taxpayer has some of their basic rate band remaining any gains falling into the remainder can be taxed at 10%. All other gains must be taxed at 20%.

Task 12 (6 marks)

(a)   **Complete the following sentences that relate to inheritance tax (IHT).**

If appropriate, enter your answer in whole pounds only. If your answer is zero, enter '0'.   **(4 marks)**

∇ Drop down list for task 1.12 (a) – box 1 & 2

would
would not

∇ Drop down list for task 1.12 (a) – box 3

carried back to be used in the previous tax year only
carried forward to be used in the next tax year only
carried forward indefinitely

Richard transferred the ownership of a boat into his wife's name in May 2015. In December 2018, Richard died. The transfer of the boat

would ∇

be exempt from IHT on Richard's death.

Samantha received £10,000 from her grandfather on the occasion of her marriage on 22 March 2019. The maximum value of the transfer that may be liable to IHT when her grandfather dies is

£	7,500

Hugo transferred a valuable painting to a charity in April 2015. In January 2019, Hugo died. The painting | would ∇ | be exempt from IHT on Hugo's death.

Where a person does not use all of their annual exempt amount in a tax year, the unused excess can be

carried forward to be used in the next tax year only. ∇

Notes

Transfers between spouses/civil partners are always exempt from IHT.

Where a gift is in consideration of marriage an exemption of £2,500 is available where the gift is from a grandparent.

Transfers to charities are always exempt from IHT.

The AEA can never be carried back and can only be carried forward for one tax year.

(b)   Tick to show if the following statements are true or false.

(2 marks)

Statement	True	False
Partnerships are treated as chargeable persons for IHT purposes.		✓
The £250 small gift exemption is per transferee per tax year.	✓	

(Total: 6 marks)

Task 13 (6 marks)

Ian died on 12 January 2019 leaving an estate valued in total at £1,550,000. This included his home which was valued at £420,000.

His will shows that the entire estate is to be left to his grandchildren and he made no gifts during his lifetime.

Ian's wife died on 22 September 2012. Her estate on death used 30% of the nil rate tax band.

Calculate the inheritance tax payable on Ian's estate, entering your answer and workings into the blank table below. You have been given more space than you will need.   **(6 marks)**

	Workings	£
Chargeable estate		1,550,000
Nil rate band	Ian	325,000
	Ian's wife (£325,000 × 70%)	227,500
		552,500
Residence nil rate band	Ian	125,000
	Ian's wife	125,000
		802,500
Taxable	£1,550,000 – £802,500	747,500
Tax payable	@ 40%	299,000

(Total: 6 marks)

Notes

As Ian's spouse has died it is possible to claim the unused proportion of her nil rate band on Ian's death.

As Ian left his residence in his death estate to a direct descendant the residence nil rate band is available. As his spouse died before 6 April 2017 a full RNRB is available to transfer to Ian.

KAPLAN PUBLISHING

SAMPLE ASSESSMENT 2
AQ 2016

1 Sample Assessment 2 Questions

This assessment has been provided by AAT and has enhanced answers prepared by Kaplan Publishing.

You have 2 hours and 30 minutes to complete this practice assessment.

This assessment contains 13 TASKS and you should attempt to complete every task.

Each task is independent. You will not need to refer to your answers to previous tasks.

Read each task carefully to make sure you understand what is required.

Task 1 requires extended writing as part of your response to the question. You should make sure you allow adequate time to complete this task.

Where the date is relevant, it is given in the task data.

You may use minus signs or brackets to indicate negative numbers unless task instructions say otherwise.

You must use a full stop to indicate a decimal point.

For example, write 100.57 NOT 100,57 or 100 57

You may use a comma to indicate a number in the thousands, but you don't have to.

For example, 10000 and 10,000 are both acceptable.

If your answer requires rounding, apply normal mathematical rounding rules unless the task instructions say otherwise. If your answer is a calculation of VAT and requires rounding, apply the relevant VAT rounding rules.

Task 1 (10 marks)

You work for DBQ, a small firm of accountants. The managing partner is concerned over recent publicity into high profile organisations accused of tax irregularities. They have asked you to produce information for distribution to DBQ's clients.

Explain the following three terms and give an example of each of them to help DBQ's clients understand the difference between them.

(10 marks)

Tax planning

Tax avoidance

Tax evasion

(Total: 10 marks)

Task 2 (8 marks)

Jack was provided with the use of a company car for the whole of the tax year 2018/19. His employer also paid for the running costs of the car, including all private fuel. The car was registered on 1 October 2017. The table below shows all of the necessary information in respect of the car.

Car	List price £	Cost price £	Fuel type	CO2 emissions g/km
Car Z	79,000	62,000	Diesel	168

The car was certified to the Real Driving Emissions 2 (RDE2) standard.

Contributions paid by James are as follows:

- £6,000 towards the original cost of the car

- £10 per month towards the cost of private fuel.

(a) **Complete the following table below to calculate the assessable benefit in kind for Car Z for 2018/19. Show your monetary answers in whole pounds only.** (6 marks)

	Scale charge %	Amount £
The scale charge percentage		
Taxable benefit on the provision of the car		
Taxable benefit on the provision of fuel		
Total taxable benefit		

(b) **Complete the following sentence in relation to Jack's benefit in kind for 2018/19.** (1 marks)

∇ Drop down list for task 1.2(b): (both boxes)

Increased
Decreased
Made no difference to

If Jack had not made an annual contribution of £120 towards the cost of private fuel and had, instead, increased his capital contribution to £6,120 towards the cost of the care, this would have [∇] Jack's assessable benefit in kind for 2018/19.

Margaret had the sole use of a company van throughout 2018/19. The van is electric and has zero emissions. Her employer pays all running costs and 50% of the mileage is for private usage.

(c) Calculate Margaret's benefit in kind for 2018/19. **(1 marks)**

£ [   ]

(Total: 8 marks)

Task 3 (8 marks)

Foday has employment income of £19,000 for the 2018/19 tax year. In addition, he has received the following employment benefits.

Date	Details
30 June 2018	Foday attended the financial year end staff party costing the employer £120 per employee.
July 2018	During the month, Foday worked away in the UK for five nights in a row. He received payments of £4, £9, £3, £4 and £4, respectively, from his employer for incidental expenses.
1 August 2018	Foday received an interest-free loan of £4,000 from his employer.
15 December 2018	Foday attended the staff Christmas party costing the employer £100 per employee.
1 January 2019	His employer wrote off the loan Foday had received in August.
Whole year	For 52 weeks, Foday received £60 per week in childcare vouchers for his son. This arrangement had been in force since April 2016.

Complete the table below to calculate Foday's total employment income for 2018/19. If your answer is zero, enter '0'. Enter your answers to the nearest whole pound. **(8 marks)**

Details	Amount £
Employment income	19,000
Staff parties	
Incidental expenses	
Loan	
Childcare vouchers	
Total employment income	

(Total: 8 marks)

Task 4 (6 marks)

In the 2018/19 tax year Samuel has employment income of £18,000. The only other income he received is the following investment income which was paid directly into his bank account.

Source of income	Amount £
Interest from a bank account	1,200
Interest from an ISA account	2,800
Interest from a building society account	2,000
Dividends	9,900

Calculate the tax payable by Samuel on his investment income by completing the table below. If your answer is zero, enter '0'. Enter your answer to the nearest whole pound. **(6 marks)**

Sources of income	Tax payable £
Interest from bank and building society accounts	
Interest from an ISA account	
Dividends	

(Total: 6 marks)

Task 5 (6 marks)

Mary rents out three properties.

For the 2018/19 tax year, the details of each property are provided in the table below.

	29 Main Road	35 London Street	4 Green Drive
Income:			
Monthly Rental Income payable in cash on 1st of each month	£300	See below	£550
Expenditure:			
Replacement of a boiler which was no longer working	£500		
Extension to the back of the house		£3,200	
Water rates			£1,170

Additional information:

Tenants occupied 29 Main Road and 4 Green Drive for the whole of 2018/19.

35 London Street:

The first tenants occupied the property from 1 April 2018 to 10 June 2018. They left owing rent for June which Mary was unable to recover. The second tenants paid £500 on the 1st of each month and occupied the property from 1 November 2018 for the remainder of the 2018/19 tax year.

Mary claims all possible allowances.

Mary has not made any elections.

Complete the table below to show the net income chargeable to tax for each of the properties for the tax year 2018/19. Enter your answers to the nearest whole pound. (6 marks)

Property	Net income chargeable to tax £
29 Main Road	
35 London Street	
4 Green Drive	

(Total: 6 marks)

Task 6 (12 marks)

Two taxpayers, Jonas and James, received the following income in the 2018/19 tax year.

	Jonas £	James £
Income from employment	49,000	14,000
Profits from property	15,000	Nil
Income from pension	Nil	8,500
Bank interest received	900	550
Building society interest received	800	1,200
Dividends received	11,700	2,250

Calculate both Jonas's and James's total income tax liabilities for 2018/19, entering your answer and workings into the blank table below. **(12 marks)**

Enter your answer to the nearest whole pound.

You have been given more space than you will need.

Jonas

KAPLAN PUBLISHING

James

(Total: 12 marks)

Task 7 (4 marks)

Bob is a sole trader and employs Joan as his secretary. She is Bob's only employee.

Joan earns a salary of £16,000 in the 2018/19 tax year. She is not an apprentice and does not receive any benefits in kind.

Complete the following sentences by placing your answer, to the nearest whole pound, in the boxes provided. If your answer is zero, enter '0'. **(4 marks)**

The total Class 1 National Insurance contributions payable by Joan in 2018/19 are:

£ [   ]

The total employer Class 1 National Insurance contributions payable in 2018/19 are:

£ [   ]

(Total: 4 marks)

Task 8 (7 marks)

During the 2018/19 tax year, Ben has employment income of £25,000. In addition to this, Ben has £200,000 invested in a building society account from which he received £8,000 interest during 2018/19. He also has £20,000 invested in shares from which he received £750 in dividends during 2018/19.

During the 2018/19 tax year, Ben receives the following benefits in kind:

- The private use of a company car. Ben paid £10 per month towards the use of the car. Ben paid nothing towards the fuel of the car, which is paid for by his employer at a cost of £25 per month.

- An interest-free loan of £4,000 in the tax year 2015/16 and an interest-free loan of £7,000 in the 2017/18 tax year. These are the only beneficial loans Ben has received from his employer. On 10 April 2018, Ben made his first capital repayment of £2,000 off the second loan.

- Incidental expenses of £3, £2, £10, £4 and £5 for five consecutive nights away from home in the UK.

Identify the effect on Ben's tax liability for 2018/19 if he had made each of the following changes. Assume that each of the seven changes are the only change that Ben makes to the situation as detailed above. **(7 marks)**

Changes	Increase	Decrease	Have no effect
If Ben had paid £10 per month to his employer towards the cost of private fuel instead of towards the use of his car.			
If Ben had paid £25 per month to cover all the cost of private fuel.			
If Ben had repaid the £2,000 off the second loan one week earlier.			
If Ben had paid 1% interest to his employer on the second loan.			
If Ben had claimed £5 instead of £10 in incidental expenses on the third night away from home.			

KAPLAN PUBLISHING

If Ben had invested £5,000 from his building society account into more shares. He estimates that he will receive additional dividends of £200 from these shares.			
If Ben had reduced his investment in his building society by £5,000 but invested this instead as the only payment into an ISA account in the 2018/19 tax year.			

(Total: 7 marks)

Task 9 (10 marks)

Jim made a number of disposals of capital assets during the 2018/19 tax year which are detailed in the table below.

(a) **Calculate the amount chargeable to capital gains tax (CGT) in the 2018/19 tax year and insert your answer in the table below. If your answer is zero, enter '0'.** **(8 marks)**

Capital asset	Date	Details	Amount chargeable to CGT (£)
House	30 May 2018	Jim sold his principle house. He owned the house for 100 months but bought a new apartment 12 months before he sold the house. The apartment became his principle residence as soon as he bought it. The house cost Jim £120,000 and he sold it for £395,000.	
Car	20 June 2018	Jim sold his car as he was about to receive a company car. The car cost Jim £16,400 and he sold it to a neighbour for £17,000.	

Painting	10 October 2018	Jim bought a watercolour painting at an auction for £4,000. He paid 2% auctioneers fees. Jim paid £500 to restore the painting and sold it to an unknown buyer in a private sale for £8,500.	
Antique table	12 December 2018	The table was bought by Jim for £4,750 and he sold it to a friend for £6,300.	
Land	12 March 2019	Jim bought a small piece of land five years ago for £15,000. Jim sold the land to his father for £4,000. At the time of the sale it was worth £17,500.	

Ceris bought 20 acres of land for £45,900. In the 2018/19 tax year, she sold five acres for £50,000 and the remaining 15 acres were valued at £400,000.

(b)   **Calculate the gain on the sale of the land. Show your answer to the nearest whole pound.**   **(2 marks)**

£ [   ]

(Total: 10 marks)

Task 10 (10 marks)

Mahesh holds shares in RSB Ltd and has made a number of transactions over the years.

Details are as follows:

Event date	Detail
13 May 2014	Mahesh bought 1,000 shares at £10 per share.
12 December 2015	There was a 1 for 10 bonus issue when the shares had a market value of £12 each.
10 September 2016	Mahesh sold 55 shares for £15 per share.
25 April 2017	Mahesh bought 595 shares for £11 per share.
10 April 2018	Mahesh sold 330 shares for £20 per share.

(a) **Clearly showing the balance of shares and their value to carry forward, calculate the gain Mahesh made on the sale of the shares for 2018/19.**

  All workings must be shown in your calculations. **(8 marks)**

Assume that Mahesh had bought a further 500 shares in RSB for £15 per share on 30 April 2018.

(b)   Calculate the gain Mahesh would have made if he had made this additional purchase on 30 April 2018.

All workings must be shown in your calculations.   (2 marks)

(Total: 10 marks)

Task 11 (7 marks)

Precious has the following capital gains and losses in the 2018/19 tax year.

Sale	Chargeable gain (£)	Allowable Loss (£)
Mirror	6,120	
Antique		14,600
Shares	12,600	
Painting	16,210	

(a)   Calculate the amount of capital gains tax payable by Precious assuming all capital gains are taxed at the basic rate.

Your answer must be in whole pounds only. If your answer is zero, enter '0'.   (2 marks)

The amount of capital against tax payable by Precious is:

£	

(b) Identify whether the following statement is true or false. (1 mark)

Statement	True	False
Taxpayers will have to pay their 2018/19 capital gains tax liability by 31 January 2019.		

Thomas has the following capital gains and losses in the last few years. He wishes to relieve his losses at the earliest opportunity.

Year	Annual exempt amount (£)	Capital gains (£)	Capital losses (£)
2016/17	11,100	26,500	15,700
2017/18	11,300	31,800	46,500
2018/19	11,700	46,300	27,500

(c) Complete the following sentences by inserting the answers in the boxes provided. Your answer must be in whole pounds only. If you answer is zero, enter '0'. **(4 marks)**

The amount that Thomas will have to pay capital gains tax in 2018/19 is:

£ [   ]

The amount of losses (if any) Thomas can carry forward to the 2019/20 tax year is:

£ [   ]

(Total: 7 marks)

Task 12 (6 marks)

Mabel, who is 95 and lives in the UK, made a number of gifts to her granddaughter, Martha, in recent years. These are the only gifts Mabel has made.

Complete the table to show whether each of the gifts below is a chargeable lifetime transfer (CLT), an exempt transfer (ET) or a potential exempt transfer (PET).   **(6 marks)**

∇ Drop down list for task 1.12(a): (all boxes)

CLT
ET
PET

Date	Details of the gift	Value (£)	Type of transfer
20 May 2016	Cash gift	2,000	∇
6 April 2017	Cash gift	7,000	∇
10 July 2017	Wedding gift given on the day of Martha's wedding	2,500	∇
30 August 2018	Holiday home in Spain	41,000	∇
10 September 2018	Cash gift for Martha's birthday	500	∇
25 December 2018	Family jewellery as a Christmas present	18,200	∇

(Total: 6 marks)

Task 13 (6 marks)

Stanley died on 10 April 2018 leaving an estate at death of £300,000 to his brother. In the 10 years leading up to his death, the only gift he made was to a friend, Emily. The gift, a house, was made on 22 December 2011 when it was valued at £341,000.

(a) Calculate the inheritance tax payable by Emily on Stanley's gift at the time of his death, entering your answer and workings into the blank table below. You have been given more space than you will need. **(4 marks)**

(b) Calculate the inheritance tax payable on Stanley's estate, entering your answer and workings into the blank table below. **(2 marks)**

(Total: 6 marks)

1 Sample Assessment 2 Answers

Task 1 (10 marks)

You work for DBQ, a small firm of accountants. The managing partner is concerned over recent publicity into high profile organisations accused of tax irregularities. They have asked you to produce information for distribution to DBQ's clients.

Explain the following three terms and give an example of each of them to help DBQ's clients understand the difference between them.

(10 marks)

Tax planning

Tax planning should involve the payment of the correct amount of tax (but no more), when it is due and following the spirit of the law (i.e. being tax complaint).

Tax planning involves the taxpayer using lawful provisions when calculating their tax liability. An example would be where a taxpayer declares property income and uses all available tax allowances in the computation of a tax payable.

The main difference between tax planning and tax avoidance activities is the intent of the taxpayer. In tax planning the taxpayer seeks to pay the correct amount of tax (albeit the lowest amount possible) whereas tax avoidance seeks to exploit unintended loopholes or conflicts in different tax laws to avoid paying the correct amount of tax.

Tax avoidance

Tax avoidance is seeking to legally minimise a tax liability. However, it is in a way not intended by Parliament. When challenged, many high profile organisations make a public statement that 'They have complied with the law' and this they have even though they have worked against the spirit of the law by sometimes diverting monies to countries with more advantageous tax rates. This may be termed exploiting loopholes in the law for their own advantage – i.e. to reduce their tax liability.

Tax evasion

Tax evasion is illegal and if you are found guilty, you may face penalties under civil or criminal law.

Tax evasion results in an under- or non-payment of taxes usually as a result of a false, inaccurate declaration or indeed making no declaration at all.

An example would be where a person has multiple businesses but declares only some of these businesses or a business may deflate income or inflate expenses to reduce the amount taxable.

(Total: 10 marks)

Task 2 (8 marks)

(a) **Complete the following table below to calculate the assessable benefit in kind for Car Z for 2018/19. Show your monetary answers in whole pounds only.** **(6 marks)**

	Scale charge %	Amount £
The scale charge percentage	34	
Taxable benefit on the provision of the car		25,160
Taxable benefit on the provision of fuel		7,956
Total taxable benefit		33,116

Workings

The scale charge percentage is calculated as 20% + (165-95) × 1/5= 34%

The taxable benefit is calculated as (£79,000 – £5,000) × 34%= £25,160

The taxable fuel benefit is calculated as £23,400× 34%= £7,956

Notes

Car benefits are calculated as follows:

- Appropriate percentage × List price × n/12

- Where n = number of months the car is available in the tax year.

The scale percentage is found from the following calculation:

- 20% + (CO_2 emissions – 95) × 1/5

- CO_2 emissions are rounded down to the next number ending in 0 or 5

- Diesel cars attract an extra 4% except where they meet RDE2 standards

- Maximum scale percentage is 37%.

Fuel benefit is calculated as follows:

- Appropriate percentage × £23,400 × n/12

- Where n = number of months the benefit is available in the tax year.

If an employee contributes towards the running costs of the car this is an allowable deduction, but partial contributions towards the cost of private fuel are NOT an allowable deduction.

If an employee contributes towards the capital cost of the car this is an allowable deduction from the list price up to a maximum of £5,000.

(b) Complete the following sentences in relation to Jack's benefit in kind for 2018/19.   (2 marks)

If Jack had not made an annual contribution of £120 towards the cost of private fuel and had, instead, increased his capital contribution to £6,120 towards the cost of the care, this would have

| Made no difference to ∇ | Jack's assessable benefit in kind for

2018/19.

Margaret had the sole use of a company van throughout 2018/19. The van is electric and has zero emissions. Her employer pays all running costs and 50% of the mileage is for private usage.

(c) Calculate Margaret's benefit in kind for 2018/19   (1 marks)

| £ | 1340 |

Notes

A private use benefit for a company van has an annual benefit of £3,350. This is multiplied by 40% when the van has zero emissions.

(Total: 8 marks)

Task 3 (8 marks)

Complete the table below to calculate Foday's total employment income for 2018/19. If your answer is zero, enter '0'. Enter your answers to the nearest whole pound. **(8 marks)**

Details	Amount £
Employment income	19,000
Staff parties	100
Incidental expenses	0
Loan	4,000
Childcare vouchers	260
Total employment income	23,360

(Total: 8 marks)

Workings

Childcare vouchers= 52 × (£60 – £55) = £260

Notes

(i)   Staff parties are an exempt benefit up to £150 per head per year. If the total amount of parties exceeds £150 during the tax year then the taxpayer can exempt the events that total the most which are covered by the £150 exemption. The year end staff party was £120 per head whereas the Christmas party was £100 so it is better to use the exemption to cover the year end party.

(ii) Incidental expenses when working elsewhere in the UK an exempt benefit up to £5 per night. The payments can be averaged out on a trip that contains a number of nights. As the trip was for five nights then up to £25 could have been exempt.

(iii) Interest free loans with a balance of no more than £10,000 throughout the tax year represent an exempt benefit. However, when any amount of loan is written off the write off amount gives rise to taxable employment income.

(iv) Where an approved childcare arrangement has been entered into prior to 6 April 2017 £55 per week of vouchers is an exempt benefit for a basic rate taxpayer.

Task 4 (6 marks)

Calculate the tax payable by Samuel on his investment income by completing the table below. If your answer is zero, enter '0'. Enter your answer to the nearest whole pound. (6 marks)

Sources of income	Tax payable £
Interest from bank and building society accounts	440
Interest from an ISA account	0
Dividends	592 or 593

(Total: 6 marks)

(This model answer shows both rounded up and rounded down options. Both options are equally valid for the purposes of this assessment.)

Workings

(i)

	£
Taxable investment income	3,200
£1,000 × 0%	0.00
£2,200 × 20%	440.00
Income tax liability	440.00

(iii)

	£
Taxable dividend income	9,900
£2,000 × 0%	0.00
£7,900 × 7.5%	592.50
Income tax liability	592.50

Notes

(i) As Samuel is a basic rate taxpayer he is entitled to a personal savings allowance of £1,000.

(ii) All taxpayers are entitled to a dividend allowance of £2,000.

Task 5 (6 marks)

Complete the table below to show the net income chargeable to tax for each of the properties for the tax year 2018/19. Enter your answers to the nearest whole pound. **(6 marks)**

Property	Net income chargeable to tax £
29 Main Road	3,100
35 London Street	3,450
4 Green Drive	5,430

(Total: 6 marks)

Workings

29 Main Road		£
Rent	300 × 12	3,600
Boiler		(500)
Property income		3,100

35 London Street		£
Rent	450 + (500 × 6)	3,450
Extension		–
Property income		3,450

4 Green Drive		£
Rent	550 × 12	6,600
Water rates		(1,170)
Property income		5,430

Notes

As Mary has gross rents of no more than £150,000 she will use the cash basis to prepare her property income assessment.

Under the cash basis it is rent received that is included in the assessment. For 29 Main Road and 4 Green Drive 12 months' worth of rent has been received in the tax year. For 35 London Street the April rent was received in 2017/18 and so should not be included. June should also not be included as it was never received. The new tenants start paying on 1 November 2018 and so six months of rent have been received from them during 2018/19.

A replacement of a boiler that no longer works is classed as a repair and so will be an allowable expense.

An extension is enhancing the value of the asset and so is not an allowable expense.

Task 6 (12 marks)

Calculate both Jonas's and James's total income tax liabilities for 2018/19, entering your answer and workings into the blank table below. **(12 marks)**

Enter your answer to the nearest whole pound.

You have been given more space than you will need.

Jonas

	Workings:	£
Employment income		49,000
Property income		15,000
Interest		1,700
Dividends		11,700
		77,400
Personal allowance		(11,850)
		65,550
Basic rate:	£34,500 × 20%	6,900
Higher rate: (£49,000 + £15,000 – £11,850 – £34,500)	£17,650 × 40%	7,060
Savings	£500 × 0%	0
Savings:	£1,200 × 40%	480
Dividends:	£2,000 × 0%	0
Dividends:	£9,700 × 32.5%	3,152 or 3,153
		17,592 or 17,593

James

	Workings:	£
Employment income		14,000
Pension income		8,500
Interest		1,750
Dividends		2,250
		26,500
Personal allowance		(11,850)
		14,650
	(£14,000 + £8,500 – £11,850)	
Basic rate:	£10,650 × 20%	2,130
Savings:	£1,000 × 0%	0
Savings:	£750 × 20%	150
Dividends:	£2,000 × 0%	0
Dividends:	£250 × 7.5%	19
		2,299

(Total: 12 marks)

Notes

(i)   All taxpayers are entitled to a dividend allowance of £2,000.

(ii)   Jonas is a higher rate taxpayer and so is entitled to a personal savings allowance of £500.

(iii) James is a basic rate taxpayer and so is entitled to a personal savings allowance of £1,000.

Task 7 (4 marks)

Complete the following sentences by placing your answer, to the nearest whole pound, in the boxes provided. If your answer is zero, enter '0'. **(4 marks)**

The total Class 1 National Insurance contributions payable by Joan in 2018/19 are:

£	909 or 910

The total employer Class 1 National Insurance contributions payable in 2018/19 are:

£	0

(Total: 4 marks)

This model answer shows both rounded up and rounded down options. Both options are equally valid for the purposes of this assessment.

Workings

Employee National Insurance= (£16,000 – £8,424) × 12%= 909.12

Employer National Insurance= (£16,000 – £8,424) × 13.8%= 1,045.49

Notes

Every business receives an employment allowance of £3,000 to set off against their Class 1 employers National Insurance liability. As Joan is Bob's only employee then the employer's National Insurance liability for her would be covered by the employment allowance and so nothing is payable.

Task 8 (7 marks)

Identify the effect on Ben's tax liability for 2018/19 if he had made each of the following changes. Assume that each of the seven changes are the only change that Ben makes to the situation as detailed above.   (7 marks)

Changes	Increase	Decrease	Have no effect
If Ben had paid £10 per month to his employer towards the cost of private fuel instead of towards the use of his car.	✓		
If Ben had paid £25 per month to cover all the cost of private fuel.		✓	
If Ben had repaid the £2,000 off the second loan on week earlier.		✓	
If Ben had paid 1% interest to his employer on the second loan.		✓	
If Ben had claimed £5 instead of £10 in incidental expenses on the third night away from home.			✓
If Ben had invested £5,000 from his building society account into more shares. He estimates that he will receive additional dividends of £200 from these shares.		✓	
If Ben had reduced his investment in his building society by £5,000 but invested this instead as the only payment into an ISA account in the 2018/19 tax year.		✓	

(Total: 7 marks)

Notes

(i)   Partial contributions towards private fuel cannot be deducted from the benefit amount. They will therefore make no difference to the taxable income.

(ii)   If the employee covers the cost of private fuel in full then no taxable benefit will arise.

(iii)   If the loan repayment had been made one week earlier it would have been made in 2017/18. This would mean that throughout the 2018/19 tax year the total beneficial loan balance would be less than £10,000 making it an exempt benefit.

(iv)   The benefit for a beneficial loan is calculated as the loan balance multiplied by the official rate of interest less any interest paid. Therefore paying 1% would reduce the taxable benefit.

(v)   Where incidental expenses are paid for consecutive nights on a trip the payment amounts can be averaged when comparing to the £5 per night exempt limit. As the total for the trip is £24 it is already exempt and so claiming less would make no difference to taxable income.

(vi)   Ben currently only has £750 of dividends and is not making full use of his £2,000 dividend allowance. Receiving £200 more dividends would be covered by the allowance and taxed at 0%.

(vii) ISA interest is exempt from tax.

Task 9 (10 marks)

(a) Calculate the amount chargeable to capital gains tax (CGT) in the 2018/19 tax year and insert your answer in the table below. If your answer is zero, enter '0'. (8 marks)

Capital asset	Date	Details	Amount chargeable to CGT (£)
House	30 May 2018	Jim sold his principle house. He owned the house for 100 months but bought a new apartment 12 months before he sold the house. The apartment became his principle residence as soon as he bought it. The house cost Jim £120,000 and he sold it for £395,000.	0
Car	20 June 2018	Jim sold his car as he was about to receive a company car. The car cost Jim £16,400 and he sold it to a neighbour for £17,000.	0
Painting	10 October 2018	Jim bought a watercolour painting at an auction for £4,000. He paid 2% auctioneers fees. Jim paid £500 to restore the painting and sold it to an unknown buyer in a private sale for £8,500.	3,920
Antique table	12 December 2018	The table was bought by Jim for £4,750 and he sold it to a friend for £6,300.	500
Land	12 March 2019	Jim bought a small piece of land five years ago for £15,000. Jim sold the land to his father for £4,000. At the time of the sale it was worth £17,500.	2,500

Notes

(i) Where a principal private residence is disposed of the gain will be exempt if the property has always been occupied or had deemed occupation to cover the whole ownership period. The last 18 months count as deemed occupation even if another property is the principal private residence at that time.

(ii) A car is an exempt asset for CGT purposes.

(iii) A gain on a non-wasting chattel should be restricted to 5/3 × (Gross proceeds – £6,000).

(iv) Parents are connected people for the purposes of CGT. When a disposal is made to a connected person market value must be used as proceeds.

Ceris bought 20 acres of land for £45,900. In the 2018/19 tax year, she sold five acres for £50,000 and the remaining 15 acres were valued at £400,000.

(b) Calculate the gain on the sale of the land. Show your answer to the nearest whole pound. **(2 marks)**

£	44,900

Workings

	£
Sales proceeds	50,000
Cost (£45,900 × £50,000/£50,000 + £400,000))	(5,100)
Gain	44,900

(Total: 10 marks)

Task 10 (10 marks)

(a)   Clearly showing the balance of shares and their value to carry forward, calculate the gain Mahesh made on the sale of the shares for 2018/19.

All workings must be shown in your calculations.   (8 marks)

		Shares:	Cost £	
13 May 2014	Purchase	1,000	10,000	
12 December 2015	Bonus Issue	100	0	
		1,100	10,000	
10 September 2016	Disposal	(55)	(500)	
		1,045	9,500	
25 April 2017	Purchase	595	6,545	
		1,640	16,045	
10 April 2018	Disposal	(330)	(3,229)	
	Share pool balance to c/f	1,310	12,816	
	2018/19 gain			
	Proceeds 330 × 20	6,600		
	Cost	3,229		
	Gain	3,371		

(b)   Calculate the gain Mahesh would have made if he had made this additional purchase on 30 April 2018.

All workings must be shown in your calculations.   (2 marks)

Amended gain		£		
Proceeds:	330 × 20	6,600		
Cost:	(330 × 15)	(4,950)		
Gain		1,650		

(Total: 10 marks)

Notes

Share matching rules must be applied when disposing of shares of the same type.

The matching rules should be applied as follows:

(i)   Shares bought on the same day

(ii)   Shares bought in the next 30 days (FIFO basis)

(iii)   Shares from the share pool.

Task 11 (7 marks)

(a)   Calculate the amount of capital gains tax payable by Precious assuming all capital gains are taxed at the basic rate.

Your answer must be in whole pounds only. If your answer is zero, enter '0'.   **(2 marks)**

The amount of capital against tax payable by Precious is:

£	863

Workings

	£
Mirror	6,120
Antique	(14,600)
Shares	12,600
Painting	16,210
	20,330
Annual exempt amount	(11,700)
Taxable gains	8,630
8,630 × 10%	863.00

(b)   Identify whether the following statement is true or false.

(1 mark)

Statement	True	False
Taxpayers will have to pay their 2018/19 capital gains tax liability by 31 January 2019.		✓

Notes

Capital gains tax is due by 31 January following the end of the tax year. For 2018/19 it is due by 31 January 2020.

(c) Complete the following sentences by inserting the answers in the boxes provided. Your answer must be in whole pounds only. If you answer is zero, enter '0'. **(4 marks)**

The amount that Thomas will have to pay capital gains tax in 2018/19 is:

£ | 0

The amount of losses (if any) Thomas can carry forward to the 2019/20 tax year is:

£ | 7,600

(Total: 7 marks)

Workings

	£
2016/17	
Gains	26,500
Current year losses	(15,700)
	10,800
Annual exempt amount – restricted	(10,800)
Taxable gains	0

	£
2017/18	
Gains	31,800
Current year losses	(31,800)
	0

Loss to c/f: (£46,500 – £31,800)	14,700

2018/19	**£**
Gains	46,300
Current year losses	(27,500)
	18,800
Brought forward capital losses – restricted	(7,100)
Taxable gains	11,700
Annual exempt amount	(11,700)
Taxable gains	0
Loss to c/f: (£14,700 – £7,100)	7,600

Task 12 (6 marks)

Complete the table to show whether each of the gifts below is a chargeable lifetime transfer (CLT), an exempt transfer (ET) or a potential exempt transfer (PET). **(6 marks)**

Date	Details of the gift	Value (£)	Type of transfer
20 May 2016	Cash gift	2,000	ET ∇
6 April 2017	Cash gift	7,000	PET ∇
10 July 2017	Wedding gift given on the day of Martha's wedding	2,500	ET ∇
30 August 2018	Holiday home in Spain	41,000	PET ∇
10 September 2018	Cash gift for Martha's birthday	500	ET ∇
25 December 2018	Family jewellery as a Christmas present	18,200	PET ∇

(Total: 6 marks)

Notes

(i) The cash gift in 2016/17 would be covered by the 2016/17 AE.

(ii) The cash gift on 6 April 2017 would utilise the £3,000 2017/18 AE and the remaining £1,000 of the 2016/17 AE leaving £3,000 which could potentially become taxable.

(iii) £2,500 of a gift in consideration of marriage can be exempt when made by a grandparent.

(iv) The holiday home would use the 2018/19 AE but the remainder would not be covered by any exemptions.

(v) The cash gift for Martha's birthday is not covered by any annual exemptions and so is a potentially exempt transfer.

(vi) There are no exemptions available for the gift of jewellery. It cannot be covered by the normal expenditure out of income as it is a gift of a physical asset.

Task 13 (6 marks)

(a) **Calculate the inheritance tax payable by Emily on Stanley's gift at the time of his death, entering your answer and workings into the blank space below. You have been given more space than you will need.** **(4 marks)**

	Workings	£
Value of the house		341,000
Annual exemption:		
2011/12		(3,000)
2010/11		(3,000)
Nil rate band		(325,000)
		10,000
Tax payable at 40%		4,000
Taper relief at 20%	Tax payable	800

Notes

As the gift was to an individual it is classed as a PET. No IHT would have been due in lifetime, however, as Stanley has died within seven years of the gift it becomes chargeable at death.

As no other gifts have been made previously then the current year and prior year annual exemptions are available as well as a full nil rate band.

Tax is payable at 40% but can be reduced by taper relief as there have been 6–7 years between the gift and date of death.

(b) **Calculate the inheritance tax payable on Stanley's estate, entering your answer and workings into the blank table below.**

(2 marks)

	£
£300,000 × 40%	120,000

Notes

No nil rate band is available for the death estate as it has been used by the lifetime gift to his friend.

(Total: 6 marks)

INDEX